INTERPRETING
MARTIN LUTHER

For Ian Gentles:
a scholar,
a Christian gentleman,
+ my friend.

Victor Shepherd

Trinity 2008.

INTERPRETING MARTIN LUTHER

An Introduction to His Life and Thought

Victor Shepherd

REGENT COLLEGE PUBLISHING
Vancouver, British Columbia

INTERPRETING MARTIN LUTHER
Copyright © 2008 Victor Shepherd

Published 2008 by
REGENT COLLEGE PUBLISHING
5800 University Boulevard
Vancouver, British Columbia
V6T 2E4 Canada
www.regentpublishing.com

Editor: Debbie Sawczak
Cover design: Robert Hand
Interior design: Rob Clements

Library and Archives Canada Cataloguing in Publication

Shepherd, Victor A., 1944-
Interpreting Martin Luther : an introduction to his life and thought /
Victor A. Shepherd.

ISBN 978-1-57383-399-8

1. Luther, Martin, 1483-1546. I. Title.

BR325.S46 2008   284.1092   C2007-902853-5

To

Glenn A. Davis

" . . . you love the Word of Christ sincerely and further it faithfully."

Letter of Martin Luther to Prince George of Anhalt
28 March 1533

CONTENTS

Acknowledgments

I am grateful to Maureen and Matthias Benfey for their encouragement, their patient and painstaking transcription work, and other valuable input. Many thanks are due also to my editor, Debbie Sawczak, whose skillful and creative efforts turned about 35 hours of interactive, sometimes repetitive, and often discursive classroom lectures into clear, readable text. And finally, a huge debt of gratitude is owed to Glenn Davis for his personal support and indispensable practical help with this project from beginning to end. Without the collaboration of each of these people, the book would not have appeared.

1

Introduction

Ever since arriving at Tyndale Seminary in 1993 I have taught the course, "Theology of Martin Luther," as often as course rotation permitted. While students in this course are required to have pursued two courses in introductory Systematic Theology, they come to the Luther course without any prior exposure to the history or thought of Luther; more broadly, without any exposure to the magisterial Reformation. Moreover, no student in the course has ever belonged to a Lutheran denomination. For this reason I can presuppose an acquaintance with elementary theological vocabulary but not with the issues that are more immediately associated with Luther and the Lutheran family of churches.

Students relate more warmly to Luther than to any other theologian I expound. John Calvin, for instance, they find measured and reserved; certainly not cold, but nonetheless lacking the radiant heat of Luther's burning heart. John Wesley, on the other hand, frequently strikes students as distant, despite his having written more about love than most. Luther, however, students see to have a heart as large as a house. His passion is unmistakeable. Like Elijah of old, Israel's greatest prophet, the "wild boar in the vineyard" knew both ecstatic height and unutterable abyss. None of this suggests that he was afflicted with bipolar mood disorder, a psychosis that moves from depression to mania and back.[1] There is no evidence of derangement in Luther. His ecstasy and agony arose not from temperamental instability but were rather the concomitants of a self-abandonment to the gospel—a gospel that brings to those who welcome it such joy as the world neither gives nor takes away nor understands, even as the selfsame gospel provokes in those who spurn it a lethal opposition whose hatred is virulent, irrational, and unrelenting.

Several students (the average age of the Tyndale Seminary student is thirty-eight) have sought pastoral counsel from me in the midst of assaults they have had to endure in the work-a-day world. In their frustration and apparent helplessness before a victimization they could not anticipate and now cannot understand; amidst the ensuing isolation that finds them alone as others slink away self-protectively; in their days of wild oscillation between raging pain and frozen numbness, these mature students have told me that Luther, and only Luther, could address their anguish. When 'best-seller' devotional writings were unavailing if not an affront, Luther alone reached them just because Luther grasps both life's complexity and the world's ceaseless turbulence and treachery. Luther alone spoke to them and sustained them in their *Anfechtung* or trial[2] as they struggled to cope with the nadir of their outer and inner existence.

Each year pours forth another avalanche of books on Luther. The reason is ready to hand: Luther is fathomless. To delve into him is quickly to find oneself admitted to intellectual and spiritual depths that

---

1.   Interestingly Henry Rack speaks of Charles Wesley as having "almost a manic-depressive personality" (Henry D. Rack in *Reasonable Enthusiast: John Wesley and the Rise of Methodism* [Nashville: Abingdon, 1992], p.252).

2.   The meaning of *Anfechtung*, so characteristic of Luther as frequently to be left untranslated in English discussions of Luther's work, will be amplified later in the book.

are not only oceanic but ultimately unsoundable. However deeply we immerse ourselves in Luther, we are no closer to exhausting the riches his mind and heart make available to us.

Interpreting Martin Luther: An Introduction to His Life and Thought discusses the assigned readings in a one-semester course. The textbook for the course is *Martin Luther's Basic Theological Writings*, assembled and edited by Timothy F. Lull.[3] It is hoped that my book will prove a helpful amplification of the Luther excerpts deemed important for the first-time reader of Luther. For this reason the page references to Luther citations follow the Lull text rather than the *Weimar Ausgabe* (German) or the American edition of *Luther's Works* (English).

Readers who wish to move through the book uninterrupted will find that they can return at their convenience and peruse the Luther works mentioned in the footnotes. In other words, *Interpreting Martin Luther: An Introduction to His Life and Thought* aims at providing an orientation to Luther through discussing major topics that he was impelled to address, together with the theological, religious, and sociopolitical context of his thought.

---

3. Lull, Timothy F., ed.; *Martin Luther's Basic Theological Writings* (Minneapolis: Fortress Press, 1989).

THE LIFE AND TIMES OF MARTIN LUTHER

1483-1546

1483	November 10	Luther is born in Eisleben to Hans and Margareta Luder.[1]
	November 11	Luther is baptized at St.Peter's Church.
1484		Luther's family moves to Mansfeld, where his father finds work in copper mines.
1492		Luther begins school in Mansfeld.
1497		Luther attends school in Magdeburg.
1498-1501		Luther attends the Latin School in Eisenach.
1501		Luther graduates with B.A. from the University of Erfurt.
1502		Wittenberg University, with which Luther and Melanchthon would be associated throughout their academic careers, is established.
1505		Luther gains M.A. degree and begins studying law. Frightened by a thunderstorm and lightning bolt, Luther vows to become a monk and enters the monastery of the Reformed Augustinian Order in Erfurt.
1506		Luther is ordained at the Cathedral in Erfurt.

1. Luther was later to turn "Luder" into "Luther." *Eleutherius* is Greek for "free man," and like all humanist-trained scholars Luther was determined to spell his name according to classical conventions. For the same reason Philip Schwarzerd ("black earth") was soon to translate his name correctly into the Greek, "Melanchthon." Thereafter Melanchthon was known by this name only.

1510-1511	Luther walks to Rome where he represents his order concerning the Observant controversy.
1511	Disillusioned, Luther returns from Rome and moves to Wittenberg.
1512	Luther gains a doctorate in theology and becomes professor of biblical theology.
	Luther lectures on the Psalms (*Dictata super Psalterium*).
1515-1516	Luther lectures on the Epistle to the Romans.
1516	Luther lectures on the Epistle to the Galatians.
1517	Luther lectures on the Epistle to the Hebrews.
	Luther disputes scholastic theology, and repudiates Aristotelianism.
	Luther posts his Ninety-Five Theses and denounces the traffic in indulgences.
	Archbishop Albrecht of Mainz denounces Luther in Rome.
	The Curia in Rome regards the Ninety-Five Theses as an attack on the authority of the pope.
1518	Luther speaks at the Heidelberg Disputation.
	After the Diet of Augsburg Cardinal Cajetan (a papal emissary) questions Luther. Luther refuses to recant. Elector Frederich (from Saxony) refuses Cajetan's request that Luther be sent to Rome or banished.
1519	Luther begins second course of lectures on the Psalms. (*Operationes in Psalmos*)
1520	Luther speaks at the Leipzig Disputation, and is supported by Carlstadt against Eck.

1521	Luther writes the three tracts by which he is most widely known: *Address to the Christian Nobility of the German Nation; The Babylonian Captivity of the Church; The Freedom of a Christian.*
	Luther is threatened with excommunication. Luther is summoned to the Diet in the city of Worms, and refuses to recant. "Kidnapped" by supporters near Eisenach on his way home, Luther is sequestered by supporters in the Wartburg Castle. An imperial ban is imposed on Luther and his followers.
	Luther translates the New Testament in eleven weeks.
1522	The German translation of the New Testament is printed.
1523	Luther resumes his lectures in Wittenberg.
1524	Luther abandons his religious habit.
	Erasmus publishes his *Concerning Free Will.*
1525	Luther publishes *Against the Robbing and Murderous Hordes of Peasants.*
	Luther marries an ex-nun, Katharina von Bora.
	Luther opposes Erasmus with *Bondage of the Will.*
1527	The princes refuse to enforce the Edict of Worms (a price had been put on Luther's head) at the Diet of Speyer.

1529		At the Marburg Colloquy Luther is unable to agree with the "South Germans" (i.e., German-speaking Swiss) on the meaning of "This is my body." The disagreement between Luther and Zwingli concerning the Lord's Supper hardens into a stand-off between Luther and Reformed Churches that remains.
1530		Fearing for Luther's well-being, his friends keep him in Cobourg, a few miles from Augsburg, while Melanchthon represents the Lutherans at the Diet in the German city.
1534 ca.		Luther's complete *German Bible* appears.
1535		Luther lectures on Genesis.
1540		Luther writes second set of lectures on *Galatians*.
		Pope Paul III recognizes the Jesuit Order ("Society of Jesus").
1543		Luther publishes *Of the Jews and Their Lies*, a tract that will prove deleterious in Germany and elsewhere for centuries. It will be quoted by Rudolf Streicher, a notorious Nazi, at his War Crimes trial in 1945.
1545		The Council of Trent, called to articulate Roman Catholic theology in the wake of "Lutheranism", is convened. It will meet intermittently for the next eighteen years.
1546	February 14	Luther preaches his last sermon, "Against the Jews," in the church in Eisleben.
	February 18	Luther dies in Eisleben.
	February 22	Philip Melanchthon preaches at Luther's funeral in the Castle church, Wittenberg.

1

Background to the Reformation

SOCIAL AND RELIGIOUS TENSION AS
THE SOIL OF THE REFORMATION

It is held by some that Luther and his people tore apart a united Christendom—that there was only one church until the sixteenth century, that the Reformers destroyed the unity of the church irrecoverably, and that they could have avoided this devastation by being patient and waiting a little longer. Is this true?

There was in fact a reformation underway before Luther, beginning with the Renaissance. The Catholic reformation, as it was called, sought to purify the church of theological, moral, and institutional abuses; it climaxed in the Council of Trent, which met in several stages over a period of eighteen years from 1545 to 1563. Regardless of the abuses the Council remedied and the theological integrity it retained, however, Luther believed that some aspects of Roman Catholic theology obscured the gospel, and that a recovery of the gospel in its inherent integrity, militancy, and efficacy required more than mere purging of ecclesiastical abuses. Ought he then to be faulted for what he did? Was the Reformation—the magisterial Reformation—immoderate after all? Was it extremist?

Consider Zwingli, born only weeks after Luther. An accomplished musician, he noticed one day in the Zürich cathedral that church music had become so fine as to be an end in itself, an aesthetic spectacle on Sunday morning that detracted from the Word. Not because it was inelegant, but precisely because it was so magnificent, it no longer served the praise and worship of God. He therefore picked up an axe and reduced the pipe organ to matchwood, earning himself the reputation of an iconoclast and culture-wrecker. In fact, Zwingli, like all the magisterial Reformers, was culturally sophisticated, but he recognized that any dimension of church life—even music, good in itself—could usurp the place of the Word.

Luther never went that far. Unlike John Calvin—a representative, like Zwingli, of the Reformed rather than the Lutheran wing of the Reformation—Luther held that anything not forbidden by Scripture was permitted. Rejecting any semblance of worship offered to Mary, he would nonetheless have entertained a statue of the Virgin in church, for instance, because Scripture does not forbid it. Even so, some have regarded his Reformation as immoderate.

Were the magisterial Reformers spiritually defective? Did they not understand the apostle Paul when he said that God will destroy whoever destroys the unity of the church? The Body of Christ is never to be dismembered; but did Luther dismember it? Or would he have said that he was criticizing what had ceased to be the Body of Christ, since it had forfeited the gospel? Were his actions then a legitimate attempt to recover the gospel's integrity?

As a matter of fact, the unity that characterized the late medieval period was more apparent than real. There were many tensions on many fronts. For instance, there was considerable political tension as princes, who often resembled warlords, fought with each other for territorial and economic gain. In the sixteenth century, Germany was not yet a nation; it would not become one until the era of Bismarck. "Germany" consisted of three hundred different principalities or fiefdoms, all of them competing with each other and frequently at war. Relations between the Emperor of the Holy Roman Empire and secular rulers were likewise strained on the eve of the Reformation. The office of Holy Roman Emperor was in its last days, and Charles V found himself competing for the people's allegiance against rising national self-consciousness in the principalities.

Tension also existed between towns, on the one hand, and rural communities governed by aristocrats on the other, as the latter found themselves threatened by an emerging entrepreneurial or middle class of increasing wealth and influence. The middle class and its attitudes and values arose with the cultural shift brought about by the Renaissance as well as the economic shift that resulted from banking and a measure of industrialization. By the time of Luther's Reformation, the social structure of feudalism was ready to be overturned.

One example of the huge social shift accompanying the change in economy is particularly worth looking at. The fourteenth century was distinguished by the rise of institutions that are still with us today—banks, universities, and parliament—but another thing that marked the fourteenth century was not an institution at all but an invention: the clock. With the shift from a relatively primitive agricultural economy to an urban entrepreneurial economy came a completely different attitude towards time. Prior to the clock, life was regulated by the sun and by the seasons; people rose when it was light and retired when it was dark. While this worked fine as long as activities revolved around the land, it did not mesh with the activities of the rising entrepreneurial middle class. If you went to the office to start work at daybreak and left at nightfall, little banking would be done in the dead of winter, while in the summer the employees would be working eighteen hours a day. The life of the entrepreneurial, trading, manufacturing middle class presupposed a day regulated by the clock, and the clock therefore facilitated far-reaching cultural change.

The magisterial Reformation fed on this tension between urban and rural culture. The Reformation was largely a city phenomenon, catching fire almost exclusively among people who had left an agricultural economy for a middle-class urban economy; it was part of a social movement that gathered up the manufacturing class, and the banking class, all of whom congregated in cities.[1] In fact, each major Reformer can be associated with one or more cities: Luther with Wittenberg, Worms, Augsburg, Erfurt, and Eisenach; Calvin with Geneva; Zwingli with Zurich; Bucer with Strasbourg; and several other Reformers with Basel.

The development of an urban economy and the rise of the middle class were accompanied by upheaval in the social structure. The medieval feudal system permitted virtually no mobility between social strata; one's position was fixed by the fortune or misfortune of one's birth. Within a stratum, movement was allowed which in some cases might strike us as absurd today: a four-year-old could be appointed bishop, or a six-year-old accede to the throne, as in England, simply because this person was in line for the position and it was not an option to bring someone in from a different part of the socioeconomic spectrum. As feudal society gradually gave way to urban, entrepreneurial society, however, the whole social structure began to melt.

---

1. The Anabaptists—radicals—largely attracted people of rural background, on the other hand. They were rural dwellers with ties to the agricultural economy, although they also included a disproportionate number of physicians, for reasons that are hard to explain. A brief observation is in order here about the culture of mainstream Protestantism. There is no denying that the Protestant Reformation appealed to a fairly narrow slice of the socioeconomic spectrum, and this continues to be reflected in the Protestant church today. While the Roman Catholic church appeals equally to people of many different backgrounds and levels of cultural sophistication, from slum dwellers to CEOs of multinationals and from factory workers to literati, this is not so of mainstream Protestantism—the magisterial end of the Protestant church. It still appeals mostly to the suburban bourgeois. The legitimate Protestant emphasis on preaching and hearing has taken the form of highly abstract sermons, guaranteed to tax the attention span of those without formal education, while Roman Catholic worship is more eye-oriented. The primacy of hearing over seeing is biblical: God speaks, but is not seen, in contrast to the pagan idols. On the other hand, restoring sight to the blind was a crucial part of Jesus' ministry. The Protestant wing of the church must readdress the visual depiction of the gospel, especially as the culture we live in has become percept- rather than concept-driven.

Revolts were unfolding all over Europe. There were the Munster rebellion of the radicals and the sociopolitical thrusts of the Anabaptists. There were efforts on the part of the rising middle class to limit the financial exclusivity of the nobility—anticipating the French Revolution. And there were peasant revolts. As we shall see, Luther initially supported the peasant cause, having told the knights for years that their oppression of the poor would give rise to savage uprisings. Acknowledging that the people were mistreated and exploited, he supported their cause in the revolt of 1524—that is, until they became murderous and unrestrained, threatening a social chaos in which no one could thrive, peasants included. At that point he helped to suppress the revolt, and the Marxists will never forgive him for it. Luther, however, knew what the alternative entailed.

At the height of the Reformation, cities such as Amsterdam that owned the new movement flourished economically and developed greater social mobility, while those that resisted the Reformation did not. The latter could not readily escape the economic control of the papacy. Canadian readers will find it interesting to make a comparison here with Quebec. Right up until the Quiet Revolution, francophone Quebec society was characteristically Roman Catholic, and as such it retained the socioeconomic mindset of feudalism. In some towns (e.g., St.-Jean-Port-Joli) you can find seigneuries built as late as the early 1900s and looking as if they came right out of the Middle Ages. The seigneurie was the large residence of the seigneur—the local aristocrat—and included a mill where people in the area brought their lumber and grain. There was no real business class in Quebec at that time, at least not among francophones; the business people and bankers were Montreal anglophones transplanted from Scotland. If the francophones were educated, they were trained in law, medicine, or theology, but rarely in business or economics or accounting. Only in the wake of the Quiet Revolution in the mid-1900s, when the church's influence and its feudalistic mindset were shed, did an educated entrepreneurial class develop among francophones in Quebec. This was happening several centuries earlier in Europe in those areas that adopted the Reformation.

In addition there was tension within the church between conciliarists, who believed that church authority should be vested in church councils, and papalists, who vested church authority in the pope. The Middle Ages had seen this dispute surge back and forth, with conciliarists poised to win on the eve of the Reformation. The Church of Rome, needing strong central leadership in the face of Protestant threat, ultimately adopted papalism. Conciliarism never reappeared thereafter.

This conflict over ecclesiastical leadership was accompanied by tension between scholastics and humanists within the church. Humanists were creatures of the Renaissance; they were preoccupied with literature and language, particularly Greek and Latin, and produced a great richness in those areas, but little philosophy. While they believed literature to have enormous capacity to transform humans, they regarded philosophy as obscurantist, focusing on minutiae and intellectual game-playing. The scholastics, on the other hand, were accomplished philosophers who moved in the orbit of medieval Aristotelianism. The most famous had been Thomas Aquinas (1224-1274), the pupil of Albertus Magnus, or Albert the Great; Aquinas travelled from Italy to Cologne in order to study under Albert, but obviously became much better known than his philosophical mentor. Other medieval scholastics, both before and after Aquinas, include Thomas Bradwardine, John Duns Scotus, John Scotus Erigena, and Bonaventura. The scholastic philosophical tradition, having assumed its characteristic outlook and competence during the Middle Ages, continued into the Renaissance and gave rise to such erudite Thomists as Cardinal Suarez, whose work underlies much of the Jesuit reading of Aquinas. Renaissance humanists, however, set this tradition aside. They regarded Aristotle as a fetter inhibiting intellectual adventure, including the pursuit of natural science. This tension between the humanists and scholastics was at its height on the eve of the Reformation.

Thanks to their academic formation, all the magisterial Reformers were humanist scholars before they were theologians. They wanted to free theology from philosophy, and since the philosophy in which theology had been embedded for so long was medieval Aristotelianism, they initially sided with the humanists in this regard—though, as we shall see, their agendas eventually diverged.

Finally, a third tension within the church existed between those who wanted a life of deeper interiority—or 'spirituality' in today's vocabulary—and those who set store by such things as masses for the dead, relics, and indulgences, or what might be called exteriority. More will be said about this in the next section.

One should not imagine a unified Christendom, then, which suddenly became fragmented under Luther's hammer. Enormous tensions already riddled Christendom on the eve of the Reformation. No leader, however able, ever leads in a vacuum. The Protestant Reformation was anticipated by, among other things, the twelfth-century Franciscan movement, with its emphasis on gospel integrity and preaching; social and intellectual turmoil in the thirteenth and fourteenth centuries; the Council of Constance in the fifteenth century (1414); and, of course, related to the Council, the appearance of Jan Hus (1373-1415). We shall look at some of these in greater detail.

DEPARTURES FROM MAINSTREAM RELIGION IN THE FIFTEENTH CENTURY

As has been noted already, there was considerable tension and unrest on the eve of the Reformation. Among other things, there were more than a few rumblings of religious disquiet among the rank and file of the church. One was the movement begun by Jan Hus, most of whose teachings came from John Wycliffe (1329-1384). The Hussite movement was noteworthy in that it was a self-declaration in a national sense as well as a religious sense. The relationship between the aspiration for national self-determination and theological recovery is one that we shall note more than once in our discussion of Luther.

In terms of religious practice, the express issue for the followers of Hus—the people of Husinec, Czech Republic—was utraquism, the reception of both elements of Holy Communion by the people as well as the priests. Up to this point the priest had received bread and wine at the Eucharist, while the people received bread only. This seemingly minor item unleashed an earthquake, for if all are alike in receiving communion, an important part of the distinction between priest and people collapses—or at least, the ground of such a distinction must be rethought—and the doctrine of ordination must be rearticulated. An apparently minor matter was therefore an issue of first importance, in fact, and would soon be paralleled by a development that collapsed another aspect of the clergy-laity distinction: the right of clergy to marry. Ecclesiastical self-determination was a second issue raised by this Hussite demand, and a third was the ultimate authority of Scripture over Rome and over tradition.

On such issues the Hussites obviously showed affinity with the later magisterial Reformers. On other issues they also had affinities with the radical Reformers, the Anabaptists. Like them, the Hussites were pacifists, while the magisterial Reformers believed that the state had the right to bear arms in self-protection. The Anabaptists, who gave rise to such people as the Mennonites, also advocated withdrawal from the world and from political involvement. They flourished in rural areas, where such withdrawal was easiest to accomplish. Hus himself was more closely aligned with the thinking of the Reformers, but the Bohemian or Czechoslovakian brethren who supported him affirmed much of what later became the Anabaptist understanding of Christian life.

The Hussite movement was like an oil geyser. As oil rushes out of the ground it needs someone to harness, package, and transport it, or it will continue to spew forth unproductively. At the time, there was no one to channel the Hussite movement and make it available on a wider front; it was Luther who would later appear as its champion when he declared his theological convictions at the Diet of Worms in 1521, exclaiming, "We are Hussites!"

The Waldensians were another movement at this time, originating in the Italian-French alpine region. They trained and commissioned people as missionaries, and differed importantly from the magisterial

Reformers in this respect because the latter, including Luther, were so thoroughly preoccupied with the Reformation and the need to forge doctrine that they overlooked missions. The Waldensians cherished Scripture, routinely memorizing long passages, and expressed their faithfulness to the gospel by eschewing ostentation and pursuing a simple lifestyle. Rejecting purgatory and the remembrance of the saints as unbiblical, they nonetheless participated in the liturgy of the church. They were also sacramentarians; that is, unlike sacramentalists, they tended to look upon the sacraments as symbolic only. The Waldensians made a lasting contribution that the magisterial Reformers were able to take up, modify in key areas, and use with their more subtle intellectual equipment and their greater social opportunity.

In addition to these new movements, there was a religious semi-underground that had existed throughout the Middle Ages. These were people who rejected pretense and power, who craved greater interiority (or 'spirituality'), who understood that Christians are constituted such by faith. They regarded the triumphalism of the church as a contradiction of the gospel and repudiated the perverseness and corruption of the church. One such movement was the *Devotio Moderna*, which embraced a quasi-mystical form of interiority. Followers of this movement always knew that the work of Christ for us, on our behalf, also has to be done in us, or it profits us nothing, and they recognized that this could be done only through faith. However, the various groups under the *Devotio Moderna* were not uniform. Some were less theologically orthodox, others more concerned with moral renovation.[2]

CHALLENGES TO PAPAL POWER

Erastianism, which takes its name from Thomas Erastus, born 1524, is the notion that the state has the right to intervene and overrule in

---

2. An interesting study would be a comparison between the *Devotio Moderna* and today's charismatic movement, in terms of the range of biblical orthodoxy observable in both.

church affairs. In the sixteenth century, state control of the church was preferred over papal control of church and state, if only because the state could promote Reformational convictions and ensure compliance with them. Since the state was ordained by God no less than the church, each exercised authority in relation to the other: the state guaranteed the social order essential to the church's institutional life, while the church informed the state of God's mandate concerning it. However unacceptable many might find such an agreement today, and however eager Christians might be to insist that the only authority the church has is the peculiar authority of the gospel, it must always be kept in mind that the social situation was different in the sixteenth century when late medievalism was giving way to modernity. Living as they were on the edge of uninhabitable social chaos, the people of that era could endorse such notions as the divine right of kings, or political absolutism, because the alternative was worse.

The conviction concerning the state's authority, allied with rising political and national self-consciousness, helped unseat the notion that Rome was the God-appointed locus of church administration. The primacy of Rome was further called into question when the medieval document on which it was founded, the Donation of Constantine, was exposed as a forgery. What, then, grounded Rome's claim to primacy with respect to the church? Furthermore, in the absence of any evidence that Peter had ever been in Rome, the so-called Petrine authority of the Roman See did not rest on any actual connection between Saint Peter and that city—a point that the Reformers never failed to exploit.

Meanwhile in France and England, no little power had already been transferred from the papacy to secular rulers. There, for instance, the state was appointing bishops and priests.[3] In sixteenth-century

---

3.   As a matter of fact, the Queen still appoints the Archbishop of Canterbury. The tombstone of John Newton in England says that he was a 'clerk'; it makes no mention of his being a Church of England clergyman. That is because, to this day, all Church of England clergy are civil servants: clerks in holy orders. For centuries their living has been guaranteed by the crown.

England the state had already flexed its muscle by enacting restrictions on papal exactions, having recognized the people's resentment at the flow of money out of their country to Rome. For this reason the state's appointment of bishops and priests aroused little controversy in either England or France.

The picture was slightly different in Germany, but this was because of political fragmentation, not because of sympathy for papal power. Germany, it must be remembered, consisted of over three hundred political entities each ruled by its own prince, with no centralized government or monarchy. Although some German princes were almost as powerful as English kings, others were virtually powerless. Germany had a nationalistic drive and plenty of anticlerical sentiment, but lacked the political unity to concretize either its nationalism or its anticlericalism. When Luther arrived on the scene, he ignited kindling laid long before.

ECCLESIASTICAL CORRUPTION AND THE CHURCH'S IMAGE

Ecclesiastical corruption and the people's perception of it became another factor in the religious tension of the time. The papacy, always in need of money for its projects at home and abroad, needed effective means of financing itself. Heavy taxation provoked hostility in many; the indulgence system, an exploitation of people's fears concerning God's judgment, would become an outrage. The selling of ecclesiastical offices, or sinecures, was yet another unpopular method of raising funds. Pope Leo X (1475-1521) garnered vast amounts of money in this way. A sinecure was a lifelong appointment as priest, paid for by the appointee. It carried a guaranteed annual salary, but as this was less than the interest earned by Rome on its investment of the purchase price, the papacy made money on the arrangement. The Renaissance popes were masters at this,[4] and became superbly effective diplomats

---

4.   See Barbara Tuchman's *The March of Folly* (New York: Ballantine, 1984), chapter 3, *passim*.

and statesmen—a dazzling compend of duplicity, sophistication, genius, and, where necessary, out-and-out corruption.[5]

Dispensations were also sold profitably at this time, particularly with respect to marrying within forbidden degrees of consanguinity and confraternity. While marrying one's brother or sister, for instance, was always forbidden, marrying a blood relative or marital relative of slightly lesser degree was permitted upon the transfer of money.

Concerning religious matters, the higher clergy—bishops and cardinals—had functioned for hundreds of years as feudal overlords. Bishops were often appointed not on the strength of theological learning or Christian character but as a reward for their political support of secular rulers. Since ecclesiastical position entailed social prominence, money, and power, the higher clergy naturally tended to be preoccupied with these. They were not typically regarded as spiritual fathers or advisers; they were people of wealth and prestige, expected to pour themselves into the characteristic pursuits of the upper classes: hunting, the arts, politics, and finance. No one was surprised if a bishop was not found at his residence working at church matters. Instead, bishops drew their stipend and then hired subordinates at a lower rate to meet people and conduct services. Some, of course—men of spiritual discernment such as the Englishman John Fisher (1469-1535)—protested, but they were frequently hamstrung by a system that served both the secular powers and ambitious clerics.

Meanwhile the lower clergy at this time were poorly educated for the most part, with minimal grasp of their responsibility. They were to celebrate mass, for example, but the mass was recited in Latin, and many knew no Latin; they simply memorized the words, oblivious to

---

5. They did not have the field to themselves, however: they had to deal with political rulers such as the Hapsburgs. Politically, Rome had lost touch with European national sensitivities, never sufficiently recognizing the desire for national self-determination. While Europe was emerging from medieval feudalism into the modern world, Rome was trying to restrict it to a medieval mindset.

their meaning.[6] They had other tasks, too, such as hearing confession, but had been given little help for their work of "spiritual formation" and frequently had little time for it in any case: poorly paid, they had to supplement their income with another occupation. Needless to say, the magisterial Reformers, along with the Catholic reformation underway at the same time, would emphasize the need for remuneration adequate to obviate such "moonlighting," as well as the need for literacy and learning equal to the relentless demands of preaching and pastoral work. This is not to impugn the footsoldiers of the church; many of the lower clergy, if not most, did their work conscientiously. They merely lacked sufficient tools for the work they had taken up.

All clergy were sworn to celibacy, but many violated this vow. In the late medieval period there was a tax on the children of priests, and an extraordinary tax on the children of bishops. Many priests kept mistresses. In a small town or village the priest's mistress and his children were known to everyone and despised. As the mistress of a priest was unemployable by anyone else, she became the priest's economic prisoner. The church winked at this concubinage, reckoning it one step better than promiscuity.

THE RELIGIOUS LIFE OF THE COMMON PEOPLE

Among the common people, the prevailing mood was frequently fear. In their fragility people feared much, not least the plague.[7] The plague swept Europe between 1348 and 1352, climaxing in 1349, and in its wake one third of Europe's population disappeared; France, being more densely populated, lost almost half its population. People also

---

6.   The expression *hocus pocus*, for example, meaning "magic," is a corruption of the Latin words *hoc est meum corpus* ("This is my body") spoken quickly in consecrating the bread during the mass.

7.   For the effect of the plague in Europe see Heiko Oberman, *The Two Reformations* (New Haven: Yale University Press, 2003), chapter 5.

feared new diseases, including syphilis,[8] and they feared what we would consider ordinary sickness: lacking the medicine and surgery we now take for granted, people routinely died of pneumonia, blood poisoning, or appendicitis. Life was manifestly fragile.

Hell was a very potent source of fear as well, and this was readily exploited on the eve of the Reformation. If the people tended to see all clerical figures as something halfway between a lawyer and a judge, it was because they tended to see Christ, whose representatives these leaders were, in the same way. They regarded Christ largely in terms of his capacity as judge. Luther's articulation of the gospel would change this by magnifying Jesus' role as the Good Shepherd, the atoning sin-bearer. Luther would recover the truth that the Judge who is uncompromisingly just—for sin can never be winked at—is also Justifier, is also Father: he puts in the right with him those currently in the wrong, and so makes them his sons and daughters. On the eve of the Reformation, however, hell remained vivid in the popular imagination.

There was also a fear of Turkish (i.e., Islamic) invasion; the Ottoman Empire had been moving steadily westward. Luther was in northeast Germany, that is, Prussia, with the Turks next door. It was widely feared that an Islamic invasion was imminent, and church bells tolled regularly to summon people to pray against the threat. Europeans had not forgotten that in the seventh and eighth centuries Islamic armies had conquered everything from Spain to India. Understandably, fear of Islamic aggression was ingrained in the public consciousness.

If the religious life of the common people was permeated by fear, it was also characterized by a credulous readiness for revelations, theophanies, portents, and miraculous signs, especially visual manifestations. For example, in a village in Brandenburg it was claimed that a wafer had secreted the blood of Christ, and in no time huge pilgrimages

---

8. Named after the title character of a Latin poem by Girolamo Fracastoro, Veronese physician and poet and the supposed first victim of the disease.

were underway to see this phenomenon.[9] At one point Frederick the Wise (1463-1525), Luther's staunch protector, had seventeen thousand relics stored in the castle church: body pieces from the saints, pieces of wood from the true cross, and breast milk from the Virgin Mary.

Speaking of the Virgin: veneration of Mary was another feature of the religion of the common people. As noted already, their predominant image of Jesus was as judge coming to punish the wicked; his saving and intercessory work had receded far into the background. But every human being has an unappeasable hunger for a savior, a redeemer, an intercessor, and this role became Mary's: she was felt to be gentle and pitying and human, softer and kinder than Jesus. The Reformers were to address this matter at length, magnifying our Lord's humanity especially as our sin-bearer and intercessor. It is when the humanity of Jesus is allowed to recede, so that his effectual sin-bearing oneness with all humankind is lost to sight and his intercession on behalf of his people disappears, that Mary is handed the role of intercessor or co-redemptrix. Someone must be summoned to furnish human solidarity with sinners. Indeed, the heart of Reformation theology is Christology. While the Reformers denounced medieval Marianism frontally as idolatry, they did a great deal to dismantle it simply by their understanding of Jesus as the one who not only mediates God to humankind, but savingly represents and thereby mediates all humankind to God.

---

9.   With respect to the wafer secreting blood: it is tempting to see this as a kind of naïve silliness with some spiritual significance, but no social significance. It is important to recognize, however, that nothing in the public consciousness lacks social significance; all theological assertions have social consequences. There was a relationship between blood-secreting wafers, for example, and the medieval blood myths surrounding the Jews—that they used the blood of a slain Christian child to make matzo, or that they somehow put a hex on the blood of Christ in the Eucharist. These myths legitimized hatred of the Jews. Similarly, the reason there were so many people on hand to see Luther nail his *Ninety-Five Theses* to the door of the Wittenberg church was that he had chosen to do so on the anniversary of the promulgation of an indulgence, an occasion whose portentous character attracted large crowds.

However, it would be inaccurate to suggest that the religious outlook of the common people could be summed up definitively in this mix of fear, credulity, and Marian veneration. All the while there were evidences of deeper spirituality among the laity within the bosom of the church. The Brethren of the Common Life, chiefly in Holland and Germany, lived simply, soberly, and piously, working diligently and devotedly among the impoverished and the marginalized. Yet the greater contribution of the Brethren, perhaps, lay in their work as educators. Erasmus, the Renaissance's leading humanist, and Gabriel Biel, the theologian whose work was to be the doctrinal foil for the Reformation, were both schooled at the hands of the Brethren of the Common Life. The Brethren never wanted to overturn Roman theology, or even forge new doctrine for the church; they assumed that the current teaching was true, and found in the Roman church everything they needed spiritually. For this reason few of them sided with the Reformation. They anticipated it, however, in at least one respect: they had vernacular translations of the Bible and memorized lengthy passages of Scripture.

There was also a mystical aspect to the religious self-consciousness of this era. Whether mysticism is a good word or a bad one in your vocabulary depends on your theological predilection. According to some Protestants, mysticism, lacking the concreteness and specificity of the gospel, is "esoteric atheism" (to use the words of Karl Barth). To be sure, there is a mysticism that has nothing to do with the gospel, that tends to confuse experience of God with an experience of the creation in terms of those depths of the creation that are beyond words—the kind of moving experience one has while standing at the edge of the dock in summer, or gazing at the mountains. At the same time, there is a true and profound mysticism normed, formed, and informed by Christ, nothing less than the surge of the Holy Spirit upon a person so as to render that person vividly aware of God's immediacy and intimacy. Mystics have always known that without this, the Christian life is reduced to rationalist cerebralism or the mere shuffling of doctrinal vocabulary: another philosophy that happens to deploy theological terms. Instances of mysticism appear throughout Scripture: Paul hearing the voice and seeing the light on the Damascus road, the two disciples' encounter with Christ on the road to Emmaus, Isaiah's visitation in the temple, and the vividness of the prophets' vocation are only a few examples of experiences that were nothing if not mystical. Without them, what is the Christian life? Joy Davidman, wife of C. S. Lewis, in trying to describe her coming to faith, remarked, "How do you gather the ocean into a teacup?"[10]

Undeniably, mysticism was also part of Luther's understanding of Christian spiritual life. Protestants, in their understandable zeal for correct doctrine, characteristically undervalue the dimension of spiritual experience in the magisterial Reformers and therefore read past descriptions of the latter in their writings. So much is heard of Luther's *simul peccator, simul totus iustus*—that the believer is both wholly sinful and wholly justified at the same time. Overlooked, however, is his no less characteristic description of the believer as *simul gemitus, simul raptus*—groaning with his own and the earth's anguish, and at the same time "caught up to the third heaven" (2 Cor. 12:2) in unutterable joy. It appears again and again in Luther's writings; he lived in the Spirit and knew that theology at all times subserves an intimate, life-altering engagement with God himself. Certainly the Reformers rejected a mysticism of vague religiosity that was not Christ-normed. Still, their close reading of Scripture found them gladly acknowledging the experiential dimension of faith, the "Word in the heart".[11]

The *Devotio Moderna*, mentioned earlier, embraced mysticism, as did the Brethren of the Common Life. Their mysticism tended to be inward-looking, however; it did not direct Christians outwards nor equip them to contend with a world exponentially enlarged by the Renaissance and navigational instruments. It could not inform and

---

10.   I am unable to recover the reference concerning this aphorism that has remained with me.

11.   See Heiko Oberman, *The Reformation*, trans. by Andrew Gow (Grand Rapids: Eerdmans, 1994), chapter 4.

sustain the rising entrepreneurial class in Europe—the businessperson, the banker, the trader, the industrialist. These people wanted to be equipped as Christians for engaging the world, but to engage the world one must be theologically apprised of the nature of the world, as well as of "the fullness of the blessing of the gospel of Christ" (Rom. 15:29). The mysticism in the church on the eve of the Reformation provided little or no theological structure; in the view of the Reformers, it lacked iron. The Reformers aimed at steeling the Christian's experience of her Lord through a rereading of the gospel.

THEOLOGICAL TRENDS ON THE
EVE OF THE REFORMATION

By the end of the fifteenth century, the rich complexity of medieval scholasticism was giving way to the less nuanced nominalism of William of Occam (1280-1349). Occam and his followers emphasized God's will, but without relating God's will to God's nature. They understood will in terms of sheer power, and power as the capacity to act. In their account of God's power, God was able to do anything at all except what is by definition impossible; he could not make a square circle, since that is self-contradictory, nor annihilate himself, since he exists necessarily. But anything that was in principle possible, God could do. Grace, in turn, was understood in terms of will, that is, as subordinate to will.

The Protestant Reformers were to disagree with this on several fronts. First, they would say, grace is not subordinate to will, but will to grace. Grace is God acting in conformity to his nature—love—to enact and preserve his covenant faithfulness with sinful humankind. Such love, when it collides with sin, takes the form of mercy. Grace, then, is the loving God (love is what he is, not merely something that he does) acting effectively to rescue those whose predicament is otherwise hopeless. Grace is God's salvific act.

Secondly, the Protestant Reformers would fault nominalism because it begins with philosophical speculation: What is God able to do? What are the limits to his ability to do? The Reformers maintained that no one knows what God can or cannot do, what might be the sort of limit to what God can do. Rooted in the gospel, they insisted that we know only what God has done, as made plain by the apostles: he has incarnated himself in the one from Nazareth and given himself up to suffering, degradation, and death—specifically, the self-alienation of death in the dereliction at Calvary. This event determines our understanding of God's grace and God's will. And what of God's power? Power, for the Reformers, is not mere capacity to act but the capacity to achieve purpose. God's purpose is to restore a fallen world to its Edenic integrity, and he achieves this purpose by means of incarnation and the cross. In other words, the power of God is defined by the achievement of God wherein he acts not only most mightily but also most characteristically: the cross. To begin anywhere else, said the Reformers, or to proceed in any other direction, is to become lost in the miasma of philosophical speculation.

William of Occam hugely magnified God's will and omnipotence, but without reference to biblical logic. Omnipotence was understood as unrestricted power—power to do anything at all. But sheer power, power for its own sake, is just what Scripture means by the devil, by evil. How can it be predicated of God? God's power must surely be understood in the light of the cross. His omnipotence is the unlimited capacity to achieve his purpose, and his purpose is to save the world. Luther was later to insist, with typical pithiness, that apart from Jesus Christ, God and the devil were indistinguishable.[12]

In the light of the cross it is plain that there is no limit to God's vulnerability. This is a radical challenge to the Occamist understanding of power, and lies at the heart of Reformation theology. Luther, especially, would say that to understand the nature of omnipotence we must look at the helplessness of a baby, the helplessness of a Jew crucified between two unsavory men at the edge of the city dump. God rendered himself

---

12. See Gerhard O. Forde, *The Captivation of the Will: Luther vs. Erasmus on Freedom and Bondage* (Grand Rapids: Eerdmans, 2005), p. 45.

utterly vulnerable at the cross, and remains characteristically vulnerable. Such vulnerability—helplessness, in some respects—is not tantamount to ineffectiveness, however. On the contrary, Christ's resurrection guarantees the effectiveness of God's vulnerability. It does not transcend or terminate that vulnerability, for that will not happen until the eschaton— the day of our Lord's appearing—when his purpose is fully accomplished. Meanwhile, the risen Jesus suffers still. John's gospel records that he was raised wounded, and the rest of the New Testament tells us that the risen and ascended Jesus continues to suffer in the suffering of the world, and preeminently in the suffering of his people. When Paul is apprehended on the Damascus road, the voice he hears does not ask, "Why are you persecuting my people?" but "Why are you persecuting me?" The risen, ascended, sovereign Lord is still vulnerable.

It is not difficult to understand why Occam's nominalism, with its absolutizing of God's omnipotence, typified theology on the eve of the Reformation. If the secular authority in that politically absolutist era exercised unqualified coercive power, why would God not behave in a similar way for similar reasons?[13]

Clearly the Reformation approach to all theological matters was to be not only Christocentric (Jesus Christ as the focus of theological thought) but above all Christological (Jesus Christ understood according to the logic of the Hebrew Bible). Christology would determine the shape of all aspects of Reformation theology, not least of which was ecclesiology. When the Reformers insisted that the church is *reformata, semper reformanda* (reformed and always being reformed), they meant that the church must always interrogate its life and faith in the light of the logic of Scripture—not once only, but repeatedly. Otherwise, every denomi-

---

13. If Christians today are reluctant to surrender an unbiblical understanding of omnipotence as sheer unmodified power, perhaps it is because deep in our hearts we aspire to omnipotence ourselves. Fallen humankind relishes the capacity to coerce, and since one aspect of the Fall is to create God in the image of humankind, it is not surprising that we impute to God what we crave for ourselves, our *ersatz* worship thereby reinforcing what is actually a sign of depravity.

nation unconsciously allows extraneous elements to be superimposed upon Scripture and become a lens through which it is read. The result, said the Reformers, was the paganization of the church.

CULTURAL FORCES AIDING THE REFORMATION

The socioeconomic forces at work have already been discussed briefly. It has been noted that the Reformation was largely an urban phenomenon and that those cities which embraced it developed greater economic vitality and social mobility. But the economic vitality of pro-Reformation cities was always related to a cultural vitality. Literacy, for example, spread much more rapidly through these towns, while the flow of traders and craftsmen from one town to another resulted in new practices and new ideation.

The recently-invented printing press had a crucial role in this development. It is an exaggeration to say, as some do, that the printing press made the Reformation; nevertheless, the Reformation is inconceivable without it. The printing press was, of course, allied with the increase in literacy sponsored by both the humanists and the Reformers. Just as it served humanism by making available plentiful, inexpensive copies of ancient texts, it supported the Reformation through the production of three types of documents.

The first type was major theological writings, the tomes that everyone associates with the Reformation. Although Luther did not write a systematic theology, he did write voluminously and tellingly; the fifty-five volumes of his *Works*, still in print, attest the cruciality of the print medium for the Reformation. His friend and associate Philip Melanchthon penned the first systematic theology of the Reformation, *Loci Communes* (Common Places or theological topics), which went through several editions between 1521 and 1555. It proved enormously influential: Elizabeth I memorized huge tracts of it and made it mandatory reading for Church of England clergy.[14] Another document

---

14.   Its influence is apparent in Thomas Cranmer's *Book of Common Prayer*.

of this type was John Calvin's *Institutes of the Christian Religion,* a systematic theology that underlies all Protestant thought in non-German-speaking lands. Even those critical of some aspects of it—John Wesley disagreed with the doctrine of predestination, for example—are indebted to it and exemplify its spirit far more than they contradict it. Calvin's *Institutes,* though upwards of 2,000 pages long, represents only 6.8% of all of his written output. Heinrich Bullinger, the Reformer who succeeded Ulrich Zwingli in Zurich, produced a corpus greater than that of Luther and Calvin combined. Obviously, then, the Reformers wrote much in addition to systematic theology.

The second type of printed document that advanced the Reformation was occasional writings or tracts. Through their occasional writings, which were much more likely to be read by ordinary people than the huge theological tomes, the magisterial Reformers were able to impress their convictions on vast areas of Europe. Luther was a master at this, but he was not alone. Much good theology was articulated through occasional writings, and has been since the Reformation as well: John Wesley (1703-1791) wrote no systematic theology, but produced a great number of occasional writings to address disputes on specific topics, leaving behind an enduring legacy for the church as a whole. A thinker who writes systematically may be easier to get hold of, but is not necessarily a superior thinker to the one who produces only occasional writings.

The third type of writing was the pamphlet. If relatively few people read systematic theology and more read occasional writing, far more read pamphlets. Pamphlets penetrated public consciousness. They proliferated throughout the Reformation, and had such telling effect because of their accessibility. A pamphlet written in 1523 by Heinrich von Kettenbach, for instance, drew forty-nine contrasts between the biblical ministry of Jesus and the anti-Christian behavior of the pope. One can imagine the effect that would have had among people who were never going to read Philip Melanchthon's *Loci* or Calvin's *Institutes.*

In addition to the printing press, there was the establishment of new universities. The older universities did not support the Reformation, but the newer ones proved more receptive. The University of Wittenberg, having been established in 1502, was brand new when Luther went there for the first time in 1508. His most formidable and persistent foe, John Eck (1486-1543), who opposed him at Leipzig in 1519, at Worms in 1521, and at Augsburg in 1530, belonged to the University of Ingolstadt, one of the oldest universities in Germany. The Reformation was a young person's movement and as such was supported by those universities whose newness enabled them to be more innovative and adventuresome.

Universities have traditionally been the mouthpiece of intellectual developments, which is why dictators typically shut them down. Nowadays, however, their role has changed as the whole intellectual climate has changed. Far from being centers of theological ferment, universities are increasingly less reputed for intellectual ferment in any of the humanities, and still less in the field of theology. The empiricism of the Enlightenment fostered the pre-eminence of science in the public profile of the university, followed by the elevation of the social sciences, while the liberal arts struggle to maintain intellectual rigor if not to survive. Although universities promote what is deemed a human good by facilitating scientific and social scientific research, the humanities are less visible in their promotion of a humanistic good, and the department of theology is scarcely the showpiece for any university's fundraising. In addition, while many universities were founded by churches, most have now abandoned their theological roots. Gone are the days when the president of Canada's most prestigious university—Toronto— was a clergyman. At the time of the Reformation, however, theology was a major item in the university, and a department of theology was considered essential. As a result, the universities proved crucial in the spread of the new movement.

JAN HUS

Jan Hus is important not only for his theology, which anticipated the Reformation, but also as an early rallying point for that movement in light of his treatment at the hands of the church. Having been promised a safe conduct to the Council of Constance, he was then executed by church authorities, and thus became a symbol for ecclesiastical treachery. Those who subsequently swelled the Reformation often exhorted each other to "Remember Jan Hus!" in much the same spirit that Americans once said "Remember the Alamo!"

Hus was born in 1369 of a peasant family in Husinec in Bohemia, part of what is now the Czech Republic. It was ruled at that time by King Charles, whose son Wenceslas (immortalized in the Christmas carol "Good King Wenceslas") succeeded him when Hus was an adult. A brilliant scholar at the University of Prague, Hus was ordained priest after eleven years of formal study. Near the university stood a large church known as the Bethlehem Chapel, a non-parish church built and supported by Czech nobles as a locus of protest.

This protest was twofold, addressing the lack of scriptural teaching and the inaccessibility of the Latin mass. The leaders of the Bethlehem Chapel wanted services in the vernacular and biblical preaching, both of which were to be hallmarks of the Reformation and essential to its advance. The Chapel pulpit was therefore always filled by a notable Czech preacher and scholar, scholarship being regarded as integral to good preaching. Although these preacher-scholars were *bona fide* priests, they were suspected by the ecclesiastical hierarchy because their brilliance, learning and theological orientation rendered them hard to control. The hierarchy would have liked to dismantle the Bethlehem Chapel, but were reluctant to do so in view of the pressure exerted by the nobility.

Two years after his ordination, Hus was appointed to the pulpit of the Bethlehem Chapel, where he preached scholarly evangelical sermons twice each Sunday to a large and influential congregation. Soon he was appointed chaplain to the royal court, confessor to the queen, and president of the University of Prague. As Hus was theologically informed by the work of English proto-reformer John Wycliffe, his preaching always urged reform, and his reforming zeal soon made him the target of ecclesiastical espionage. One Sunday, recognizing a spy in the congregation, Hus paused in the sermon, pointed to the man, and said, "Fellow, be sure not to miss the next sentence." In those days a clergyman and his theology could easily become the focus of public controversy, posing a threat to the powers in a way that is hard to imagine nowadays. Boldness was required.[15]

Until the Council of Constance in 1414, Hus was not legally under condemnation for proclaiming Wycliffe's doctrine, because it was only then that Wycliffe himself was condemned. Informally, however, Hus was strongly opposed by ecclesiastical authorities. Among other things, he was vocal in his objection to the traffic in indulgences, an issue that was to resurface time and time again in the church.[16] Still, he had the king and queen of Bohemia on his side. The archbishop in turn co-opted the king of Hungary, brother of the king of Bohemia, and together they decided to do their best to eliminate Hus. The archbishop secured from Rome a twofold order to be used against Hus. One was to burn Wycliffe's works, and the other was to shut down non-parish churches such as the Bethlehem Chapel. The archbishop did manage to seize and burn most of Wycliffe's books in the university library, while the clergy looked on approvingly: Wycliffe, later to be known as the "morning star" of the Reformation, was already deemed an abomination.

Hus continued to preach in his chapel, however, arguing that little weight could be placed on a papal order when there were rival claimants to the papacy, as there indeed were at that time.[17] He wondered aloud

---

15.   The incident is reminiscent of one involving Martin Niemöller (1892-1984), famed for his resistance to Hitler. One Sunday morning in his Berlin church, Niemöller noticed a member of the Gestapo planted in the congregation and said, "Could someone next to Mister Police Officer please help him find his place in the hymnbook? Someone help that spy, as he doesn't even know where Mark's gospel is." Niemöller was eventually arrested and spent eight years in prison.

16.   Even in the year 2000, Pope John Paul II facilitated a new indulgence for the millennium year. It did not receive widespread recognition, and embarrassed many Roman Catholics.

17.   Significantly, Alexander V, who was pope at the time, died mysteriously of poisoning.

how many vicars of Christ there could be. He catalysed the Bohemian nobles in protesting the twofold order at the popeless Vatican, while the civil courts ruled that the archbishop had to reimburse the university for the destroyed books. The archbishop refused, so the court seized his property. Riots broke out and a new pope was elected in 1410, John XXIII (later denounced as a nonlegitimate pope). He appointed Cardinal Colonna to handle the matter, and Colonna summoned Hus to Rome. Hus refused to go, whereupon the cardinal excommunicated him and directed the state to execute him. Hus, supported by devotees of the Bethlehem Chapel, ignored the condemnation and simply kept on preaching.

In the meantime, Pope John XXIII had declared war on Naples; note that it was not the state but the pope, head of a religious institution, that declared war. He needed money in order to wage this war, however, and the fastest way of raising it was to sell indulgences. When the indulgence sellers arrived in Prague, they were greeted in much the same way that they would be greeted in Wittenberg one hundred years later; namely, the whole matter of indulgences was hailed as a matter for university debate.

The university condemned the traffic in indulgences. When the sale continued, riots broke out. Three theology students from the University of Prague who supported Hus were beheaded, and Hus sympathizers gave them a huge funeral in the Bethlehem Chapel. Rome countered by excommunicating Hus for the second time, while the archbishop put the city under an interdict. This meant that the city was deprived of all spiritual consolation: no marriages, burials, confessions, absolutions, baptisms, last rites, or other such ceremonies could be administered according to the rubric of the church. Understandably the incident plunged people into despair and panic, dependent as they were upon the sacramental ministrations of the church for their earthly comfort and their eternal well-being.

Hus was then hidden for several years in the castles of various noblemen, as Luther would be later on. Pope John XXIII, prodded by the king, convened a general council in Constance, Switzerland. Hus was not the only matter for the council's consideration; in fact, he was a somewhat minor item on the agenda. But he felt he had to go because he wanted to reply to the charge of Wycliffite heresy. Church authorities pledged that he would not be molested if he emerged from hiding and presented himself at the council. Trusting this promise, Hus journeyed to Constance in October of 1414. Upon arrival, however, he was charged with denying transubstantiation by way of affirming that bread remained on the altar after consecration. Hus repudiated the charge, insisting that his position on the Lord's Supper was thoroughly Roman. It was, in fact, but the substance of his preached gospel was decidedly different.

Hus was arrested, chained in a dungeon, and interrogated under torture for the next several months. Back in Prague, people were incensed at the treatment their friend and hero had received, and moved closer to the soon-to-be Protestant position by receiving Holy Communion in both kinds. In the Middle Ages this was an explosive act, for, as noted already above, the reception of Holy Communion in both kinds by the laity constituted a challenge to the authority of the church. It also challenged a sacerdotal theology of ordination, as surely as did the subsequent introduction of clergy marriage. A huge step had been taken.

Hus was asked to recant. He refused. In another anticipation of the Reformation, he appealed to his conscience under the norm of Scripture, as Luther was to do at Worms in 1521. He was taken to the stake and again refused to recant, declaring, to the irritation of his accusers, "In the truth of the gospel which I have written, taught, and preached, I will die today with gladness." It was July 1415; he had gone to Constance in October 1414 and had been ill-treated for nine months. Not surprisingly, then, when Luther ventured from Wittenberg to Worms, his anxiety mounted with every mile. Hus had been promised a safe conduct to Constance, then in an unforeseeable reversal had been arrested and detained, and was dead nine months later.

Back in Bohemia, a twelve-year war broke out, fed by zeal for religious reform and national self-determination in that alliance which was to appear repeatedly in the course of the Reformation.

Despite the charge of denying transubstantiation, the real problem with Hus lay in the gospel he preached. Moreover, his work in Bethlehem Chapel escaped ecclesiastical control, and few things infuriate church authorities more than a young, able preacher whom they cannot control and whose appeal they therefore cannot curtail. This is not to suggest that Hus was in any sense a smart aleck, self-importantly flouting church authority (as Michael Servetus was to flout it next century in Calvin's Geneva). His preaching in the Bethlehem Chapel, however, fostered major ferment among his hearers, and was welcomed by a class of politically powerful nobles who were not about to be told what to do by a foreign power—as they now regarded Rome.

Hus's story is significant. He understood the importance of scholarship for weekly preaching in the local congregation; his years of rigorous academic study were essential to the theological and spiritual leadership required by the coming Reformation and exemplified the crucial role played by the universities in a movement that would attract young intellectual luminaries. Philip Melanchthon was only fourteen years old when he went off to university, and after the death of Erasmus in 1531 was the brightest star in the scholarly firmament of Europe. In Prague's Bethlehem Chapel, the preacher was always a scholar, and brought his scholarship to bear on his preaching. If theology is a minor matter in today's university and theology professors attract little attention alongside the prizewinners in molecular biology and mathematics, the church has not done much better. For the church seems to have lost confidence in the integrity of its theology, as it appears to have lost confidence in the saving power of the gospel and in its Lord as the one in whom "everything holds together" (Col. 1:17), including the subparticles of post-Einsteinian physics. Meanwhile, the notion has arisen that the 'common people' cannot appreciate teaching that is theologically rich, when the observable reality is just the opposite: ordinary parishioners hunger for greater substance and are tired of dilute fare.[18] Unfortunately, evangelical churches today are not looking for scholars to fill their pulpits, and until they do, congregations will not develop the theological iron they need to engage our society.

Another important lesson in the story of Hus is that every theological statement has psychological, social, and political consequences. Hus was not aiming to rock the authorities, but that was the direct result of the integrity of his preaching. Similarly, in Nazi Germany the confessing church (as distinct from the national church) was not out to defy political authority *per se,* but when people like Asmussen, Bonhoeffer, and Niemöller preached the gospel, defiance of Hitler was both unavoidable and unmistakable. Preaching the gospel may not appear to be a political act in itself, but it inevitably implies one. In the same way, as we shall see, the Reformers a century after Hus were to affect virtually every aspect of society as the gospel they preached became the vehicle of the sovereign Lord's claim upon and restoration of the entire creation.

---

18. Often these are older people schooled in a different generation, while many younger people with postgraduate degrees have less appreciation of solid theological content. This may have as much to do with the quality of today's educational system as with the state of people's hearts.

2

Humanism in the Fifteenth Century

A NEW WAY OF LOOKING AT THE WORLD

Humanism is rooted in the Renaissance. The Renaissance began in the mid-1400s, by most reckonings, and was not intentionally antireligious or antiChristian at its inception. In fact, there is considerable debate as to the relationship between the Reformation and the Renaissance: were they "birds of a feather", a single phenomenon with a religious and non-religious component? Or were they ultimately antithetical, even if their mutual exclusivity was not recognized at first? Did they begin together and then diverge as each developed? And how do humanist studies relate to theological studies? Questions like these were posed in the sixteenth century and are still being addressed today.

The Renaissance was first of all a transition from a medieval worldview to a modern one. This transition had at least four major aspects: development of the scientific method; a boom in geographic exploration; cultural and intellectual exchange fostered by increased trade and commerce; and a new emphasis on the individual.

The Renaissance saw the beginnings of modern empirical science, science based on observation of what actually happened in the natural world instead of on philosophical deductions about what ought to happen. More sophisticated astronomy, for instance, and particularly the work of Copernicus and Galileo, indicated that the planets described elliptical orbits rather than the circular ones prescribed by Aristotelian physics on the basis of the circle being the perfect figure. The "macro" investigations made in astronomy were paralleled by the "micro" investigations in anatomy by Andreas Vesalius (1514-1564).

Far-reaching inquiries, burgeoning now on all fronts, spilled over into curiosity about the earth as the human environment, making geography an important discipline. The geographical explorations undertaken at this time represented a spirit of risktaking, a cutting loose from the safe and conventional so as to shed anything inhibiting or confining. The village, the province, and even the nation were simply too small; there was a notion that the human self should be extended further afield in endeavors of greater human significance. At the same time, a new impetus arose for trade and commerce, and this produced extensive cultural and intellectual cross-fertilization as traders brought their own worlds with them from one urban center to the next. Obviously, the consequences of increased trade and commerce were primarily economic, but they brought an end to cultural ghettoism as well.

Early humanism also magnified individual effort. The guild system of the late medieval period, involving coppersmiths, wheelwrights, carpenters, and other practitioners of skilled crafts, was a form of collectivity; it would be an anachronism to describe it as a collectivity in the Marxist sense, but it was a collectivity of sorts. It began to dissolve, however, as greater scope and encouragement was given to individual effort in the Renaissance.

Not surprisingly, this multifaceted shift in outlook had a political dimension. Every era is characterized by a different way of seeing the world, as reflected in sociopolitical realities. There was one way under the Greek empire, and a slightly different way under the Romans. The barbarian hordes sweeping down from the Danube in the winter of 406 certainly ushered in a very different way of perceiving the world, and the medieval period brought yet another. The Renaissance represented a still further change in worldview, manifested politically in the form of nationalism and a desire for self-determination. In Italy and Germany, the pope and emperor were strong enough to prevent a melding of nation states under one political head. But there were national forces at work everywhere in Europe as secular princes gained confidence and flexed their muscles, trying to throw off papal control. They were trying, in fact, to throw off the whole ecclesiastical mindset, for if freedom from papal taxation was sought, so was freedom from its religious underpinnings. Humanism asserted the individual's right to revolt against tyranny, against whatever inhibited the full flowering of humanity in any way. For many people, the papacy appeared to be one agency of such inhibition.

Modern democracy, related to humanism, appeared first in Europe among the Swiss city-states. It appeared later in other parts of Europe, and with shocking slowness in places such as Spain. The significance of this is that church governance followed the same pattern. Church governance reflects sociopolitical or national governance: where monarchic absolutism characterizes the state, it tends to be accompanied by episcopacy in the church, while democracy in the state is accompanied by congregationalism in the church. Those who uphold any given denomination's particular form of church government will insist that it is rooted in Scripture; the fact is, however, that the church in every age is unavoidably affected by its political and social context. All aspects of human activity are interrelated.

This interrelation is reflected further in the Renaissance by a movement in the moral realm that paralleled the political trend towards autonomy. For the humanist the meaning of human existence, and therefore of the human good, was not something to which one simply acquiesced; it had to be *forged*. There was a new vision for self-making—not the self-making of modern existentialism, but one based on different presuppositions that were recovered in part from antiquity. The movement was away from heteronomy—rule by something else—towards autonomy—rule by oneself—and religion was a part of this movement. It was thought that unquestioning submission to any authority, including that of the church, would cramp self-enhancement and self-expression. Just as there were no limits to geographical exploration, there were now no limits to the exploration of the human interior, that is, the mind and heart. The humanists spoke eloquently of self-confidence and self-worth *grounded in the creature as such*.

In so doing, they magnified the goodness of creation as they felt it had not been magnified for some time. Initially they understood the goodness of the human creature to be the goodness of God's creation as a whole, by virtue of the fact that it was *God's*. In other words, this goodness was not free-standing, existing independently of God; it was a goodness in the creation which originated with God and had survived the Fall.

The Reformers and the Renaissance humanists appeared to agree, then, on the residual goodness of creation. However distorted or corrupted, the goodness of God's creation remained. The *imago dei*—the image of God in which we are created—was *defaced* by the Fall but never *effaced*; marred, but never obliterated. For if the image of God in humankind had been effaced, humankind would have ceased to be human, and the sinner annihilated. Sinners, however, remain human (only humans sin), and are not transmogrified into another kind of being. They remain possessed of that image which they cannot forfeit regardless of the extent to which they contradict it. What highlighted the later divergence between humanist and Reformer was the question as to what extent, and to what end, the undeniable, perduring goodness of the *imago dei* was still shining forth resplendently (that is, was naturalistically recognizable) despite the Fall.

This was, certainly, a crucial divergence, and one of its most decisive marks appeared in 1525 at the debate between Luther and Erasmus on the bondage of the will. Erasmus was a linguistic genius and the most learned man of that era, but his theology never matched Luther's "extremism" where the ravages of the Fall and the novelty of the gospel were concerned. He and Luther pursued a celebrated, lengthy, and highly repetitive exchange on the righteousness of God, during which neither one was able to persuade the other. It revolved around one question: is the righteousness that is necessary to human salvation a good which we lack in ourselves and can only receive from another source, or does it inhere in the human being as such? Is righteousness an achievement, or a gift? Luther insisted that righteousness was a gift, Erasmus that it was an achievement, and from that point onward it became clear that the humanistic and religious dimensions of the Renaissance, which had seemed to be allies, were not. Thoroughgoing humanism magnified the perduring capacity of the human creature over all other considerations.

THE REVIVAL OF ANCIENT LANGUAGE, LEARNING, AND ART

We alluded earlier, in passing, to the recovery of antiquity during the Renaissance and how this fueled humanist thought. The classical view of life, the view expressed in Greek and Roman culture, was felt to be more rational than the medieval view. It was less riddled with what the humanists regarded as superstition and unnecessary guilt, less morbid, and more life-affirming. It gave greater scope for the intellect, the emotions, aesthetics, and the affirmation of the senses—sheer delight in the physicality of the body. In other words, what the humanist relished about the classical worldview was its apparent elevation of impassioned living on all fronts.

Latin had never actually perished during the Middle Ages; it was the language of every educated person. But with the Renaissance, Latin became more than just the language of religion, diplomacy, or business; it became the key to the great literary resources of antiquity, along with Greek. Humanists knew that language was the door to a culture. They knew that no translation can ever be a substitute for reading a work in the original language, if only because every language contains words that have no precise equivalent in another. They were aware that language transcends mere description to fashion a whole world into which the reader is invited to step and live thereafter. The acquisition of more sophisticated language, then, allows one to inhabit a vastly larger universe, and each additional language acquired expands one's world exponentially. The Renaissance humanists grasped this, and therefore considered the study of Latin and Greek essential in order to access the culture of antiquity.[1] In fact, they venerated these languages.

However, this embrace of classical culture did not extend to the philosophers of antiquity. The Renaissance humanists were largely anti-philosophical, reacting especially to the prevailing scholastic version of Aristotelianism, their *bête noire*. It has already been mentioned how early modern scientific inquiry had uncovered the failure of Aristotelianism to predict accurately such things as the planetary orbits. The humanists also despised the hair-splitting of scholastic philosophy and found the Aristotelian vocabulary and conceptual framework constricting. They found a greater richness in literature, to which they attributed a humanizing efficacy that philosophy could not match. It is difficult to exaggerate the extent to which humanists maintained that literary expression—especially that which was written in elegant, precise prose—could of itself better the human heart and thereby effect the Renaissance's equivalent of the "new creation."

---

1. It was considered essential especially for an appreciation of the beauty of literary form, something valuable which has largely been lost to us today. We may think of a great writer of hymns, such as the thinker Charles Wesley (1707-1788), and imagine that he simply wrote as the Holy Spirit inspired him. But Wesley spent nine years at Oxford University studying Greek and Latin poetry, learned there an appreciation for poetic form, and brought this appreciation to eighteenth-century English. One convention he borrowed from Greek poetry is *anadiplosis*: the restatement, in the first line of a stanza, of an idea expressed in the last line of the preceding stanza, both for emphasis and to increase cohesion. An example from Wesley is the hymn "And Can It Be", in which the first stanza ends with the line, *Amazing love! How can it be, that Thou, my God, shouldst die for me?* and the second stanza opens with *Tis mystery all! Th'Immortal dies....* When Charles and his brother John went to high school at the age of eleven, the assignment on Monday morning for the lower-form boys was to write a précis of the previous day's sermon. The middle-form boys wrote the précis in Latin, and the upper-form boys wrote the précis in the form of Latin verse. During the Renaissance, any scholar would have been able to do the same.

THE SPREAD OF HUMANISM

At first there was nothing apparently hostile to the church in this embrace of classical culture, with its appreciation of the emotions and the senses. In fact, the church initially looked favorably upon this development as a recovery of the goodness of the creation. The papacy, specifically, contributed actively to it. The biggest impulse in this direction was given by Pope Nicholas V, elected in 1447, who was a prodigious lover of books and founded the Vatican library. He also gathered around himself scholars and artisans with no little appreciation of beauty. Pope Julius II, elected in 1503, went even further. Stating that the head of the church should also demonstrate leadership in intellectual and cultural affairs, he instructed Michelangelo to represent him as Moses in a painting. He saw himself as leading the church out of intellectual and cultural oppression, through a wilderness, and into the Promised Land, just as Moses had brought the children of Israel out of political and religious bondage.

Notice, it was not simply that Julius II regarded himself as a leader in the field of aesthetics as such. More was at stake than this, because aesthetics, for the humanist, had unique spiritual significance as the vehicle of one's life in God; it was felt that the appreciation and enjoyment of aesthetics was a necessary route to the enjoyment of God, so that anyone who led others into an appreciation of the arts and the world of antiquity was a spiritual liberator—a savior of sorts.[2]

---

2.   Needless to say, the Protestant Reformers would eventually object to this view. While they acknowledged that God is to be enjoyed and delighted in, they denied that even the profoundest appreciation of aesthetics, of culture—a *creaturely* good—could ever be a bridge to, or an aspect of, the enjoyment of *God*. They distanced themselves from any suggestion that those who are more aesthetically sophisticated are, or might be, closer to God in any sense. As mentioned in the previous chapter, when Ulrich Zwingli, an able musician and no musical philistine, perceived that church music had begun to distract from the Word instead of facilitating worship, he took an ax to the pipe organ in Zurich and reduced it to matchwood. The problem, said Zwingli, was not that the church music in Zurich was inferior or slovenly and

The papacy's appreciation of aesthetics, then, served in the beginning to promote the spread of humanism. But as humanism spread north from Italy into Germany, it met with resistance in the German universities, where scholasticism was more entrenched. It should be noted that this was not the scholasticism of Aquinas, but the late medieval scholasticism of William of Occam and Gabriel Biel. This scholasticism, while questionable at many points concerning its faithfulness to Aristotle (Philip Melanchthon, the first systematic theologian of the Reformation and Luther's colleague at the University of Wittenberg, would soon deplore the late medieval Aristotelianism of those whose ignorance of Greek meant they had to read Aristotle in a Latin translation), was scholasticism nonetheless. It insisted on a philosophical underlay to theology, with a version of Aristotelian philosophy supplying the language and logic of theology and the categories by which theology and all other matters were to be understood. It largely controlled the curriculum and outlook of the medieval German university.[3]

---

for this reason unfit to be offered to God or likely to impede the congregation in its praise of God. On the contrary, the music was resplendent. However, its very excellence, aesthetically speaking, had become an impediment to Word-inspired worship. The worshippers, entranced by the music, substituted their response to a cultural phenomenon for the response that grateful, penitent sinners owe their Redeemer and the obedience that newly-recruited soldiers owe their Lord.

3.   Although scholastic theology cherished Aristotle, there were some Roman Catholic thinkers, more humanist than the scholastics, who upheld Plato and tried to reconcile the gospel with his teaching. The greatest representative of Christian Platonism at this time was Pico della Mirandola (1463-1494). Mirandola and his followers inadvertently skewed the gospel in the direction of an ancient pagan mindset, affecting doctrine, ethics, and the understanding of what constitutes the human good. Under the Platonists, Hellenistic culture came to be regarded alongside Israel as the progenitor of Christ; that is, Plato or Socrates had at least as great a place as the Hebrew Bible.

The church, in every generation, has the task of relating the gospel to whatever is current in the intellectual environment, but at what point does this endeavor end up adulterating the gospel? Each generation draws the line in a different place. In the Middle Ages, theology was linked to the thought of Aristotle; later, in the Enlight-

Although it was a huge move, the humanists were eager to be free of the influence of Aristotle and the late medieval interpretation of his teaching, and regarded as an ally anybody who would help in the jettisoning of metaphysics. Luther appeared at first to be such an ally. Given his understanding of the inherent truth and vitality of the gospel, he considered reliance on the teaching of Aristotle to be not only superfluous but detrimental. The gospel did not need to be established or defended by philosophy, since the gospel possessed inherent integrity, cogency, and militancy. Humanly articulated, to be sure, yet empowered by the Spirit, the gospel could make its own claim for truth in the human mind and heart; appeals to philosophy as foundation or buttress of any sort only attenuated this claim. Hence Luther and the other magisterial Reformers were quick to agree with the humanists concerning the theological counterproductivity of medieval philosophy.[4]

When humanism eventually came to penetrate German universities, it did so chiefly through people trained in the schools of the Brethren of the Common Life. Two famous scholars in this tradition were Nicholas of Cusa (1401-1464) and John Wessel (1419-1489), both of whom exhorted students to master Greek and Hebrew. For the Brethren of the Common Life, humanistic learning was not a cultural enhancement to be appropriated wholesale but a tool to reform education, and educational reform was in turn the springboard to ecclesiastical and social reform. (They did succeed in this agenda to some extent, but it was really humanism under the Protestant thinker Melanchthon that later

---

enment, to the thought of John Locke or of the French *philosophes*. In our own era, theology has been linked by Rudolf Bultmann (1884-1976) and his followers to the philosophy of Heidegger, and in North America, it has been linked to popular liberalism. As a result, of course, the gospel has been skewed in each case.

4.   Nevertheless, as each of the several editions of Melanchthon's *Loci Communes* appeared from 1521 to 1555, more Aristotle found its way into the next edition. Luther was dismayed by this. Having begun by extolling the authority of Melanchthon's *Loci Communes* as second only to Scripture, the later Luther admitted he scarcely recognized what (he thought) Melanchthon had become.

produced public education in Germany.) Plainly there was an intimate connection between humanism and public education.

The best known of the urban German humanists was Willibald Pirckheimer (1470-1530). Pirckheimer was as well-equipped as the best of the Italian humanists, but unlike many of them he cared as much about ecclesiastical reform as he did about political reform. He supported the Reformation in its earlier stages, and stood by Luther at Leipzig in 1519; significantly, however, he never joined the Lutheran church after it ceased to recognize Rome. This pattern recurred numerous times: the humanist thinkers wanted a Roman Catholic church reformed in several respects, but not a Reformation church. The Catholic reformation had already been underway for at least a century, and humanist thinkers supported it. While they were enthusiastic about remedying abuses in the church, they saw little need for doctrinal differentiation; above all, they abhorred the sundering of Christendom. When faced with humanist reluctance to support the Reformation in all its aspects, the Reformers characteristically insisted that no remedying of institutional or moral deficits in the church would affect a theology that obscured the gospel.

Some of the other urban German humanists, such as Hans Holbein (1460-1524) and Albrecht Dürer (1471-1528), were poets, teachers, or painters. These men did not extol ancient paganism and aesthetics, but they did insist that all aspects of human existence should be elevated, since all of it, in its God-given multidimensionality, is God-honoring.

One sign that the new learning had taken hold in a university was the establishment of a chair of poetry. In Germany, humanists were often simply referred to as poets; the terms 'humanist' and 'poet' were virtually synonymous. Poetry, neglected for centuries, flourished in the Renaissance. (This is not to deny that philosophy continued to thrive throughout the Renaissance era, since the tradition of scholasticism perdured before, during, and after the Renaissance. As pointed out already, however, philosophy was never dear to the Renaissance *humanists*.) Disdaining the notion that poetry is arcane and abstract, somehow more complicated or 'difficult' than prose, Renaissance poets recovered the essence of poetry: it is simpler than prose, more elemental, more concrete. Poetry, after all, is the natural idiom of primitive people and children, and in its imagistic, compressed density eschews the abstract quality characteristic of philosophy.[5] Poetry was the mark of the humanist educated person, and a chair of poetry put a university on the humanist map.

The center of German humanism was Erfurt. Exposed to the best of German humanism at the university there, Luther was soon to reflect its riches in his poetical and musical contributions as hymnwriter and liturgist.

THE HUMANISM OF RUFUS MUTIANUS

Rufus Mutianus (1470-1526) was another key figure in German humanism. His teaching highlights the divergence between humanism and the gospel preached by the Reformers. He also distanced himself from the Brethren of the Common Life and the use made of humanism by that movement.

Among other things, Mutianus said that Christianity began long before the advent of Christ, but he did not mean that Christianity begins with Abraham, prototype of the person of faith. Instead he insisted that the origin of Christianity was extrabiblical. He believed that the true Christ was not the God-man, the Incarnate One, but the *discarnate* wisdom of God. Mutianus posited a historical Jesus—Jesus of Nazareth—as well as a 'supracarnate' Christ who can be found anywhere and is the secret truth of all religion, indeed of all of life. The true Christ, said Mutianus in direct contradiction to 1 John 1, cannot

---

5.   In fact, poetry can be said to be more primitive than prose, which is why it comes naturally to children. It is *non*-metaphorical discourse which is so highly sophisticated and abstract; the challenge of poetry is not its abstraction but its density. Cf. the post-Holocaust Jewish spokesperson Elie Wiesel, in his famous inversion of the usual proverb, "A poet's word is worth a thousand pictures." Northrop Frye may have gone too far in suggesting that only those who wrote poetry or fiction are real writers, but the current undervaluing of poetry is nonetheless a tremendous loss.

be seized by human hands; the true son of God is a discarnate wisdom which alights equally on Jews, Greeks, and Germans. German cultural and historical life, then, was as much the preparation for the gospel as Genesis-through-Malachi was.

Mutianus also taught that because the natural law—love of God and neighbor—is written on the human heart, all are thereby made partakers of heaven. Admittedly, the Reformers upheld natural law, but they ascribed no more to it than two non-redemptive functions: (i) a 'holding operation' whereby humankind's proclivity to treachery can be checked and sufficient social cohesion maintained to enable the gospel to be announced and heard; (ii) a condemning operation grounding humankind's inexcusability before God and thereby forestalling any suggestion that the gospel might be superfluous. In other words, natural law, written on the heart, anticipates the gospel not least by rendering everyone culpable before God. Here the Reformers claimed the support of Romans 1.

Mutianus' ahistorical view of Christ naturally went together with an ahistorical view of Scripture as fable or myth. Scripture, according to Mutianus, is a narrative without historical anchor, a tale by which we gain insight into ourselves. But the Reformers would maintain that the gospel is anchored in history: the ragtag group of slaves brought through the Red Sea were forged as God's people; Jesus was crucified 'under Pontius Pilate', date and place locatable. Scripture (or the gospel as the substance of Scripture) is not the means to insight into ourselves; it is the normative witness to God's saving act, and as such has become part of that act itself—an aspect of God's inclusion of us in his saving act. It is only in the course of that inclusion, by grace and through faith, that we ever come to the knowledge of God, and thereafter self-knowledge under God.

We would do well to be attuned to the opposition between humanists like Mutianus and those of Reformational conviction, because it has persisted into the present era: Mutianus' views are often heard in Protestant churches today.[6] Northrop Frye, who did much in our day to boost this humanistic understanding of Scripture, asserts in *The Great Code* that the Bible from Genesis to Revelation is the grand myth apart from which Western literature cannot be understood. He is right about the Bible being a key to understanding literature, and this is indeed one of the functions of overarching myth, that it unifies and explains the stories told in a culture. In that sense the biblical narrative is rightly called a myth. But this is not the same as saying that it is not historical. In the words of C. S. Lewis, the story of God and humankind in the Bible is "the one true myth", that is, the one that actually *happened*. Frye, on the other hand, felt that the very *logic* of Scripture, regardless of what the church has tried to make of it, is inherently myth. In this he adopted the approach of many humanists.

There is only one God or Goddess, continued Rufus Mutianus, but many forms and many names: Jupiter, Sol, Apollo, Moses, Luna, Proserpina, Mary. Humanists could grasp this, but those with inferior intellectual powers needed to be told fables. The gospel was merely illustrative matter for people who could not quite grasp intellectual subtleties.[7]

But notice that in Hebrew, the name of God is written YHWH, with no vowels. A word with no vowels cannot be uttered, and a word that cannot be uttered cannot be translated. There is no substitute for a word that cannot be translated. There is therefore no substitute for the Holy One of Israel. He, Yahweh, is not Allah, Krishna, or Gitchi Manitou, but only the one revealed under the name YHWH in the

---

6.   I have observed that when the church derails theologically, it often does so by way of the teaching offered to children. Sunday School literature and children's sermons are typically filled with moralistic bromides in place of the gospel, because the assumption is that children cannot understand the gospel; they can be taught not to steal, they can be taught not to swear, but they cannot understand the gospel. This is a serious misjudgment.

7. Note that this 'pictorial' role for the gospel was philosophically articulated by Hegel. For a thorough exposition and criticism of it see Emil Fackenheim, *The Religious Dimension of Hegel's Thought* (Bloomington: Indiana University Press, 1967).

Bible. That is why, in Jewish circles to this day, the name of God is not pronounced. Jewish literature in Hebrew will refer to 'the Holy One, blessed be He,' but not 'YHWH' or 'Yahweh'. Even references to God in English are spelled 'G-d', without the vowel in the middle, so as to be unpronounceable and therefore untranslatable. Christians do utter the name of God to avoid awkwardness, but always keeping in mind that the God we are speaking of is not to be confused with anything creaturely or religious, nor with any other deity. Zeus is not the same, Thor is not the same, as the God who is Father of our Lord Jesus Christ.

Like many other humanists, Mutianus denounced those things that he regarded as superstitions and accretions in the church, but never wanted to break decisively with the church. He denounced the veneration of relics, for instance, as well as fasts, auricular confession (that is, confession to a priest), and masses for the dead. But he had no interest in the question which preoccupied Luther and the other Reformers, namely, how do we come to be rightly related to God? The question of righteousness in its totality—not only imputed righteousness or justification but righteousness imputed, imparted, and exemplified—was the question of the Reformation. Mutianus, like so many other university humanists, wanted to be rid of the intellectual straitjacket of the church but regarded the question of righteousness as relatively narrow and shallow—as little more than a tempest in a teapot. The humanists could never understand why the Reformers attributed such capital importance to this question.

HUMANIST SUPPORT OF LUTHER

Ulrich von Hutten (1488-1523), an important ally of Luther, was an intellectually precocious humanist who drank deeply at the fount of Italian humanism. Above all he wanted a united Germany under a reformed emperor, although he was never specific about the theological shape of his vision. As a supporter of anything that might curb papal power and stop the papacy from siphoning money out of Germany, he regarded himself as Luther's ally even after the Leipzig debate in 1519, when most other humanists parted company with the Wittenberger. He was far removed from Luther's theology, however; he could never understand, for example, why Luther was so agitated by the indulgence controversy. If a few thousand people found help in something that rescinded the temporal penalty for sin, why could Luther not allow them its comfort? Why should an ecclesiastical dispute concerning someone's supersensitive conscience occupy the time and talent of a sophisticated intellectual? Luther, of course, insisted that the whole concept of indulgences was a major issue; people's eternal salvation and present spiritual well-being were at stake. In the end, von Hutten could only shake his head sadly at Luther's passion.

Luther always knew the gospel to be qualitatively different from the kind of richness offered by humanism. To be sure, humanism offers glorious cultural riches, whereas the gospel is rich with the singular mercy of God. Humanist riches have a similarity to *religious* richness, but Luther and the other Reformers regarded 'religion' as a human invention and cultural artifact; it was neither faith nor the preparation for faith. Here they anticipated two colossal thinkers in twentieth century theology, Buber and Barth. Martin Buber maintained that modernity was open to religion but closed to faith, while Barth, even more pointedly, spoke of religion as "...the realm of man's attempt to justify and to sanctify himself before an arbitrary and capricious picture of God."[8] The Hebrew prophets also found the Israelite people open to religion (less the religion of their non-Israelite neighbors than the self-serving idolatry that arose *within* Israel) but closed to faith, and Luther found the same to be true of European society on the eve of the Reformation. Religious riches are humanistic in the sense that religion is an expression of culture. The gospel, on the other hand, is not, regardless of the cultural 'bed' in which it is laid. What is the rela-

---

8.   See Martin Buber, *Eclipse of God* (New York: Harper, 1957), and Karl Barth, *Church Dogmatics*, trans. by G. Bromiley and T. F. Torrance (Edinburgh: T & T Clark, 1975), Vol. I, Part 2, p. 280.

tionship, then, of the gospel to religion, including *Christian* 'religion'? The Reformers addressed this question relentlessly.

The humanists who gathered around Luther represented the last of three generations in the spread and development of humanism. In each of the major countries of the north there was first a generation of pioneer humanists who acquired classical learning and a classical mindset. This was followed by a generation of consolidators who put to use the tools developed by the pioneers and integrated the rich materials dug up from antiquity. This second generation represented the high point of Renaissance humanism. The third generation was a younger cohort. Not content merely to understand or critique society, they wanted to change it, and saw humanistic training as a means to this end. Between 1510 and 1520 many of these third-generation humanists rallied around Luther, wanting to correct ecclesiastical and social abuses, and it was they who did most to boost the Reformation. They were, for example, the runners who disseminated Luther's *Ninety-Five Theses* throughout Germany.

This third generation of humanists was aware that the Reformation was a young person's movement. By 1517, nearly all of Luther's followers in Wittenberg were younger than he, while nearly all his theological opponents, except Eck, were older. (Calvin was twenty-six years old when he wrote the first edition of the *Institutes*. The crown jewel of the shorter Reformation writings, the *Heidelberg Catechism*, was written by two young men in 1563: Kaspar Olevianus and Ursinus Zacharias, both under thirty years of age.[9])

There were numerous affinities between Luther and the humanists, although in each case there was an unmistakable divergence at a deeper level. One such affinity, already alluded to, was the rejection of scholasticism. The humanists found scholastic theology unnecessarily

---

9.   Of course, the same point can be made about most reforming movements. Seventeenth-century Puritanism, for example, was also a young person's movement: nearly all the Puritan leaders were young men, while their Anglican opponents were much older men.

subtle and complex to the point of being unintelligible, and felt that it obscured the riches of antiquity. They were interested in a theological formulation that was more elegant, in the logical sense of drawing a conclusion from the fewest number of premises. Luther, on the other hand, opposed scholastic theology not because it was unintelligible, but for the opposite reason: its intelligibility exposed it as anti-gospel.

The humanists also appreciated Luther's return to Scripture, though for different reasons. They valued the Scriptures as documents of antiquity, meriting as much attention as any other ancient document. Luther, however, went to Scripture to recover the unique content of the gospel. Along with other Protestant Reformers, he maintained that when the Holy Spirit vivifies Scripture, the living person of Jesus Christ emerges and stands forth as compellingly as he did for the people on the road to Emmaus. In fact, Luther insisted that when Scripture is preached Sunday by Sunday and the Holy Spirit acts, the sermon, so far from being a speech, is nothing less than Christ coming to his people. The humanists were never prepared to speak of Scripture in this manner. Both Reformer and humanist endorsed *sola scriptura*, but they did not mean the same thing by it.[10] For the humanist it meant "not without Scripture": Scripture, as part of the rich literary deposit of antiquity, was never to be slighted. For Luther, on the other hand, *sola scriptura* meant Scripture as the unnormed, normative witness to Jesus Christ and the occasion of Christ's rendering himself contemporaneous with the reader.

Third, Luther and the humanists had in common a desire to return to patristics. The humanists regarded patristics as a simple, understandable statement of Christian faith, free of fruitless speculation and scholastic obfuscation. Luther cherished patristics as being closer to the New Testament era than medieval formulations of faith, and hence less distorted by centuries of nonbiblical speculation. Since the

---

10. See Alister McGrath, *Reformation Thought*, 3rd ed. (Oxford: Blackwell, 1999), pp. 60-63.

humanists esteemed antiquity for its own sake, all the church fathers were on an equal footing; they did not elevate any one over another.[11] But for the Wittenberg theologian, and indeed for all the Reformers, Augustine was preeminent.[12]

Rhetoric was another shared interest: the humanists pursued rhetoric, like eloquence, as a form of cultural excellence, recognizing its aesthetic significance. For Luther, on the other hand, rhetoric was worthwhile chiefly as a tool to facilitate the preaching and understanding of the gospel. Rhetoric was the art of persuasion, as contrasted with dialectic, the art of refutation; dialectical skill is needed in order to refute theological opponents, but a refuted opponent is not necessarily won over to the truth. Luther accorded rhetoric the place he did because he knew that the ultimate category, in the church's encounter with the world, is not argument but witness.

After 1520, the Reformation stood in starker and starker contrast with humanism. The humanists loved Luther's devotional writings and had agreed with his educational views, but they were alienated by what they regarded as the extreme character of his Pauline—actually

---

11.   Erasmus was the exception to this impartial approach; he always elevated Jerome above the other church fathers.

12.   Augustine is the most quoted thinker in the work of Thomas Aquinas, if not in the work of every medieval Christian thinker, but this fact does not detract from the particular use that the Reformers made of his teaching. Other church fathers were preeminent in Eastern Orthodoxy: Athanasius first of all, with John Chrysostom ranking a very close second. Interestingly, John Wesley, though a son of the Reformation and cherishing the doctrine of justification by faith, preferred the eastern fathers over the western. Apart from being put off by Augustine's rigid predestinarianism, he also felt that the eastern church fathers had a better grasp of the biblical subtlety of sanctification. The emphasis in the western church from the Reformation onward, without denying transformation, has been transaction: the work of the Cross is a transaction whereby our guilt and shame are transferred to Christ, and his righteousness and acquittal are transferred to us. The eastern church does the opposite; without denying transaction, it emphasizes transformation. If the Protestant Reformers preferred the western church fathers, it was perhaps because doctrine was at stake in the sixteenth century the way it was not in the eighteenth century.

his scriptural—convictions. The gospel has to do with death and resurrection, with condemnation and acquittal, with an ultimacy that relativizes everything else. The 'extremism' of the Reformers' gospel—it had nothing to do with human self-enhancement, however profound— made it unattractive to many humanists. They were also repelled by the vehemence of Luther's expression of it. Luther not only possessed fine theological instinct, but articulated it with such force as to make his verbal torrents, not infrequently couched in a vernacular that was out-and-out vulgar, offensive to those who considered themselves more refined.

By way of summary: those humanists who became Reformers were university-trained, exposed to classical culture, intellectually adventuresome, and averse to scholasticism—although many of the youngest had not even been exposed to it, as universities who embraced humanism ceased to feature scholasticism. Most of these humanist-trained Reformers served not only as theologians but as pastors, and as such they constituted the dynamic leadership of the Lutheran movement. Lutheran ministers who lacked humanist formation, on the other hand, remained ecclesiastical 'foot soldiers' who provided no leadership in the Reformation and wrote no memorable theology. One generation later, these non-humanistically trained clergy reintroduced a rigid scholastic mindset just like that of medieval scholasticism but using a Protestant vocabulary.[13]

Plainly, humanist exposure was crucial in the expansion of the Reformation. And just as plainly, it is the scholarly pastor (not the professor of theology unconnected to the pastorate) who is the true successor to the Protestant Reformer. Before the Reformers were theologians, they

---

13.   The mindset described was one of the aspects of Puritanism. Although Puritanism did not depart from the doctrines of justification by faith or the normativity of Scripture, it brought Aristotle back as a philosophical buttress for theology. This was a return to scholasticism with Protestant vocabulary. The Continental and English Reformers had insisted that theology, whose essence is the gospel, does not need a philosophical buttress.

were exegetes—all wrote more commentary than theology—and before they were exegetes, they were pastors. Luther preached every week, if not every day, and Calvin preached daily. On top of their relentless preaching schedule, these men had to sort out all manner of pastoral problems. In Geneva, for example, there were four churches, and their pastors were better paid than those in rural congregations. It was a source of contention: the rural pastors, who had the same training, did the same work, bore the same responsibility, and preached the same gospel, felt they ought to be paid the same. The urban pastors argued, as some urban pastors do today, that in order to retain credibility with their sophisticated congregations they had to be paid a salary commensurate with that earned by their parishioners. Calvin had to deal with scores of such issues. In addition, the leaders of the Reformation exercised enormous civic responsibilities. Pastor, exegete, theologian, town councillor—the magisterial Reformers were able to honor the demands on their gifts in large part because they had first drunk deeply from the fountains of Renaissance humanism.

The lesson here is that the intellectual training gained through humanistic studies is invaluable to the believer, providing the tools for a lifetime of independent learning not only in theology but in all areas of life and service and in turn benefiting the church as a whole. That includes the study of languages: recall that Melanchthon, whose commentary on Romans undergirds many of the eighty commentaries of the Reformation era, was the finest Greek scholar in Europe after Erasmus. Melanchthon objected to teaching theology at Wittenberg because he preferred to spend his time teaching the humanities. And even Melanchthon was able to expound the Greek testament for soon-to-be preachers only because of the work Erasmus had done with respect to the *Textus Receptus*, making a usable, dependable Greek text available to those whose passion was the gospel.

ERASMUS

Luther described Erasmus as the most intelligent man of the Reformation, but it is debatable whether Erasmus *was* in fact a man of the

Reformation. Did he manage to hold together the diverging outlooks of the Reformation and the Renaissance, or did he sacrifice the former to the latter? Through his philological gifts he made a unique contribution to the Reformation, but was he ever part of it? Scathing in his contempt for what he regarded as indefensible superstitions and institutional abuses, he managed to avoid criticizing the church's doctrine. Having lampooned Pope Julius II, he later disavowed his earlier mockery. He claimed to have lived and died "old church". Yet Erasmus is usually 'claimed' as a Reformer, however different he may have been from Luther. He is just as frequently held up as a model for what could have been a different kind of 'Reformation', one that would have avoided the legacy of the seemingly anti-Roman churches of European Christendom. In this regard it is still heard lamented that the Reformation did not proceed "along Erasmian lines."

Erasmus was born in Rotterdam in 1466. His father became a priest, orphaning him, and Erasmus was raised by relatives who gave him his name. He was well educated at a famous Dutch school of the Brethren of the Common Life, and was deeply rooted in that movement. He became an accomplished Latinist. At the age of seventeen he was sent by his guardians to study under a monk, who exposed him to the writings of Saint Jerome. Erasmus came to admire Jerome as his favorite patristic thinker, but was even more entranced by the Latin classics. Latin, he said, should be learned not by appropriating the rules of grammar but by immersion in the usage of the greatest Latinists, from Cicero to Quintilian.

Erasmus was consummately able in both Latin and Greek. The vernacular languages, on the other hand, never had as much appeal for him. That is not to say that he was not adept in them—in addition to his native Dutch, he spoke several other European languages. Although he always deprecated his skill in French, he was able to appreciate the subtleties of pub humor in that language, proof of his fluency even in colloquialisms and puns. He was, moreover, appointed professor of theology at Cambridge University, and must have used some English in this post as well as Latin.

Adept as he was at Latin, Erasmus was even more in love with Greek, finding it to be the deepest mine he had explored. Indeed, he said, "I can hardly refrain from exclaiming, 'Socrates, pray for me!'"—a statement that tells us something about Erasmus' view of classical antiquity rather than Israel as the preparation for the gospel. This was a view typical of humanists, as we have seen, and one of its enormous consequences was an anti-Judaism (a disdain for Jewish worship and theology) that moved eventually into anti-Semitism (contempt for the Jewish people).[14] Luther and the other Reformers are castigated to this day for their alleged anti-Semitism—really better described as anti-Judaism—yet anything the Reformers uttered in this regard was characteristically less extreme compared to the humanists. Despite the humanists' embrace of tolerance, gentility, and broad-mindedness, and despite their belief in a universal world spirit, their anti-Semitism was pronounced. Erasmus was particularly noteworthy in this regard. He said that he always liked going to Paris because not one living, breathing Jew could be found there. (It was not true; Paris had a large Jewish population at that time and had had one for centuries.) Unlike Luther and Calvin, Erasmus knew relatively little Hebrew and did not regard it as essential to either the theological or the humanist project.[15] He considered the Old Testament "Jewish nonsense," a judgment that rings rather ominously in view of later events in Europe.

Neither was Erasmus much concerned with the inventions and discoveries of the age that were enthralling so many thoughtful people. Nor did he care about the quest for national or political self-determination. What Erasmus wanted was an undogmatic religion, by which he meant religion without theological controversy and without theological rigor, with an ethical piety grounded in the Sermon on the Mount. In 1497 he wrote to a friend, "Theology itself I have always

---

14. See chapter 12 for a more detailed exposition of the difference.

15. Erasmus feared that the Reformers' emphasis on the study of Hebrew might lead to a revival in Judaism. See J.C. Olin, ed., *Christian Humanism and the Reformation: Selected Writings of Erasmus* (New York: Harper and Row, 1965), p. 80.

singularly cultivated, but the theologians of our age are characterized by the murkiness of their brains, the barbarity of their speech,
the stupidity of their natures, the hypocrisy of their lives, the violence
of their language, and the blackness of their hearts."[16] Theology, for
Erasmus, was a compend of what he called the philosophy of Christ
and the philosophy of the Greeks. By the philosophy of Christ he meant
the Sermon on the Mount read as an ethical treatise, largely devoid of
theological significance.

In 1499, Erasmus published *Adages*, a collection of pithy sayings
culled from Christian and pagan antiquity. It was a runaway bestseller
and became a status symbol. He published another little book in 1520,
The Dagger of the Christian Knight, also a bestseller. It was used by
some of the major Reformers to attack gross superstitions and medieval
practices such as the worship of saints. Those who shared Erasmus'
approach to what was supposedly silly, false, and deleterious felt that to
expose something to ridicule would cause it to wither.

Erasmus traveled to England at least six times, and in 1499 was
introduced to Sir Thomas More, the inveterate foe of William Tyndale
and writer of the tract *Utopia*. While Erasmus is considered a Reformer
and Thomas More certainly not, the two had a great deal in common.
What Erasmus could never understand, however, is why More, as a
matter of principle, would suffer execution rather than recognize the
king as head of the church. No truth ever seemed to be that important
to Erasmus.

In 1509 Erasmus made his third trip to England and was given a
professorship of divinity at Cambridge, where, incidentally, William
Tyndale was among his pupils. During that time Erasmus made a visit
to Canterbury with John Colet, and the two of them saw the relics of
Saint Thomas à Beckett. They continued their little anti-pilgrimage,
stopping next at the shrine of Our Lady of Walsingham, where pilgrims

---

16.   E.S. Lautenschlaeger, unpublished lectures, "Church History: The Reformation," Lecture 3, Emmanuel College, University of Toronto, 1969, p. 2.

could see Peter's knuckle, the Virgin's milk, and the statue of Mary nod. Erasmus failed to see any such thing. He subsequently wrote about them in such a way as to mock them without drawing accusations of blasphemy, heresy, or disloyalty to the church. The price of heresy was execution, after all, and Erasmus would never imperil his own safety. Did he ever comment theologically on these practices or the presuppositions which underlay them? He was content to laugh.

Erasmus claimed to have "always singularly cultivated theology", but one might well question his claim. After completing a doctorate in theology at the University of Turin, he returned to England and wrote his most famous book, *The Praise of Folly*, still found in bookstores. It was a waggish, finger-poking mockery of indulgences, but once again Erasmus made no trenchant (and therefore dangerous) theological comment. Similarly, although he knew as surely as anyone of the woeful ill-behavior of Pope Julius II, Erasmus never made a frontal attack on papal wickedness or questioned theologically the institution of the papacy. All he did was comment humorously on it. Luther, on the other hand, could never make light of these matters. He was impelled to target the abuses he could not deny, as well as excoriate the popes for their failure to fulfill the mandate of their office. This latter point is crucial. Contrary to popular opinion, so far from denouncing the papal office in principle, Luther regarded it as crucial to the gospel-saturation of the church. He deplored, rather, the fact that pope after pope failed to school the church and its priests in Scripture, preferring instead to be judge over Scripture.[17] Unlike Erasmus, Luther was willing to incur the wrath of the church and pay whatever price it exacted.

Once Luther had published *The Babylonian Captivity of the Church* in 1520, a tract arguing against the church's misbegotten understanding of the sacraments, Erasmus never supported the Reformation publicly again. By 1525, the year of his debate with Luther on the latter's

---

17. For a detailed articulation of this point see Scott Hendrix, *Luther and the Papacy* (Philadelphia: Fortress Press, 1981), chapter 5.

Bondage of the Will, the two of them recognized that they were not theological allies at all.

The logic of Erasmus' "philosophy of Christ" never approached the logic of the gospel; he remained a religious moralist. He never grasped the Reformers' perception that no matter how many institutional and moral abuses were remedied, the gospel would remain obscured by elements of Roman theology unless these were refuted. He never agreed with Luther's understanding of human depravity, and therefore never apprehended why Luther insisted that moral people sin as surely in their morality as the immoral do in their immorality. He saw no point in doctrinal disagreement and eschewed theological contention, since contention, he believed, could yield no edification. Luther was convinced that truth had been forfeited; he commented, "I fear he [Erasmus] does not sufficiently reveal Christ and the grace of God, for human considerations prevail with him much more than divine."[18] While Erasmus' philological skill and his efforts at promoting Christian civility were not without merit, he missed the theological issue that moved the Reformer.

As mentioned already, Erasmus' single greatest contribution to the Reformation was his assembling of the documents that made up the *Textus Receptus*, the edition of the Greek testament apart from which the Reformation would not have assumed the form it did. Yet remarkably, despite his skill in Greek and his facility with vernacular languages, he never produced a vernacular translation of the New Testament—probably because deep down he despised common people as much as Luther loved them. Such a near-sacred object as books were to humanists would be spoiled by the overindulgence of common people. It is widely thought that Erasmus worked assiduously to produce a better Greek text not because he wanted an accurate vernacular translation for the people, but rather because he wanted a better Latin translation than the Vulgate. Despite his seemingly egalitarian remark

---

18.   Lautenschlaeger, "Church History: The Reformation," p.5.

that no one was to be denied access to the New Testament, regardless of social position, Erasmus' New Testament *Paraphrases* were written and published in Latin. The Protestant Reformers, on the other hand, saw that without the Scriptures in the vernacular, the Reformation could not proceed.

THE PHILOSOPHY OF ERASMUS *vs* THE THEOLOGY OF THE REFORMERS

1. Erasmus identifies the content of pagan morality with Christian exhortation.

Both pagan morality and Christian exhortation instruct us to be kind to our neighbor, but they start from different presuppositions. The difference is between self-willed conformity to a moral code on the one hand, and on the other the faith-bond to Jesus Christ who continues to shape us through our living relationship with him and our aspiration to obey him. A code is abstract and impersonal, whereas we are claimed, formed, and informed by a *person*, Jesus Christ. Our discipleship is the expression of our relationship with him.

The Reformers differed markedly from Erasmus with respect to ethical instruction. They said that God's characteristic work is not the dissemination of instruction; God is not an ethicist. He gives himself to us in grace, then insists that we give ourselves to him in gratitude. Instead of mere conformity to a code, he seeks the heart-obedience of those whom he has called into personal relationship with himself. For Luther, this had to do with what he called first-commandment righteousness.

What is the first commandment? "Thou shalt have no other gods before me." For non-Lutherans this is the first commandment, but for Luther, and the Lutheran church to this day, the first commandment includes what the rest of us call the preface to the Decalogue: "I am the Lord your God who brought you out of the land of Egypt, out of the house of slavery. You shall have no other gods before me." The implication is that the command to have no other gods proceeds out of the relationship established by God when he brought Israel out of slavery, and all the other commandments in turn follow logically from that first one: if you keep the first commandment, you keep them all. The ten commandments are not a moral code. They structure the life of a person-to-person relationship born of gratitude to God for God's redemptive, life-giving mercy.

According to Luther, our understanding of and obedience to all the commandments is controlled by our approach to the first. "You were slaves in Egypt, I rescued you, and now you shall have no other gods before me." Consider the commandment forbidding theft. If we refrain from stealing, have we kept the commandment? Luther would deny that we had. Unless our obedience flows from a recognition of the relationship with God our Redeemer and Lord, we have violated the commandment as surely as the one who steals, because the commandment forbidding theft can only be kept *in faith*, kept in the light of the first commandment. If we have made ourselves our own lords—the essence of unbelief—and out of that position have refrained from stealing, our not stealing is an expression of autonomy, of defiance towards God. If we obey the commandment of God but withhold our heart's love from him and our heart's trust in him, we have sinned as much as the person who flagrantly violates the commandment. Morality, Luther knew, is an enemy of faith, never a vestibule to the Kingdom or a condition of entering it.

2. Erasmus looks upon the New Testament as a sourcebook for ethics, rather than the culmination of redemptive history.

The New Testament itself, according to the Reformers, does not support this understanding. The heart of the New Testament is the Cross; it is not a compendium of ethical teaching. To miss this is to miss the point of the gospel.

The other side of Erasmus' view, however, was that the New Testament stood on its own and could be understood independently of the Old. There are many reasons why he undervalued the Old Testament, one of which was probably simple anti-Semitism. In any case, as mentioned earlier, the consequence of neglecting the Old Testament is a lethal distortion of our understanding of God and his interaction with people. The living person of God the Father—the God who grieves, weeps, snorts, spits, and suffers—is forfeited, because it is in the Old Testament that we meet the passion of God most dramatically. And without this appreciation of the personhood of God, the nature of obedience as an expression of relationship with that God cannot be understood.

Also lost is history as the primary locus of God's activity. God delivers a people from slavery in Egypt; he reconciles a wayward creation on a gibbet at the garbage dump of Jerusalem in a year that can be specified and under the jurisdiction of someone whom the historian will never forget. Only then does God act in the subordinate locus, the human heart, sensitizing heart and mind to recognize his activity, welcome it, and understand it more profoundly. He was at work throughout the history of Israel, molding a covenant people and preparing the world for the Incarnation. In fact, without the Old Testament the place of Israel in the economy of salvation disappears completely, and the typical result is anti-Semitism.[19] All of these consequences of neglecting the Old Testament can be seen in Erasmus.

The magisterial Reformers, by contrast, all of whom were exegetes, cherished the Old Testament[20] not because it was a handy compendium of items available to illustrate a theological or spiritual point that could readily be gained elsewhere; they cherished the Old Testament precisely because they knew that apart from it the point of their theology—specifically, their Christology—could never be gained.

---

19. For the consequences of the church's neglect of the Old Testament see the appendix to this chapter.

20. Calvin wrote twice as much on the Old Testament as on the New.

3. Erasmus seldom speaks of grace, and shies away from the teaching of 'total depravity.'

The people for whom grace is the operative term in their understanding of the Christian life are those who believe in the bondage of the will. Because the will is in bondage, according to Luther, we cannot help willing ourselves to be our own lord; we cannot will otherwise. The only solution to the will's being *in se curvatus* is the initiative of grace. Erasmus did not believe in the bondage of the will, and maintained that the righteousness which sinners need did not have to be the sheer gift of God. For this reason he grasped neither the Reformers' understanding of grace nor their insistence on it as the source of everything in Christian faith and conduct.

The bondage of the will is an aspect of total depravity, a doctrine the Reformers upheld not because of their so-called pessimistic view of humanity and its prospects, but rather on account of their understanding of grace. The incursion of God upon and within the person "dead [not merely ill or weakened] in trespasses and sins" (Eph. 2:1) necessitated an understanding of sin that humanists labeled extreme but that Reformers maintained was realistic. The point is that "total depravity" was not a moral category, nor was it arrived at through observation. It was upheld as the implicate of redemption: knowledge of God the Redeemer generated knowledge of the sinner as helpless and hopeless before him. Disagreeing with the Reformers concerning their doctrine of redemption, Erasmus consistently disagreed with them on total depravity.

Total depravity does not mean that we are all as bad as we can be; if we were, society would be unendurable. However badly we behave, we could behave worse if we tried. Total depravity means that the *scope* of the Fall is total, in the sense that no human activity is exempt from its effects; every human undertaking is tainted by sin, including theology. Moreover, every aspect of the human *being*, including reason, will, and the emotions, is corrupt; there is no dimension of the human person left intact by which we can restore ourselves. We can still reason, for example, or we would not be human; but while the structure of reason survives the Fall, its integrity is lost with respect to the knowledge of the divine and the human. Reason now subserves the wrong purpose, applying itself to self-aggrandizement or to rationalization. Similarly we can still exercise the will, and can even will moral, cultural, or intellectual good; but we cannot will *the* good, the Kingdom of God. We cannot will ourselves out of our sinnership, and any attempt to do so only confirms our depravity. And while we are still affective beings who can love, the integrity of our love has been lost so that it is riddled with self-interest. Our affections are misaligned so that we love what we ought to hate and hate what we ought to love. At the very least, we love the creature above the Creator, allowing lesser loves such as nation or family to usurp our love for God.

If every human undertaking is tainted and no aspect of the human creature retains its integrity, then society as a whole is also corrupt. Not only can individuals not save society, but the society cannot save the individual. Economics cannot correct what sociologists identify as the human problem, and sociology cannot correct what economists identify as the human problem. Marx reduces all considerations to the dialectical laws of materialism, and Freud to intrapsychic unconscious conflict, but the doctrine of total depravity exposes both as one-sided and short-sighted. Culture, however rich, is not the Kingdom of God, nor even an anticipation of that Kingdom; it remains a creaturely good, but is fallen. Cultural sophistication gets people no closer to the Kingdom than moral behavior does; since we are helpless to restore ourselves or to merit restoration, God must restore us by his grace. Erasmus seemed not to perceive this.

For the Reformers, humankind is not merely sick but dead; we need resurrection, not assistance. Although Jesus is rightly described as the Great Physician, the ultimate categories in Scripture are not sickness and health, or weakness and strengthening, but death and resurrection.

4. Erasmus misses the redemptive character of revelation.

For the Reformers, the content of revelation is redemption, and redemption is the starting point for knowledge of God. Scripture may begin with the creation stories, but logically it begins with the Exodus: Israel is always aware that it knows God as the One who has rescued it. Beginning from this knowledge Israel fills in, as it were, the doctrine of God the Creator. For the apostles and their descendants, knowledge of God arises through the cross, God's definitive redemptive act. Only as we are acquainted with God the Redeemer do we consequently know that we are not God: God alone is God, and is Creator. While God must create before there is anything to redeem, knowledge of God the Creator is an implicate of knowledge of God the Redeemer.

Another way of saying this is that the *ordo salutis* governs the *ordo cognoscendi*: the order of salvation governs the order of knowing. God acts on our behalf; we by grace are included in that action, and by this inclusion we know the existence and nature of the God who so includes us. If knowledge of God is an implicate of salvation, then as salvation is wholly from God to us, so is knowledge of God. It is received by grace, not by natural theology or speculative theology.

Erasmus' view that humanity has the wherewithal to generate its own righteousness keeps him from seeing the primacy and centrality of redemption, because redemption is largely superfluous. For him, Scripture (specifically, the New Testament, as he had little use for the Old) is a guide for those who are otherwise morally confused or unsure of themselves. Its content is primarily ethical. Knowledge of God becomes something that can be achieved not only by study of the 'philosophy of Christ' and the endeavor to govern one's life by that philosophy, but by study of the creation.

5. The Reformers see religion as the enemy.

As mentioned earlier, the Reformers carefully distinguished faith and religion. Religion, in their understanding, is the last self-built fort in which we hide and tell God we do not need him. Far from being the vestibule or antechamber of the Kingdom, it is the contradiction of the gospel, a monument to humankind's defiance of God.[21] Religion is one more meritocracy, one more form of self-salvation, and therefore inherently antithetical to the gospel.

6. The Reformers distinguish the sphere of God and the sphere of humankind ontologically.

Finally, the Reformers differed from Erasmus and other humanists, as well as from the scholastics, in insisting that the sphere of God and the sphere of humankind are united by grace and not by ontology. God exists non-contingently, while the world, including human beings, exists contingently; that is, the Being of God is necessary and infinite, while the being of the creation is contingent and finite (however vast). For this reason God is not bound to the world through a supposed commonality of being. God is bound to the world only by grace, only by his incomprehensible mercy. Where philosophers spoke of a metaphysical category of "Being itself" or the "Ground of Being" as the link between God and the world, the Reformers saw that if "Being itself" encompassed both God and humankind, it would possess the ultimacy that God would manifestly lack. The true god would then be not a person at all but a philosophical principle. For the Reformers, any notion of "Being itself" was idolatrous and therefore an expression of unbelief.

The great contribution of Erasmus and other humanists to the Reformation must be and has been acknowledged. In fact, the Reformation would not have occurred without the Renaissance. There are interpretations of Erasmus which see a greater convergence between him and the Reformers, and the humanists themselves saw in the gospel an enormous convergence between humanistic learning, culture, and religion. Nevertheless it eventually became clear to the Reformers that they and the humanists were on different tracks. Early in his career as Reformer Luther recognized the chasm between himself and Erasmus.

---

21.   See reference to Barth and Buber on page 15.

As the logic of the Reformation and the logic of Erasmus' Christian philosophy are probed, the divergence becomes undeniable.

The Reformers were therefore in the position of having to articulate the relationship of the gospel to the substance of humanism, the prevailing worldview of their day. There are unquestionable riches in humanistic learning. It will always be the task of the church to articulate how such riches serve the proclamation of the gospel and the edification of God's people.

APPENDIX:
THE CONSEQUENCES OF UNDERVALUING
THE OLDER TESTAMENT

1. Jesus becomes a wax figure whom we can mold as we wish.

Invariably we end up fashioning him after our own image. Consider the assorted "Jesuses" that have appeared in the 20th century: the idealist philosopher, the businessman, the existentialist, the liberal humanitarian, the social conservative, the supporter of Nazi ideology. It is most significant that the only physical description the apostles give us of Jesus is that he was circumcised; it matters not to our faith what he looked like, but it matters supremely that he is a son of Israel.

2. The gospel becomes ideation rather than the power of God unto salvation (Rom. 1:16).

"The power of God unto salvation" is God himself acting to effect our salvation. The gospel, then, is not primarily a report but is rather God himself acting; it is first inherently an event, and then the "good news" of that event.

3. We become anti-Semites.

The history of the church's interface with the synagogue is the sorriest chapter in the church's entire history.

4. We undervalue the people of God and fail to understand the church as the people of God.

In the wake of this failure the church is understood principally in terms of the clergy or in terms of an institution.

5. We undervalue history as the theatre of God's revelation and our discipleship.

The result is a pietistic distortion that promotes religious intentionality and sentimentality but neglects public witness and obedience.

6. We undervalue the Fall.

The story of the Fall occurs only in the Older Testament and is a presupposition of everything that follows it in Scripture. Insofar as we neglect it we adopt a roseate view of human nature, ourselves, and the world in which the Christian mission unfolds.

7. We substitute religious evolution for God's promise and its subsequent fulfillment.

As we replace the biblical category of promise with the worldly category of evolution, we adopt the North American myth of progress concerning world-occurrence instead of recognizing and underlining the patience, faithfulness, and undeflectability of God. In turn we undervalue the need for faithfulness and consistency in our discipleship and assume that developments in western civilization are coterminous with the Kingdom of God.

8. We lose the Hebrew affirmation of the material.

We deny the earthly, the earthy, and the bodily, the pleasures of food, drink, sex, and physicality, and appropriate the contradiction of all of this in the philosophy of Plato.

9. We fail to grasp the central scriptural motif of holiness, both God's and ours.

Scripture, cover to cover, attests God's reaffirming *his* holiness in the wake of our denial of his, as well as God's re-establishing *our* holiness, his peoples', in the wake of our contradiction of ours.

3

Gabriel Biel and
Late Medieval Scholasticism

INTRODUCTION

Gabriel Biel typifies late medieval scholastic thinking, and in this way serves as a foil for the Protestant Reformers.[1] He differed from Aquinas in that the latter was a realist, preoccupied with the concept of being, whereas Biel was a nominalist and preoccupied with the concepts of will and power. Aquinas, who baptized Aristotle into the Christian community,[2] understood God chiefly in terms of existence: God is that which is, whose essence is his existence, and who alone exists necessarily, while everything and everyone else exists contingently. Realist thought, however, gave way gradually to nominalism.

---

1.   For a thorough exposition of the whole of Biel's theology see Heiko A. Oberman, *The Harvest of Medieval Theology* (Grand Rapids: Baker Academic, 1983).

2.   Avicenna and Averroes, in the eleventh and twelfth centuries respectively, had previously "baptized" Aristotle into the Islamic community, and Maimonides, a twelfth-century Jewish thinker, likewise brought Aristotelian teaching into the Jewish community. Obviously, Aristotle looms large in the history of theology.

Occam, the first major representative of nominalism, was always less concerned than Aquinas with metaphysics and with reasoning towards God. For the nominalist, faith is not established on that which reason can demonstrate; theology is not the second storey of a structure built on a philosophical or metaphysical foundation. Faith is built, rather, on what God has willed. Of course, this understanding undercuts the scholastic way of relating theology to philosophy—that is, the notion of nature perfected by grace; if philosophy is no longer what demonstrates the existence and believability of God, then the bridge between philosophy and theology is demolished and natural theology is radically devalued. God's will determines our faith, not God's being, or our reasoning with respect to God's being. The command of God, in turn, is grounded only in the will of God, not in the nature of God.

There has been lively debate about whether Luther was a nominalist, and he certainly did have some things in common with the nominalists. He agreed with their denial of natural theology, for example. Along with the other Protestant Reformers, he repudiated the theological method of scholasticism and affirmed a God whose being, nature, and purpose are known independently of philosophy and metaphysics. Today's metaphysic gives way to a different one tomorrow; if the understanding of God is to be anchored to a particular philosophy, whose philosophy will it be? And how long will it last?

However, there are other crucial ways in which Luther contrasts markedly with the nominalists. He rejected their insistence that God is to be understood chiefly in terms of power, believing with the other Reformers that God is to be understood in terms of the self-giving of the Crucified One. He disagreed, moreover, with the idea that God's command is rooted only in God's will. Unless God's will is his nature, Luther would say, it is only the capricious exertion of sheer power, and indistinguishable from the satanic.

Whenever theology is founded on philosophy or metaphysics, features of the philosophy invariably encroach on the theology, like weeds growing up out of the ground, and distort it. Such a two-storey scheme is in fact the definition of scholasticism. The interesting thing is that while we associate it chiefly with medieval Catholicism, it resurfaces in a Protestant form, with Protestant vocabulary, a mere hundred years after the Reformation.[3] In other words, the logic of the Reformation lasted only seventy or eighty years before it gave way in the seventeenth century to the scholasticism which the Protestant Reformers had opposed. It is hard for people to let the gospel stand alone as the living, lordly presence of Jesus Christ in his self-utterance; the temptation is always to buttress the gospel with a philosophical underlay, only to distort the gospel and even obscure it thereby.

GABRIEL BIEL: INTRODUCTION

Gabriel Biel was born at Speyer during the first quarter of the fifteenth century; the exact date is not known, and in fact almost nothing is known about his childhood, youth, or early adulthood. He was ordained to the priesthood in 1432 and thereupon entered Heidelberg University, where he distinguished himself academically and became an instructor in the Faculty of Arts. He completed further studies in 1442 and 1443 at the University of Erfurt, where he absorbed relatively little of the humanist worldview there even though Erfurt was the stronghold of German humanism. In 1453 Biel enrolled in the Faculty of Theology at the University of Cologne, twenty-one years after his ordination—a fact which reveals something about how ministry at that time was understood exclusively in terms of priestly function rather than teaching or preaching. The Protestant Reformers were to overturn this view, emphasizing instead a learned and doctrinally informed ministry whose major function was teaching, not priestly activity.

At the University of Cologne, made famous in the thirteenth century by Thomas Aquinas' teacher Albertus Magnus, Biel immersed himself in the nominalist thought of Occam. Occam had by that time begun

---

3.   Examples are Francis Gomar and Jacobus Arminius. People often place Wesley and Arminius in the same category, but Wesley is not a scholastic thinker.

to eclipse the earlier thought of Aquinas, Duns Scotus, and Albertus Magnus. In middle age, as cathedral preacher in Mainz, Biel was engaged chiefly in day-to-day matters of church life. He associated himself with the Brethren of the Common Life and thereafter remained a member. The Brethren of the Common Life, it will be remembered, were primarily educators. They pursued spiritual interiority, ethical rigor, and purity in the church, but had no disagreement with the church's theology or doctrinal articulation.

In 1484 Biel was appointed professor of theology at the University of Tübingen, and five years later became its rector—or president, as we would say now. By that time he was approximately 75 years old. He died in 1495, having spent his last years exclusively among the Brethren of the Common Life.

Notably, one of Biel's theological grandsons, later to become Luther's tireless and most formidable opponent, was Johann Eck.[4]

BIEL ON JUSTIFICATION

Justification was, in a way, *the* issue of the Protestant Reformation, and was the center of enormous controversy. The statement on justification forged by the Roman church in the Council of Trent (1545-1563) was six thousand words, vastly longer than the writing on any other issue addressed by that Council.[5]

---

4.   Eck debated Luther at the disputations of Leipzig in 1519, at Worms in 1521, and at Augsburg in 1530. On the first two occasions they met face to face, after which Luther was sequestered in the Wartburg Castle in Eisenach for nine months, disguised for his own safety and occupying himself with Bible translation. In 1530, Luther and Eck did not meet, strictly speaking; Luther was represented at Augsburg by Philip Melanchthon while staying a short distance away in Castle Coburg, because it was felt that his actual presence on the site in Augsburg would have been inflammatory. Philip Melanchthon, on the other hand, was a much more irenic individual who rarely lost his temper. It was in 1530, of course, that the Augsburg Confession was forged, still the doctrinal benchmark for worldwide Lutheranism to this day.

5.   The Council of Trent set the doctrinal norms for Roman Catholicism until Vatican II; Vatican I intervened in 1870, but effected very little change. Vatican II, in

Gabriel Biel's theology of justification presupposes a nominalist understanding of God in terms of will or power, and a nominalist understanding of grace characterized by power. We saw in Chapter 2 that the starting point for nominalism was speculation about the limits of God's ability to do things. The nominalists, including Biel, believed that God is in principle able to do anything that is not a logical contradiction. God cannot make a square circle or lift an unliftable stone, but since such things are intrinsically nonsense, they represent no limitation on his power. In the same way, said Biel, God cannot annihilate himself, since he exists necessarily. Anything that is not a logical contradiction, however, God can do.

This unlimited power, God's metaphysical freedom to do anything at all that is not self-contradictory, was known as *potentia absoluta*. It was by *potentia absoluta* that God willed to create. He was under no necessity to do so, and could just as easily have not created anything at all.

God has a second kind of power, on the other hand, which the nominalists called *potentia ordinata*: a self-limited, ordained power or freedom which arises from the exercise of his unlimited power. Having created a finite, orderly world through his unlimited power, God is thenceforth bound by the self-imposed order of that world, or he will be inconsistent. For example, God has willed that pain follow injury. He could just as easily have willed that pleasure follow injury, or that injury be followed by no sensation at all. But once he has willed pain to follow injury, that order becomes a limitation that God must honor; if he does not, he will be inconsistent and his creation chaotic. *Potentia ordinata*, then, is the power that God exercises under this self-imposed limitation. Note that the limitation is self-imposed, for the nominalists always stressed what they called the freedom of God, by which they meant that absolutely any kind of action was open to God. (Freedom,

1962, changed a great deal.

like power and grace, was a concept that would be completely redefined by the Protestant Reformers.)

This account of God's power and will forms the backdrop for Biel's nominalist doctrine of justification. God could have put the universe together in any way he wanted by *potentia absoluta*, but having put it together in the way we have it, he has freely imposed upon himself a pattern (*potentia ordinata*) of dealing with us as creatures—or more critically, as sinful creatures, for the doctrine of justification pertains to how God deals with sinful creatures. Specifically, how do sinners come to be rightly related to a holy God?

Biel casts his answer to this question in terms of the respective roles played by God and humankind. Our role has chiefly to do with the nature of the human act, which can be evaluated in every case with respect to its goodness, or *bonitas*. It is important to note that when Biel speaks of goodness, he is thinking (in contrast to the Reformers) of a moral act; goodness for him is a moral category, not a theological one. Upon such a moral act, or *bonitas*, God gratuitously confers merit or worthiness, elevating it to *dignitas*. It is crucial for Biel that this is a free act of grace on the part of God. Once an act is elevated by grace to *dignitas*, however, God is under a metaphysical necessity to reward it with salvation.

We can see at once how this fits into the nominalist notion of divine power. The good moral act, in and of itself, could never oblige God to do anything. Once elevated by God's own grace, however, it gives the human agent a claim on eternal salvation—a claim which corresponds to a self-imposed limitation of God by an order he himself has created. In other words, it is by an exercise of *potentia absoluta* that God elevates our moral act or *bonitas* to the level of *dignitas*, whereupon he is obliged to grant eternal salvation through an act of *potentia ordinata*.

Nominalist theology devoted considerable time and energy to finessing the difference between congruent merit and condign merit in this scheme. Congruent merit is the merit of the morally good act of a human, conferred on it freely and graciously by God through *potentia absoluta.* Condign merit is the resulting claim of *dignitas* to salvation through an act of God's *potentia ordinata*, that is, under the self-imposed order whereby he has obligated himself. The elevation of *bonitas* to *dignitas* is a question of mercy, not justice. Once *bonitas* has been elevated to *dignitas*, however, strict justice applies: God must grant eternal salvation to *dignitas* or he denies himself, and that is impossible.

This is the heart of Biel's doctrine of justification. What are the presuppositions?

The first presupposition is that in its natural state, trying its utmost, humankind can love God more than anything else. If we will ourselves to love God, we can, and if we will ourselves to love God more than anything else in the world, we can do that, too. In other words, people have within themselves the capacity and even the desire to love God above all else.

The second presupposition is that in its natural state humankind has the capacity to choose good and evil. Without this capacity, we would cease to be human.

The third presupposition is that the will, which is this capacity for choice, is blind and must be guided by reason. According to Biel, reason is not significantly impaired, if at all. It informs and advises the will, presenting it with alternatives for moral action, and on the strength of this information the will produces a morally good act. Our morally good act, therefore, which is the first step in the process of justification, is one which we ourselves have willed on the strength of the information brought to us by reason.

Now, Biel acknowledges that no human act of moral goodness or *bonitas* is ever good enough to meet the requirements of God, and therefore such a moral act needs to be graced by God. It is God himself who makes the act worthy, converting it into *dignitas*. Note, however, that in Biel's scheme it is not any and every human act that is freely infused by grace. It is only the morally good act which God freely and graciously chooses to elevate, for the seed of grace needs to be planted in fertile soil. The person devoid of moral goodness presents only stony soil, while the moral act, arising from an inherent moral capacity, is the fertile ground which grace can inseminate.

As we saw in our discussion of Erasmus, the Protestant Reformers would disagree with this from the outset, since they believed that every faculty of the human creature was fundamentally impaired by the Fall: the will is not merely blind but downright corrupt, while its supposed informant, reason, now functions primarily as rationalization for rebellion.

For Biel, however, sin has not made it impossible for humankind to act rightly without the aid of grace. According to him, failure to act rightly is a result of improper cognition or misinformation; it is rooted in ignorance. The primary task of the church, therefore, is informational. It is not primarily to be the vehicle of God's grace (as the Reformers would say), since God himself adds grace to *bonitas* with or without the church; it is to provide people with the proper moral information so they will know which acts are genuinely good.

This information, Biel believed, was a compend of two kinds of knowledge. It was partly a natural knowledge of God and his will—although a much more attenuated natural knowledge than that propounded by Thomas Aquinas—and partly a revealed knowledge accepted on the authority of the church or one of its ministers. This combined knowledge Biel described as "acquired faith." He did not pretend that acquired faith could meet the requirements of God; even in Biel's view, we always need grace. To the suggestion that his theology of justification was merely a moralistic scheme without reference to grace, Biel would reply that, on the contrary, grace is the crucial term, apart from which our morally good act does not merit salvation or eternal life. It is only grace that elevates *bonitas* to *dignitas* so as to meet the requirements of God.

A key theological term in all of this is *iustitia*, which most of the medievalists understood as "justice." For Gabriel Biel, *iustitia* operates on the move from *dignitas* to eternal life, while grace operates at the level of *bonitas*. In fact, the concepts of *iustitia* and grace are opposites for Biel. The Protestant Reformers radically reinterpreted both *iustitia* and grace; they understood *iustitia* as "justification," or that which makes us just and right. Insofar as it is not based on our own merit, it is not in opposition to grace. And it cannot be based on our own merit, because our moral acts are no more meritorious than our immoral ones; both alike merit only condemnation. Moral acts are no more "fertile soil" for grace than immoral ones.

Biel would argue that even though our moral acts may be more impure than not, the simple initiative of pursuing *bonitas*, even if it is not achieved, will be graced. God in his mercy graces the human intent or aspiration to do good—a teaching not very different from what is regularly heard in some churches today. Biel adduces scriptural support for this idea in the form of such verses as Zechariah 1:3: "'Return to me,' says the Lord of hosts, 'and I will return to you.'" A similar one is James 4:8, "Draw near to God and he will draw near to you," and a third is Revelation 3:20, "Behold I stand at the door and knock; if anyone hears my voice and opens the door, I will come in to him and eat with him and he with me." Biel reads these texts to mean that if we take the first step, even if it is nothing more than aspiration, God will recognize and elevate it, out of sheer grace, to something that merits eternal salvation on the basis of justice. Grace is the key that works with our moral aspiration so that it will ultimately satisfy justice on the basis of condign merit. Of course, the whole distinction between condign and congruent merit will be swept away by the Reformers' exclusive appeal to the merit of Jesus Christ the crucified One.

The essence of Christianity, then, for Biel, is the gratuitous elevation of our moral goodness by God. God is under no obligation to do this, but does so out of his overflowing kindness. The mere aspiration to be a better moral creature is an implicit plea for God's mercy, and this plea never goes unnoticed; God unfailingly bestows the mercy for which we plead. Justification, then, is twofold: it is by grace alone, because no matter how much *bonitas* we have, only God can elevate it to *dignitas*; but it is also by works, because we must do our best.

Whenever this twofold scheme is proposed—by grace and by works—the emphasis always falls on works. In other words, the grace portion is a rational outer structure whose inner content is nonetheless works. The congruence between this and much of contemporary Protestantism is notable. It is not that grace or its sufficiency is denied; there is the assurance that if we do our best, God will supply *by grace* what is lacking in our effort and bestow upon us what we otherwise would not merit. But our part is to aspire to morality and produce moral behavior, through fear of judgment and the hope of salvation. And this work of ours inevitably becomes the focus of the church's preaching in such a scheme.

If Biel's notion of justification is not thoroughly Pelagian, the logic of Pelagianism can certainly be recognized in it. He explicitly rejects the Reformers' teaching of justification by grace alone as an error of carnal and idle men, as a scorning of God's justice. We are not saved by grace alone, says Biel; we are saved by grace *on the way* to being saved by God's justice on the basis of condign merit. Genuine love for God is within the reach of all of us, he contends; it is up to us, therefore, to take the initiative. What he is proposing as the basis of salvation is essentially our own moral achievement injected with something called grace: morality on steroids, as it were. Notice that in Biel's theology, God's allegedly overflowing mercy does not flow to those who produce no *bonitas*; they are not eligible. (If that is the case, if one must be eligible to receive mercy, how is it an expression of grace?)

Notice also that the cross is seriously undervalued in this theology. For Biel, the cross has something to do with grace, certainly; it is that which renders the grace of God available. However, the grace of God thus rendered available is not effective without our moral aspiration or achievement.

What does it mean to say, with the Reformers, that the cross is *sufficient*? We say that justification is by grace, through faith, on account of what Christ did on the cross. Does this not suggest the necessity of faith? How can we say both that faith is necessary and that the cross is sufficient for salvation? What we mean is that it is the efficacy of the cross that forges even the faith in our hearts. It is not that we generate this faith and add it to what the cross has accomplished, for that too would be a form of Pelagianism. Admittedly, faith is a human act or affirmation or event, or it is nothing; but it is only because of the efficacy and the sufficiency of the cross that faith is a *gift* to be *exercised.*

Biel was sincere and devout, a man of moral rectitude. As a member of the Brethren of the Common Life he was concerned with greater spiritual genuineness and integrity, and certainly would have approved of the cleanup of the church of his era. Yet he was far from the Reformation understanding of the gospel. This is significant, because it is easy nowadays to secure an admission that the church on the eve of the Reformation needed institutional and moral cleansing. What people are less willing to concede today is that even if the church had been thoroughly 'cleaned up', its theology obscured the gospel, according to the Reformers. Many today—Protestants included—espouse a theology similar to Biel's.

Consider the parable of the Pharisee and the publican in Luke 18. When the two men go up to the temple to pray, the Pharisee lists his virtues while the publican can only say that he is a sinner. Yet it is the publican who goes home justified. This parable is so often preached in such a way as to miss the point completely: the Pharisee, it is said, believes himself to be a moral paragon, but is not; he is really a proud hypocrite who has not achieved genuine moral rectitude at all. But the parable is without force unless the Pharisee is in fact a man of genuine, profound moral achievement. For the point is that *the man whose life is truly moral nevertheless goes home unjustified.* This is just as difficult to accept now as it was in Jesus' day, or in Biel's—this idea that the moral person is as far from the Kingdom as the immoral person. Deep down, we want to believe that there is *something* of our salvation that we merit. The tendency is to look upon morality as a step in a spiritual progression in which we move from immorality to morality to salvation; in other words, morality is halfway to the Kingdom. The truth uncovered by the Reformers, however, is that the moral person and the immoral person are equidistant from the Kingdom. Indeed, neither is even within the orbit of the Kingdom.

THE REFORMERS' DISAGREEMENTS WITH BIEL

1. Outside the state of grace, humankind cannot love God at all, let alone above all.

To be outside the state of grace is to be in a state of nature, and for the Protestant Reformers a state of nature presupposes a state of *fallen* nature. Biel would acknowledge that we are fallen creatures, but in his medieval scholastic framework the damage arising from the Fall is not as thoroughgoing as the Protestant Reformers claim it is; according to the medieval scholastics, even in the wake of the Fall there is a residual moral goodness by which we can reorient ourselves to God. While the Protestant Reformers never deny this residual moral goodness, they insist that it has no salvific significance. Outside the state of grace, we cannot love God at all, let alone above all, since our affect is as thoroughly devastated by the Fall as our reason and our will. We do not seek God; we flee him, but are pursued and overtaken by him.

What passes for love of God, in this fallen state, is religion. The Reformers recognize that fallen humankind may be deeply religious, but they distinguish religion from faith. Religiosity is only idolatry, a barrier behind which we flee from God in the guise of seeking him. Religion is our attempt to justify ourselves before a God who is arbitrary and capricious. Faith, by contrast, is a recognition that God in his grace has already justified us.[6]

The Bible in its entirety exposes the idolatry of religion; Martin Buber's description of modernity, quoted earlier, as "open to religion but closed to faith" is an understanding obtained from the Bible. We must be sure, however, when exposing religiosity as a posture of

---

6.   See Karl Barth, *Church Dogmatics*, I, 2, para. 17: "The Revelation of God as the Abolition of Religion."

human defiance and self-justification, that we include *Christian* religiosity. Christians are as religious as anybody else, because religiosity is ingrained in us. Jacob Jocz, a theologian preoccupied with the theological problem of religion, once said to me, "It isn't enough that the gospel exposes religiosity for what it is. The problem is that religiosity is endemic; not even the gospel can root it out of us. Therefore it has to be *converted* by the gospel."[7]

2. Instead of reason guiding the will, the will warps reason.

Not only our affect is devastated by the Fall; so is our will. The Reformers use the phrase *in se curvatus*—bent in on itself—to describe our will. We are afflicted with concupiscence, a spiritual narcissism in which we make ourselves the measure of everything. We profess to be able to will ourselves at least part of the way to God, not realizing that our attempt to do so amounts to disdain for his having already come all the way to us in Jesus Christ. We end up willing our ingratitude and blindness—which is to say, our sin, our continued alienation. As Augustine said, "What can the evil will will besides evil? Nothing."

The will, as understood in the time of the Reformation, corresponds to what the Hebrew Bible calls the 'heart': the control center of the personality. According to the Reformers, our fallen will warps our reason. In the wake of the Fall, our reason is perverted with respect to God, and is largely of the order of rationalization. Even if reason had survived the Fall intact, there is no logical bridge whereby we can reason from finite, contingent being to the necessary, non-contingent being of God. All the more certainly, then, our fallen reason can never inform us of the gospel or the truth of the cross. Notice that when people who are unaware of the gospel speculate about God, they never speculate about the humility of the manger and the humiliation of the cross. They char-

---

7. Jacob Jocz was professor of theology at Wycliffe College, Toronto, from 1960-1976. See his *The Spiritual History of Israel* (London: Eyre & Spottiswoode, 1961).

acterize God chiefly in terms of limitless, unmodified power. Yet it is at Calvary that God reconciles a recalcitrant world to himself, loving us out of the infinite resources of love that he is. He thus carries out his mightiest and most characteristic act when from a human perspective he appears most helpless. Such a God never occurs to human reason, let alone fallen reason.

A natural knowledge of God is affirmed by all the Protestant Reformers, but it is of a kind that serves one purpose only, namely, to render humankind inexcusable. It can never inform us of the gospel or of the will of God for our lives; it only silences the person who says, "I need no Savior." Calvin has a particularly vivid metaphor for this. It is as if we are walking across a muddy, rocky, and treacherous moor at night in a thunderstorm when a flash of lightning illuminates the terrain. For a millisecond we can see bog, rock, and precipice, but before we can take one step to avoid anything, or one step towards home, the lightning flash disappears.[8] The natural knowledge we have of God is like the lightning flash, says Calvin, acquainting us with the horror but unable to help us find our way out of it or do anything about it. Only the Spirit does that. With no little vehemence Luther comments, "Reason is the Devil's greatest whore; by nature and manner of being she is a noxious whore; she is a prostitute, the Devil's appointed whore; whore eaten by scab and leprosy who ought to be trodden under foot and destroyed, she and her wisdom."[9] Many people have adduced this as evidence of his anti-intellectualism, but a writer of fifty-five tomes is hardly an anti-intellectual. What Luther means by 'reason' in this statement is philosophical speculation. His point is that no amount of philosophical speculation can acquaint us with the gospel of the wretched, God-rejected Crucified, whom we apprehend only by faith.

Though never anti-rational, the Reformers were anti-rationalistic. To be *rational* is simply to possess and exercise the faculty of reason,

---

8. For an amplification of this notion, see Calvin, *Institutes,* 1.3-4.

9. For an extended discussion of this point see Martin Luther, *Works* (Erlangen Edition), Vol. 16, pp. 142-168.

but *rationalism* is the belief that by reason we gain access to ultimate reality. The Reformers would say that it is not reason, but spirit—that is, the Holy Spirit suffusing the human spirit—that grants us access to ultimate reality. What we mean by spirit is our capacity for relationship with God. This is what defines the essence of humanness, and it includes our rationality; reason is included in and subordinate to spirit, and must therefore, in the wake of the Fall, be corrected and restored to integrity by grace. Human knowledge of God obviously presupposes humanness—hence the engagement of spirit—but is only received through the work of God's Spirit. The gospel of the cross does not contradict *rationality*, because the gospel can be understood; but it contradicts *rationalism* and puts an end to speculation, because it can only be understood by faith as our reason is restored to its integrity through the action of the Holy Spirit.

When it comes to reason, then, the Reformers had the same disagreement with Biel's nominalism that they had with humanism. They maintained that the structure of reason—without which we would not be human—remains despite the Fall, but its integrity with respect to spiritual matters is devastated so that it serves the interest of sin by rationalization. When our hearts are seized by temptation, does not the thing to which we are tempted become, in that moment, the most reasonable thing in the world, and is that not after all why we do it? One of the slogans of Alcoholics Anonymous is "It's not your drinking, it's your stinking thinking." In other words, alcoholism is rooted in a characteristic pattern of thinking which is entirely rational, but which serves unconsciously to legitimate the addiction. The unwelcome truth, however, is that we are *all* beset by 'stinking thinking'. Part of sin's appeal and addictiveness is that sin brings with it the most cogent reasoning for engaging in it and continuing in it. If we rely on our reason to deliver us from temptation, therefore, we are only drawn more deeply into it, for our will has warped our reason.

3. While a morally good act or aspiration is always possible (and may even be actual), it is neither a sign of grace nor a step towards grace.

For the Reformers, morality has the same significance as religion: it is an abomination to God. Morality and religion make common cause in reinforcing our sin, that is, our unbelief and our contempt of God. We are capable of moral behavior, but morality is not a sign of grace, nor is it an invitation to grace. Why do the prostitutes and tax collectors enter the Kingdom ahead of the morally upright? It is because they are not hiding behind a smoke screen of morality or religion.

4. The entire discussion of condign versus congruent merit contradicts the logic of Scripture.

Condign and congruent merit are features of human acts or aspirations. For the Reformers, however, we do not plead our own merit at all, however elevated. The only merit is that of Jesus Christ, whose obedience to his Father, wherein he has made atonement for sin, is imputed to those who cling to him in faith. The distinction between congruent and condign merit, therefore, which loomed large in the Middle Ages, falls completely outside the Reformers' understanding of the gospel.

5. It is not merely out of misinformation or improper cognition that we fail to act rightly.

The root human problem, according to the Reformers, is not ignorance but perverseness. Humankind wills to be its own lord. In Genesis 3, the serpent asks, "Did God say ...?" "Are you sure God said ...?" God *did* say, speaking to the creature from his position as Lord. The very fact that God is distinct from what he has created, that it owes its existence to him as Creator, makes God Lord over the creature. But we will to make ourselves our own lord, the essence of sin.

"You will be like gods, knowing good and evil," the serpent promised in Genesis 3:5. We were given what we wanted, a knowledge of good and evil, but that knowledge is itself curse. Many people misunderstand this, thinking that a knowledge of good and evil is the ability to distinguish, intellectually, between good on the one hand and evil on the other. But to "know" here means knowing in the biblical sense of immersing oneself personally, and "good and evil" is a Hebraic expression meaning "everything", the sum total of possibility. To "know good and evil", then, is to be intimately acquainted with much that cannot bless us but can only ruin us. It means that we extend our lives into areas that bring down curse, areas that have been marked "off limits" by God to spare us disaster.

What we need in the midst of this ruin is not information, for no amount of information can overturn the human predicament. Our root problem is not that we have been deprived of knowledge, since on the contrary we obtained what we wanted, an intimate acquaintance with precisely what God has forbidden. The result, however, is that we are depraved, and we need someone to overcome this depravity.

6. *The primary task of the church, therefore, is not to provide people with moral information about God and goodness but to set forth Jesus Christ.*

The gospel has content, and this content must be announced and declared with all possible cogency; the gospel is not, after all, gobbledygook or superstition. In view of what has been said above, however, the benefit of the gospel is not ultimately informational. It is the *power of God* for salvation (Romans 1:16). In articulating the truth content of the gospel, therefore, the Reformers are not providing information on the basis of which we initiate a process of salvation based on merit. For one thing, the truth of the gospel is intelligible only through the activity of the Holy Spirit. And for another, as we have seen from all that has been said so far in response to Biel, we are helpless to initiate anything with salvific effect. It is not information that is the solution to the human predicament, but deliverance.

The primary task of the church, then, is to set forth Jesus Christ, the Deliverer. And who is he? He is the one attested by prophet and apostle. In the words of Luther, "Scripture is the manger in which the child is laid." Manger and child are categorically distinct, as are Scripture and

Christ, but we do not have one without the other. We cannot have the child without the manger, nor Christ without Scripture. It is the Christ of Scripture that the church is to set forth.

There is no articulation or setting forth of Christ which is not replete with content, with substantive information. But which subserves which? What is means and what is end? Ultimately, the purpose of the church is to be the vehicle of grace by setting forth Jesus Christ in the power of the Spirit, to be received by faith.[10]

7. There is no distinction between the grace of Jesus Christ and the grace of God; grace is God's action in Jesus Christ.

The medieval scholastics distinguished between the grace of Christ and the grace of God. In Biel's account, the grace of Christ operates only in the elevation of *bonitas* to *dignitas*, whereas the grace of God is what devised the whole scheme in the first place. For the Reformers, on the other hand, the grace of Christ *is* the grace of God. The grace of God is his effectual presence: God himself acting graciously in Christ. This understanding also disallows any reification of grace, as if it were an entity added to something else like an infusion. Grace is not a tonic or booster; it is the gracious action of the person of God in Christ upon us sinners.

8. Iustitia (justice) is neither (i) an abstract standard or code by which we are measured, nor (ii) the metaphysical necessity of God's rewarding dignitas.

Justice, say the Reformers, is not a quality or abstraction, but the act of justifying. God's justice is his act of putting us in the right with himself, thereby vindicating himself and his people, relieving the oppressed,

---

10. Reflecting the conviction of the sixteenth-century Reformers John Wesley used to end his day by writing four simple words in his diary: "I offered them Christ."

and clearing the opprobrium heaped on those deemed "beyond the pale." This is the way the word is used in the Older Testament.

Hitzdiq, in Hebrew, is the causative of *zadaq*: *zadaq* means "to be righteousness" and *hitzdiq* means "to make righteous." The two are morphologically and semantically related. In Greek, any verb ending in *-oun* is likewise causative; *dikaioun*, in the New Testament, means not "to be right" or "to do right", but "to *make* right," and is the verb used to express our being made righteous by God in Christ. Luther and the other Reformers read extensively in the Old Testament, particularly the Psalms, Deuteronomy, and the latter part of Isaiah. As they did, they came to see that *hitzdiq*—the causative of *zadaq*—always has to do with the action God takes to vindicate, save, and restore people. They noticed that the same word was translated *dikaioun* in the New Testament, and that these Hebrew and Greek words provided the underlay for the Latin word *iustitia*. *Iustitia* has to do, therefore, not with courtroom justice, the judge giving us what we deserve, but with the action of the judge (who is also and primarily savior) in making us just or right. In this process of justification, of restoring us to favor and to himself, the judge becomes our father. This was one of the Copernican revolutions of the Reformation.

9. "Doing one's best" is not begging for mercy. It is the opposite of begging for mercy.

The Reformers argue that the greater and more sincere our moral effort, the stronger the bastion built by our pride in defiance of Jesus Christ. The person whose life is morally faultless is the last to surrender to the gospel, saying, "I don't need it; point out some defect in my life." The defect in his life is that he is defiant of God, but he sees no defect because he is operating out of a moral framework rather than a spiritual one. From a moral standpoint his life is defect-free, but from a spiritual perspective it is wholly defective because he is offering his own goodness under his own lordship. To do one's best is to disdain the mercy God has enacted in the Son and visited upon his people through the Spirit.

10. Fallen humankind cannot "unlock the door" to God.

Biel read Revelation 3:20 as an invitation to the sinful human being to unlock the door and let God in. For the Reformers, however, no unlocking is possible by fallen humankind; any unlocking of the door is only by grace, that is, through the action of the Holy Spirit. The reformed tradition will invoke a doctrine of election here, whereas the Wesleyan tradition will invoke a doctrine of prevenient grace, but they amount to the same thing for purposes of contrast with Biel. The point is that the initiative must be taken by God. (Rev. 3:20, in any case, has to do with the Christians in Lacodicea; it is not directed at unbelievers.)

11. In the wake of the Fall, no one seeks God. We flee God.

Modernity, drunk on what it calls spirituality, has much in common with Biel's theology here. It is assumed that the quest for spirituality is a quest for God. But if our quest for spirituality can be satisfied by tree-hugging or whale-saving, or by some form of altruism, then it is not a quest for God. As a matter of fact, all fallen humankind flees God under the guise of seeking him. This is contrary to much preaching in the church today which assumes that all humankind seeks at least latently for God and that religious people seek him overtly. We think we are seeking God as we try to deal with the dis-ease in our innermost heart, but we are really running in the opposite direction.

God is sought only in faith. That is to say, it is once we come to faith in Jesus Christ that we genuinely and ardently pursue God from within that reality. We do not pursue God into faith, however; it is he who has pursued us. The gospel is the declaration that the God who never was lost or difficult to locate has in his mercy sought and found us. God seeks a rebellious race, a race that does not seek him, although we characteristically eagerly seek elsewhere some solution to our predicament.

12. There is no natural knowledge of God. The apprehension of God available through the creation serves only to condemn us.

Reading of the hardships endured by Paul and the other apostles in the cause of preaching the gospel, can we imagine that they believed a saving knowledge of God was naturally available through the creation? Such a knowledge would render their preaching superfluous. The apostles endured what they did because they knew that the gospel supplied what was available nowhere else. No part of the gospel is available through a natural knowledge of God. On the contrary, the "knowledge" we obtain through the creation serves only to condemn us.

13. There is no natural knowledge of sin.

If there is no natural knowledge of God, there is no natural knowledge of sin either, because knowledge of God is what generates a knowledge of sin. We often take for granted that the nature and existence of God must be revealed to us, while failing to recognize that the same is true of the nature and existence of sin. Those who believe there is a natural knowledge of sin typically define sin as immorality; as we have already seen, however, sin includes both morality and immorality in equal measure. Or perhaps what we mistake for a natural knowledge of sin is instead a natural knowledge of *Angst*, of innermost disquiet. In any case, it is only through the action of the Holy Spirit, giving rise to an understanding of grace, that we are able to know sin as unbelief and defiance of God. If grace is God's overtaking us, then sin is our flight from God. If grace is God's gratuitous pardon, sin must be our otherwise ineradicable guilt.

Another way of saying this is that only the existence of a relationship with God—faith—acquaints us with the nature of a defective relationship. When the psalmist cries, "Against thee only have I sinned" (Psalm 51:4), he is not denying that sin violates others besides God; when we sin against God, we also violate our neighbor. He is acknowledging, however, that sin is defined by reference to God and is revealed to be sin by God's self-disclosure. Until we know God, we cannot know the nature of a defective relationship with him. In the presence of Jesus Christ, the cure for sin, the ailment can finally be seen for what it is; otherwise, sin is misunderstood as immorality, vice, or the violation of taboo.

Some people confuse conscience with a natural knowledge of sin, but conscience is a tricky thing. It is as thoroughly fallen as any other human faculty and equally in need of correction and restoration. The natural conscience, to the extent that it is not altogether deadened, condemns us without reprieve and tells us we are worthless. We tend to think of conscience as the voice of God whispering to us, but Luther says it is the voice of the devil, the voice of despair.

The question of conscience raises the issue of morality again. The fact that there is no natural knowledge of sin does not mean that we have no natural knowledge of right and wrong, any more than our total depravity means that we are all as bad as we can be. The Reformers acknowledge that there is such a thing as moral living, and that a moral neighbor is much easier to live with than an immoral one; yet that does not mean the moral neighbor is any nearer to the Kingdom. Morality is one means by which the world is preserved and kept from falling into chaos, but it has no salvific significance. Luther had a great appreciation for the residual goodness of creation, such as a mother's love or a friend's self-sacrifice. He would say that these are evidences of the creaturely human good which remains despite the Fall and makes life livable. While the goodness of creation is compromised by the Fall, it is not obliterated. This aspect of the creation is handled, however, in terms of a doctrine of providence rather than a doctrine of grace: it is God's constant preservation of the world, including those structures that promote order and livability, that accounts for what good we see around us. Nevertheless, our natural knowledge of right and wrong, and our natural morality, avail us nothing when it comes to recognizing or dealing with our basic plight.

14. Faith is not a compend of natural knowledge and revealed knowledge, nor is it "acquired".

In the first place, as already discussed above, faith is not knowledge in the sense of information, even though the gospel does obviously have information content. Rather, faith is fellowship with Jesus Christ, union with Christ, intimacy with Christ. Christ embraces us by grace, and in the power of his embrace we find ourselves both able and eager to embrace him. This brings us to the second objection of the Reformers, which is that faith is never "acquired" in any case, but is rather always a gift. Faith is the grace-facilitated response to the action of Christ.[11] Preaching that aids this response in people is not mere exhortation to have faith, therefore, but the announcement of the grace of Christ.

15. To affirm salvation by faith alone is not to scorn God's justice (i.e., his judgment) but to submit to it, recognizing that we can only receive what he has fashioned for us in our need.

Biel accused the Reformers of scorning the justice of God, and even today people raise this objection. The Reformers would reply that an insistence on salvation by grace alone in fact upholds the justice of God, because it means that God's judgment on my sin has been exercised and is now an item of the past. The future judgment, which none of us can escape, has been brought forward into the present, and acquittal has been pronounced. This acquittal is not a suspension of judgment; judgment on us sinners *has* been rendered, in the cross, and absorbed there.

---

11.   The Reformers did not present it in exactly this light. Rightly reading Scripture, they insisted that faith is a gift, but undervalued the human exercise of that gift, as though faith were something granted over our heads or behind our backs without engaging us as human persons. It is a weakness of the Reformation that it failed to emphasize faith as a gift which quickens in us a genuinely human affirmation and activity, as described here. While the Reformers saw correctly that faith is never our contribution, faith is ever our commitment, and as such essential.

God's justifying us *always* includes his judging us, for his judgment is not the antithesis of his mercy but its converse: God's judgment serves the work of his mercy.[12] He bothers to judge us only because he longs to save us. *Sola fide* ("by faith alone"), then—an acknowledgment that we can only receive what God has fashioned for us in our need, namely, his provision of righteousness—endorses God's judgment rather than subverting it.

16. The will is not free to choose; it is bound.

The Reformers would not deny that we can choose among creaturely goods, such as to eat hot dogs rather than hamburgers, to study rather than watch TV, or to take the bus rather than drive. We can even choose moral goods. But inasmuch as we are fallen creatures, our will is bound with respect to spiritual good, the Kingdom of God, and of course the King himself, that Son with whom the Father is pleased. We cannot will ourselves out of our depravity into the righteousness of God, nor can we choose Jesus Christ except as a result of his having first chosen us. What we most sorely need must be accomplished for us and pressed upon us, for we cannot will to effect it in ourselves. Indeed, apart from grace, we cannot even recognize either the true good—Christ's righteousness—or our lack of it, because there is no natural knowledge of sin. Hence there can never be a natural willing of ourselves out of sin. The very attempt to please God or to undo our depravity only confirms and intensifies our depravity, our defiance of God and the provision he has made in the Cross. The structure of the will survives the Fall, recall, or we would not be human; but the integrity of the will is forfeited. The Reformers would acknowledge that the fallen human can will moral

---

12. Elie Wiesel makes the point repeatedly that the opposite of love is not hate but indifference, since hate still takes the person seriously, whereas indifference writes the person off as insignificant. In the Bible, the 'hatred' of God is God's judgment serving his mercy: if he did not love us, he would not judge us but would be indifferent towards us. See Elie Wiesel, *Night* (New York: Hill and Wang, 2006) and *From the Kingdom of Memory* (New York: Summit Books, 1990), *passim*.

good, including the highest moral good of self-sacrifice, but their distinction between sin and immorality, and between righteousness and morality, must be kept in mind. All that the fallen will can will, in terms of spiritual concerns, is sin.

17. The distinction between an outer structure of grace and an inner content of (meritorious) work is unbiblical and therefore impermissible.

It is not possible to have an outer structure of grace and an inner content of meritorious work. This is a misunderstanding, again, of grace. Grace is not a feature added to something; grace is the work of God. If we are saved by grace, we are saved by God alone. We are not saved by our own work somehow infused by the grace of God.

18. To be a beneficiary of Christ's righteousness is at the same time to be the beneficiary of God's righteousness; i.e., justification in the present forms the stable basis and not the uncertain goal of the Christian life.

The medieval scholastics distinguished not only between the grace of God and the grace of Christ, but between the righteousness of God and the righteousness of Christ: *iustitia Dei* and *iustitia Christi*. They said that the righteousness of Christ is that righteousness—highly moralized—which is ours now, whereas the righteousness of God is the future pronouncement of God upon us on the day of judgment. But if these two are different, objected the Reformers, how do we know that the righteousness of Christ, while better than none at all, will be sufficient to secure a favorable judgment from God at the end of time? Moreover, they argued, the Father and Son possessing the same nature, the righteousness of Father and Son must be the same. Therefore *iustitia Christi* equals *iustitia Dei*, and the righteousness of Christ pronounced upon the believer now *is* the righteousness of God at the end of time. To be justified by faith now means that the future judgment of God upon us has been brought forward into the present and we are pronounced acquitted.

The Reformers' point was that justification forms the stable basis of the believer's present life and not the uncertain goal of the future. That everyone must face the day of judgment is undeniable, but for us the day of judgment has already been anticipated. On that day we will undoubtedly learn things about ourselves that we do not know now, things that will horrify us, but we will not learn to our surprise that we are condemned. Instead we will find confirmed then what we know now: that since by faith we are found in Jesus Christ, the Son with whom the Father is ever pleased, the Father is pleased with us. We can therefore anticipate with confidence the verdict that will be rendered on the day of judgment. That is the Reformer's gospel.

In what sense, then, will we be judged according to our works? The Reformers would say that the final judgment has a purgatorial dimension. There is a great deal of spiritual garbage in us, known and as yet mostly unknown to us, that will be exposed on the day of judgment and purged as if by fire. In the words of Wesley, two hundred years after the Protestant Reformers, "Justification gives us the right to heaven; sanctification makes us fit for heaven."[13] He said this in the context of our spiritual formation in this life, but the end of this process occurs at the judgment. If someone who has been given a free ticket to the symphony cannot abide classical music, she has the right to attend, but will find the concert a torment. Similarly, justified sinners have the right to heaven, but insofar as heaven is where God's will is done perfectly and there is a great deal in us which does not yet reflect God's will, our presence in heaven would be torment unless we were first purged. We will survive the judgment, however, because "no condemnation" has been vouchsafed to us in the present.

In other words, the Reformers would not deny that there is an ongoing work of sanctification in the believer, which ought even to proceed faster than it does. They would not deny that works of wood,

---

13.   John Wesley, ed. by Frank Baker. *A Plain Account of Christian Perfection* (London: Epworth Press, 1991), p. 31. Wesley makes the same point in his "On the Wedding Garment," *Works of John Wesley* (Nashville: Abingdon Press, 1987).

hay, and stubble—to use the metaphor in 1 Corinthians 3—will need to be scorched out of us. Their point is that the issue of acquittal or condemnation does not await the believer, for it has been brought forward into the present and acquittal is already pronounced.

THE HUMAN PREDICAMENT REVISITED

The thinking of the Reformers involves a distinction between what we might call, today, the human condition and the human situation. The human *situation* is the set of problems which can be described by the sociologist, the psychologist, the biologist, the anthropologist, the novelist, or the economist, but they are only the symptoms. Their cause is the human *condition*, our predicament before God: we are creatures, made in God's image, who are profoundly perverted. Our condition can only be diagnosed by the gospel, and the only remedy for it is grace; that is, reconstitution at the hands of Jesus Christ. Our recognition of our predicament is the effect of God's remedy. Without the gospel we may understand our situation—the creaturely reasons for our unhappiness—but we do not realize that our root problem goes much deeper.

To express the same distinction in another way: the word that describes who we are—who we have become in the wake of the Fall—is *Sin*, and this gives rise to what we do, namely, *sins*. The relation between Sin and sins is subtle and profound, and runs all through Reformation theology. The Reformation's understanding of Romans 1 is that sins are the conduct to which God consigns us in order to expose our Sin and drive us to accept his provision for us in our predicament. The words "God gave them up" (Romans 1:24, 26, 28) do not mean the same as "God gave up on them;" again, God's judgment serves his mercy. The outcropping of horrible sins is the result of God allowing the character of Sin—of unbelief and defiance—to manifest itself fully in order to confront us with our wretchedness.

Much Christian preaching talks about sins without ever mentioning Sin, and the effect is to moralize the human predicament. On the other hand, to speak of Sin in isolation from concrete sins renders the human predicament abstract, with the effect of trivializing it. Both "Sin" and "sins" are necessary terms and concepts, but today's preaching is heavily weighted towards moralization. We often assume, in the church, that sins, such as theft, murder, and adultery, are what provoke God's anger. They do so, however, only because he is *primarily* angry with Sin: our defiance, our unbelief, our self-lordship. The gospel always addresses Sin primarily, and sins derivatively.

The Reformation will always seem unrealistically extreme unless we understand what the Reformers meant by morality, the judgment of God, and the righteousness of God. Most of us have a rather shallow understanding of the human condition. We believe in our own basic decency and civility, not realizing how thin a veneer it is and how quickly it would disappear under the right circumstances. To have an inkling of our depravity, one has only to read William Golding's *Lord of the Flies*, count the number of armed conflicts going on in the world, or notice what happens in a world-class city when the police are on strike for one night. Yet even the worst sins we commit and witness are not the root problem; they arise from the root problem, Sin. In contrast to both the humanists and the scholastics, the Reformers had a severer appreciation of our predicament. If the remedy for our predicament was the incarnation and death of the Son of God himself, what effort could be too extreme in recovering that gospel apart from which humankind is sealed in its alienation from God?

4

The Early Luther

Luther's tract *Disputation Against Scholastic Theology* was written in the early fall of 1517, and was almost immediately followed by the Halloween manifesto of the *Ninety-Five Theses*. It is not possible here to look at all of Luther's disputations against scholastic theology, of which there are hundreds. Instead we shall probe those that have proved controversial and that continue to reverberate in formal academic contexts and in informal conversations.

One of these is the fifth: "It is false to state that man's inclination is free to choose between either of two opposites. Indeed, the inclination is not free, but captive. This is said in opposition to common opinion."[1] Luther never denies our freedom to choose between creaturely goods. We can choose to play volleyball or read a book, to eat salad or meat. In saying that the inclination is captive, or the will bound, he is not suggesting that no choices are possible. He means that we cannot will ourselves into fellowship with Jesus Christ or out of our own depravity;

---

1. Timothy F. Lull, ed. *Martin Luther's Basic Theological Writings* (Minneapolis: Fortress Press, 1989), p. 13.

we cannot will away our fallen human nature. He amplifies this in the fifteenth disputation, saying, with reference to the will: "Indeed, it is peculiar to it that it can only conform to erroneous and not to correct precept." Even as we hear the command of God, we cannot will ourselves to obey it; we can will only its contradiction. In other words, although sin is not necessary—for nothing outside us constrains us to sin—it is inevitable.

Luther is distinguishing, of course, between original Sin and sins, between our systemic sinnership and its manifestation. Sin, the root problem, is what the Bible calls unbelief. To us modern people, unbelief is a cerebral condition: an unbeliever is a person who disagrees with what others have in their heads. In Scripture, however, unbelief is fundamentally a posture of the heart, a defiant, disdainful, and disobedient positioning of ourselves before God. Luther is speaking here from a theological standpoint, not a moral one. He would never deny that we can make moral choices as fallen human beings, that our conduct can even be morally exemplary. His point rather is that we cannot will ourselves out of our systemic sinnership or unrighteousness. That is a condition analogous to blood poisoning in that it infects and contaminates every last part of us equally, with the result that no one aspect of our being can save the rest.

By "free" in the fifth disputation, Luther means, then, "without any impediment to behaving in conformity with our true nature." If our true nature is to be a son or daughter of God, then insofar as we can live in full conformity with that appointment, we are free. Insofar as we cannot, we are bound, regardless of what creaturely goods we can choose. Similarly, when Paul says in Galatians 5:1, "For freedom Christ has set you free," he does not mean that we have been made able to choose whether to obey Christ or not. He means that there is no longer any impediment to obedience, to acting in accord with our true nature as sons and daughters of God. And since obedience must be glad and eager if it is the obedience God requires of us, the impediment to freedom Luther has in mind includes the desire to disobey. In other words, "freedom" means that any alternative to obedience is inconceivable.

Luther's famous debate with Erasmus in 1525, *The Bondage of the Will*, was read by arch-predestinarians as a defence of predestination. Luther, however, is not concerned to defend predestination as a form of philosophical determinism. His real point is twofold: first, that the righteousness we all need is given rather than achieved; and second, that the essence of the gospel is promise. This promise of God surges over and within us, despite the recalcitrance of our hearts, the folly of our heads, our weak-kneed discipleship, even despite our unbelief, and dispels all impediments to its appropriation. In other words, if justification by faith is the nub of the gospel from a human perspective, predestination is the nub of the gospel from a divine perspective. When Luther speaks of predestination, we must not read back into him a rigidly deterministic understanding with a twofold, symmetrical decree of reprobation and election. Luther does not have nearly so elaborate a scheme.

When Luther was still a monk and much troubled by predestination, he went to see his friend Johann von Staupitz, head of the Reformed Augustinian order in Germany, and Staupitz said to him, "You're troubled by predestination? Contemplate the wounds of Christ." The advice was profound (and therefore fruitful: the immediate outcome was comfort for the troubled monk, and the long-term outcome was Luther's "Theology of the Cross"). Staupitz was alluding to John 12:32: "And I, if I be lifted up, will draw all men and women to me." For Luther, predestination is simply the efficacy of the crucified and risen Lord Jesus Christ surging over us in the power of the Spirit in such a way as to fulfill his promise and thereby eclipse our unbelief.

An important point is made in the eighth disputation: "It does not, however, follow that the will is by nature evil, that is, essentially evil, as the Manicheans maintain." Luther, following Augustine, says that the bound will is evil, but he does not mean that the will is *essentially* evil. Since the will is part and parcel of our humanity, to say that the human will is essentially evil would be to say that the human being is essentially evil, leaving us with three problems. First, the human being could not be redeemed; any "remedy" would necessarily render us non-human. Second, if the will were essentially evil, then the evil of humankind would be traceable not to the Fall but to Creation, making God the author of sin and evil; the only way to avoid such a conclusion would be to posit some other deity, resulting in a Manichean dualism. Third, if to be human were to be essentially evil, then the Incarnation would be impossible. In the Incarnation the Son of God assumes our human nature, under the conditions of the Fall, for (as the church fathers were fond of saying) the unassumed is the unhealed; that is, any part of our humanity not assumed by Christ is not healed by him. The Eternal Word of God becomes flesh and assumes our human nature under the conditions of the Fall, yet remains without sin himself. This would be by definition impossible if humanity were essentially evil. The human will is perverted in the Fall, but the goodness of God's creation perdures throughout the Fall even though distorted.[2]

In Disputation 17, Luther writes: "Man is by nature unable to want God to be God. Indeed, he himself wants to be God, and does not want God to be God." This is a description of our fallen nature, not of our created nature. The root temptation, the primal temptation, is Genesis 3:5: "You shall be as gods, knowing good and evil." Recall that, for the Reformers, unbelief is not an absence of the right intellectual furniture but the installation of ourselves as our own lord and our own god. And in wanting to be our own gods, we all break the first commandment: "You shall have no other gods before me." No one, apart from grace, can fulfill that commandment, says Luther, because we always will deities other than God; ultimately we will ourselves to be judge and lord of ourselves—and of everyone else as well.

It has already been discussed in an earlier chapter how Luther regards the first commandment: to keep that one is to keep all ten, and to break

---

2.   In fact, Luther was soon opposed by some gnesio-Lutherans (the Greek root *gnesio* has to do with rightness or correctness), who said that the will is, in the wake of the Fall, essentially evil. The import of this statement is that the human being became essentially evil in the wake of the Fall, i.e., no longer really human. The most celebrated gnesio-Lutheran was Matthias Flacius Illyricus.

it is to break all ten. In reply to the protest, "I'm not a thief, I'm not an adulterer," Luther would say that the first commandment ("You shall have no other gods before me") can obviously be kept only in faith. Since the first commandment characterizes the remaining nine, the same is true of them. If we merely will ourselves not to steal, for instance, our non-stealing falls short of fulfilling the seventh commandment, because the commandment forbids theft as an expression of our glad and grateful love for our Lord; mere ethical conformity is qualitatively distinct from the logic of the commandment and the obedience it enjoins. The one who refrains from stealing out of mere adherence to a moral code, rather than as an expression of faith in Jesus Christ and love for God, violates the commandment as surely as the one who steals. Luther refers to this concept as "first-commandment righteousness", and amplifies it throughout his work, not least in his *Large Catechism*.

The gospel as promise restores first-commandment righteousness. It is the reassertion of the covenant expressed in Exodus 6:7: "I will be your God, and you will be my people." Our primal sin is to say, "I will be my own god. I will position myself before you as my own lord." This distortion is, therefore, what the gospel addresses. The primal disobedience, says Luther, is to will our self as our own lord, and the primal promise is that God will be our Lord. In our self-lordship there is curse, but in his Lordship there is blessing.

Luther's cry, in reasserting the gospel, was always, "Let God be God." It is evidence of our primal disobedience that even within the church we incline towards theologies that fail to let God be God. One of these is classical liberal theology. By definition, its presupposition is that the self-understanding of the world is the starting point, substance, and controlling principle of the self-understanding of the church. If this is the case, the church is simply the world repeating the world back to itself, and that is exactly what is evident in liberal theologies.

Paul Tillich advances another such theology. He claims that revelation is always dovetailed to the profoundest question generated by humankind out of its own (primarily cultural) resources. Here the presupposition is that whatever our question of God is, generated out of the profoundest introspection, it is always the right question. Surely, however, it is better to say that revelation discloses not only the answer of God, but even the proper question to be asked of God; it is only in the light of God's revelation that we know what question about God we should have asked but could not. Clearly, the deity whom we think we know or seek based on our cultural self-analysis is always going to be a highly acculturated one. How could it not be? Yet Tillich maintains that revelation must meet the question raised by humankind or it could not be revelation; it would fall on deaf ears and would never be appropriated. Plainly, then, according to this theology the question we generate controls the answer that can be given.

Similarly, Rudolf Bultmann so linked his theology to the philosophy of Martin Heidegger that the New Testament says to human modernity precisely what Heidegger allows it to say. All of this is another form, to use Luther's words, of not letting God be God. Luther correctly insists that in the wake of revelation, the questions we put about God or to God are radically transfigured so as to cease to be pseudo-questions.

Yet another form of theological idolatry can be found in some forms of metaphysics. Such metaphysicians maintain that there are two spheres of being, divine and creaturely. What then links these two ontologically distinct spheres is not grace but a metaphysical continuum, "Being" itself, linking divine and creaturely being and comprehending them both. If this were the case, however, this principle of Being would transcend God and thereby be the deity to be worshipped instead of God.

Luther always related the call to let God be God, and the promise of the gospel, to first-commandment righteousness: "You shall have no other gods before me." While the Puritans greatly magnified the idea that all the commandments of God are covered promises, this notion was already understood by the Reformers a hundred years earlier, although they did not articulate it in the same way. "You shall have no other gods before me" is God's way of saying, "I rescued you by my outstretched arm when you were hopeless slaves in Egypt; therefore you need no other gods. Am I not God enough, having brought you out of a land of bondage? Is life in my company, at my initiative, not pure blessing? You will in fact come to embrace no other gods, therefore, because you will not need them; they will be superfluous." For Luther the command of God is always the veiled promise of God, and can only be rightly heard and obeyed in light of the gospel's reassertion of that promise. The alternative is the moralism that continues to haunt the church, not least in its addresses to children. (The Sunday morning "Children's Moment" is frequently where the gospel is denatured into moralism.)

In the twentieth disputation, Luther writes, "An act of friendship is done, not according to nature, but according to prevenient grace. This is in opposition to Gabriel Biel." The word "friendship" here refers to friendship with God, whose prototypical example is Abraham, and an act of friendship with God can be understood as a movement towards God. Biel, as we saw in the previous chapter, regarded grace as operating only after we have exerted ourselves morally. At most such "grace" merely facilitates self-righteousness. For Luther and the other Protestant Reformers, however, grace is always prevenient by definition; it not only anticipates our response to God but is the origin of that response.

Earlier we noted Luther's idea of predestination in connection with his belief regarding the bondage of the will. Disputation 29 contains another reference to predestination: "The best and infallible preparation for grace and the sole disposition toward grace is the eternal election and predestination of God." He means that we are primordially turned out of our sinnership and towards God only by God's grace. We cannot prepare ourselves for grace or predispose ourselves to it; contrary to some aspects of the medieval tradition, there is no penitential process or technique that will accomplish this. God alone can predispose us towards himself, and to recognize this is to let God be God. His promise, greater than our recalcitrant hearts and surging over us in the power of the Holy Spirit, generates our faith in Jesus Christ.

This disputation is more relevant to evangelicalism today than commonly recognized. The notion that one needed to prepare oneself for the gospel by the cultivation of a certain inner disposition is often paralleled today by reliance on psychological and emotional preparation: we have replaced the medieval penitential scheme with a psychological technique that we think prepares people to receive the gospel. But only the power of the gospel fosters a surrender to the gospel. Our unending responsibility as Christian witnesses, therefore, is simply to announce the gospel, not to induce a "convertogenic" psychological or emotional state.

Disputation 33 is crucial: "And this is false, that doing all that one is able to do can remove the obstacles to grace. This is in opposition to several authorities." Doing all that we are able to do means that we are still our own lord. The medieval expression (actually, Augustine coined it) was *facere quod in se est*: to do what lies within oneself. Luther repudiates this notion utterly. Far from predisposing us towards grace, doing what lies within ourselves predisposes us towards judgment, since it is still an expression of our self-willed lordship no matter how noble or magnificent the effort or how sincere the motive. Therefore, whereas it was looked upon almost as a truism that *facere quod in se est* was the starting point of the life of faith, Luther viewed it as the endless contradiction of faith—an act of unbelief. The medieval mystical tradition affirmed that one of the things lying within a person was a form of self-purgation, that on our way to grace we could will away the detritus and contamination in our heart as a condition for friendship with God. Yet even in the attempt, says Luther, we are willing ourselves to be our own savior. Only God, in the power of the gospel, can get rid us of the sludge in our lives. Our responsibility is to recognize and affirm this, and thank him for it.

Although Luther's view counsels neither quietism nor antinomianism, it was misunderstood: he was accused by the radicals of encouraging irresponsible discipleship. Nothing could be farther from the truth, however. Luther's point here is that we cannot will the contamination out of our hearts, because apart from grace we fail even to recognize it. We think the contamination is our moral compromise, when really it is our self-willed lordship—one aspect of which is our moral compromise while the other is our moral triumph with its attendant self-satisfaction. Our virtue, in other words, is as much an instance of self-willed lordship as our vice. By ridding ourselves of vice we have not predisposed ourselves towards grace, therefore, but have only magnified our own self-lordship and sinnership.

In Disputation 39, Luther says, "We are not masters of our actions, from beginning to end, but servants. This in opposition to the philosophers." Luther was fond of the "master" metaphor. He was fond of saying that we are always a horse ridden by one of two riders, either God or the devil. Either Jesus Christ is master or someone else is, but we are never masters of ourselves. There is an obvious contrast here with some expressions of humanism which hold that the self is autonomous. For Luther, the self is most corrupt when it seeks autonomy; only as we surrender by grace to the Lordship of Christ do we become most profoundly our self and possess our self most truly. This notion irritates modernity as well as postmodernity, especially in the suburbanite "yuppie" culture where the self is an achievement and the whole purpose of coming to church is to enhance one's self-achievement.

When Luther speaks "in opposition to the philosophers," he is thinking chiefly of Plato and Aristotle. Plato, who believed in an eternal world of forms from which all things in this world are copied, would declare that the self is most fully self when it apprehends that eternal world of forms. Aristotle would say that the self is rooted in its rationality, since that is what renders it human in distinction from other animals. But Luther, in opposition to both, would say that our humanity is constituted by our orientation to God, the *imago Dei* in which we were created, or the fact of God's addressing us together with our consequent capacity to address God—one aspect of which is our rationality. We are most ourselves, then, when we surrender to the Lordship of Christ.

Disputation 41 likewise critiques the use of philosophy as a foundation. "Virtually the entire *Ethics* of Aristotle is the worst enemy of grace," states Luther categorically. Having taught Aristotle's *Ethics* himself at one point, he knew whereof he was speaking. By now it must be clear why he makes this statement, believing as he did that moral achievement and effort are merely expressions of self-lordship.[3]

In Disputation 57 we encounter something new. "It is dangerous to say that the law commands that an act of obeying the commandment be done in the grace of God," writes Luther. "This in opposition to the Cardinal and Gabriel." At first blush, Disputation 57 seems to contradict all that has been said so far about the relationship of grace to the commandment—namely, that the commandment of God can be fulfilled only in grace, by grace. This is true, of course; the commandment cannot be fulfilled other than by grace. But Luther is about to make a rather subtle point here. For an unbeliever, alien to the life of grace, the law of God remains the law of God nonetheless; it is not rescinded. In other writings to be looked at later, Luther will speak of two functions of the law: the first is to order the public good and promote social order, and the second is to break down our self-confidence and impel us to seek refuge in the gospel. Disputation 57 means that if someone repudiates grace, leaving the law of God unfulfilled, that law does not cease to be operative or to assert a claim. It will not save the person, and it should have been fulfilled in grace, but it remains operative; it is not repealed. The alternative would be to deny that the law is of God and so to precipitate social chaos. This point is important for Luther; in his discussion of Law and Gospel (see below) he insists that the mark of a theologian is precisely the ability to articulate the distinction between Law and Gospel.

Disputation 72 says more about the inability of the fallen will to fulfill the law: "What the law wants, the will never wants, unless it pretends to want it out of fear or love." The law, as we know from Romans 7:12, is holy, just, and good, but the will is not. The law aims at conformity

---

3.   This is only perpetuated by viewing ethics as moral principle apart from the gospel. It is odd that in every seminary, courses in ethics are offered not by the department of systematic theology but by the department of philosophy. Surely what we call ethics, from the Christian point of view, describes the converse side of the gospel: the command and claim of God, seizing us in the light of his promise to us. Thought of in this way, ethics belongs in the theology department.

to Jesus Christ, but the will of fallen humankind aims only at conformity to our fallen human nature. Nonetheless, Luther says, the will is dishonest and sometimes pretends to will conformity to Jesus Christ out of fear or love, by which he means self-love; that is, we conform outwardly to the law in order to avoid the consequences of disobedience or to serve our own interests. This, however, is by no means the same as wanting what the law wants.

"Every deed of the law without the grace of God appears good outwardly, but inwardly it is sin," asserts Luther in Disputation 76. In Romans 14:23 Paul declares that whatever does not proceed from faith is sin. Only as we are rightly related to God is our obedience to his law good in the sense of godly, as opposed to merely morally circumspect. Faith alone relates us rightly to God, and grace alone quickens faith. Therefore every deed of the law wrought apart from the grace of God arises from disobedience, and therefore is sin.

We will continue to meet this scandalous but fundamental concept again and again in Luther's writings—that any attempt to conform to the law apart from grace is sin and serves only to entrench us more deeply in our alienation from God. In fact, Disputation 79 contains another restatement: "Condemned are all those who do the works of the law." We are manifestly condemned if we fail to do the works of the law, but we are equally condemned if we do them, insofar as they were not done in faith as an expression of loving relationship to God but as an expression of autonomy and self-sufficiency—that is, sin.

Notice that there is still a place in Luther's theology for the exercise of our will. The will is the innermost control center of the human being, what the Hebrew Bible calls the "heart." Restored by grace through the power of the Spirit, the will is reoriented to God. By grace alone, we are made able to will conformity to Jesus Christ, and it would be anomalous then if we did not do so. Restoration to true humanity is not something done over our heads or behind our backs, without our participation; the effect of the Cross, of grace acting upon us, is to quicken a response of faith in us and put us into right relationship to God. (This faith is both a gift of God and a gift that we must exercise, or else "faith," so-called, ceases to be an event in the life of a human agent.) Out of that faith and that relationship we begin to will what God wills.

One last point from Luther's Disputations demands our attention. In Disputation 47 he writes, "No syllogistic form is valid when applied to divine terms. This is in opposition to the Cardinal." When it comes to aspects of the human person, most of the disputations discussed so far have had to do directly or indirectly with the will. This one, however, has to do with reason. It is not that Luther is opposed to the use of rational argument in theology; his fifty-five volumes demonstrate the contrary. His objection is to some medieval approaches that were not only highly sophistic but whose premises appeared drawn from philosophical specu-lation. Can philosophy yield premises that adequately reflect the nature and truth and grace of God? Luther would say, No. In his "Theology of the Cross," he asserts that the gospel everywhere contradicts the starting point of human theological understanding and reasoning. At the Cross the world sees shame, while the church, in the light of God's revelation, sees glory. The world sees helplessness, while the church sees almighti-ness: what could be mightier, after all, than God redeeming the world and reconciling it to himself? Luther's point is that the world's under-standing, and some aspects of scholastic theology—built as they are on a foundation of philosophy—never grasp the logic of the gospel, and only move farther away from it.

Luther would also say that to understand the gospel, we must shut our eyes and open our ears to the voice of the Spirit, because every day the gospel is contradicted by what we see around us and within us. When a pharmaceutical tragedy haunted hundreds of pregnant women in the West, a banner was found hanging over the door of an Oxford University theology residence: "Last year God so loved the world that twenty-five thousand thalidomide babies were born." It had been painted and hung by humanist students. What we see around us often belies the truth that God loves us (and in giving up his Son for us might even be said to love us more than he loves himself.) We cannot found our belief in God's mercy on world occurrence or on reasoning based on it.

THE *NINETY-FIVE THESES,* OR *DISPUTATION ON THE POWER AND EFFICACY OF INDULGENCES*

The *Ninety-Five Theses* are the famous, highly provocative, manifesto-like document that Luther nailed to the door of the church in Wittenberg in 1517. No study of Luther's early writings would be complete without at least a brief look at some of the theses.

"When our Lord and Master Jesus Christ said, 'Repent,'[4] he willed the entire life of believers to be one of repentance," declares Luther in the first thesis. The Latin Vulgate used an expression best translated "do penance," but for Luther, "do penance" suggested self-purgation, works-righteousness. It also encouraged people to think of penance atomistically, in terms of discrete or isolated acts: one carried out a specific act one day that constituted penance; next day, another one. Luther, however, regarded penitence not as something one did but as a re-alignment with God, an "about-face" that characterized the believer.

We commit the same error nowadays, with the superficial difference that we have changed penance into a psychological or emotional work of self-purgation rather than a physical one. Luther insisted that although repentance is something we will for ourselves, we can do so only because God has first willed it for us and in us. Moreover, it is to be lifelong and "lifewide", inasmuch as sin is lifelong and lifewide. Repentance is not an atomistic act we perform to compensate for an atomistic sin. Even in the hearts of believers there is a residual depravity so deep that we cannot see it; we have an inkling as to when and how we have sinned, but it is only an inkling. In fact, our whole existence is tinged with this residual sinfulness; hence our whole existence—our "entire life" in Luther's words—must be repentant.

Luther was an Old Testament scholar first of all, and repentance in the Hebrew Bible always has the sense of making a 180-degree turn. The Hebrew Bible uses three major images of repentance. One is the

---

4.   Matthew 4:17.

unfaithful wife returning to her husband. She has disgraced herself and violated her husband, and returns to longstanding love, patience, and acceptance. The second is the idolater turning from the worship of idols to the worship of the true and living God. On the one hand, idols are nothing—the Hebrew word for them is literally "the nothings." But on the other hand, they have great power, just as a vacuum has power to suck everything into it and a lie (to which nothing in actuality corresponds) is able to destroy a person. The idolater who repents turns from nothing to something, from unreality to the reality that is the Holy One of Israel. In the third image of repentance, rebellious subjects return to their rightful ruler. They have brought chaos upon themselves and on the wider world, and as they turn back to proper authority, the chaos is dispelled.

Luther was familiar with all of these images. In saying that Jesus willed the entire life of believers to be one of repentance, he was acknowledging repentance as reorientation to the love and service of Jesus Christ, as that resetting of the compass we must will for ourselves with every new day. Apart from such re-alignment we merely blunder farther into disobedience.

The sixteenth thesis revolves around the concept of proper fear. "Hell, purgatory, and heaven seem to differ the same as despair, fear, and assurance of salvation," writes Luther. First of all, notice the reference to purgatory. This is Luther in 1517; he subsequently abandoned the idea of purgatory. Nonetheless most Christians would admit that there is a purgatorial dimension to heaven in the sense that we must be purged of everything in us that is not fit for heaven. In this sixteenth thesis, however, Luther is speaking of purgatory as a distinct, intermediate state, in contrast to hell and heaven, where we undergo a fiery cleansing that qualifies us for heaven. Luther insists on giving full weight to the present possession of ultimate blessing attested in John 3:36: "Whoever believes in the Son *has* eternal life." He wants to make the point that our eternal blessedness is not in doubt and not delayed.

Notice, too, that at this stage of his theological development Luther associates fear with purgatory. He and other Reformers will distinguish servile fear from filial fear, however. Servile fear is the sheer cowering

terror of the unbeliever faced with the prospect of judgment, whereas
filial fear is the awe and reverence of the son or daughter who dreads
displeasing a father. It is an important distinction which we would do
well to retain, and which is in danger of being lost in the church today in
favor of a shallow understanding of both love and fear. As Ronald Ward,
former professor of New Testament at Wycliffe College in Toronto, liked
to tell his students, "Insofar as we fear God, we shall never have to be
afraid of him."[5] That is, if we conduct ourselves with filial fear towards
God, we shall never have to grovel or cower before him.

Following Luther, Calvin's amplification of the notion of piety
exhibited a similar understanding of the fear of God. Piety has become
a bad word in the church today, but in the Reformation it was a noble
word. Calvin described it as the fear of God combined with a love of
God induced by a knowledge of God's benefits or acts of grace.[6] Fear
of God is reverence, respect, or awe, and must always accompany love
for God. Fear alone degenerates into terror; love alone, into presumption. Many Christians today view fear and love as mutually exclusive,
when in fact the two presuppose and imply each other. The fear that is
cast out by love according to 1 John 4:18 is servile fear, while the fear
that the Reformers intend is the corollary of love. To love someone profoundly is always to fear offending that person.

"Fear God" is an exceedingly common command in Scripture, and
yet the most frequent command of Jesus is "Fear not." This reflects
exactly the true state of affairs: insofar as we fear God, we need not be
afraid of what might happen to us. As John Wesley frequently pointed
out, if we fear God we fear nothing else; if we do not fear God, we fear
everything else.[7] But the one option we do not have is to fear nothing
and no one at all.

---

5.   See R. A. Ward, *The Pattern of our Salvation* (Grand Rapids: Eerdmans, 1978),
p. 154.

6.   Calvin, *Institutes*, 1.2.1.

7.   Wesley makes this point repeatedly in his *Sermons on Several Occasions*.
See, e.g., *The Works of John Wesley* (Nashville: Abingdon, 1984), Vol. 1, pp. 633-4; Vol.

In the medieval theological schema, contrition was the first step in dealing with the fear of judgment. It was the way to purge oneself in preparation for grace—despite the inherent contradiction in that formula. But in the thirtieth thesis, Luther makes an important point about contrition with respect to self-knowledge and grace: "No one is sure of the integrity of his own contrition, much less of having received plenary remission." The thesis should be understood within the framework of the church's theology at the time, according to which contrition was the self-purgation that predisposed a person towards grace. Luther is saying, with remarkable insight, that we do not have privileged access to ourselves. When we decide that we are genuinely remorseful for sin, how do we know we have even apprehended the totality of the sin for which remorse is due? And what makes us think our contrition is adequate, given sin's enormity? To think it is is to fail to come to terms with our systemic sinnership. "I am not aware of anything against myself," says Paul in 1 Corinthians 4:4, "but I am not thereby acquitted." We are not fully aware of what is in us, and therefore cannot assume that our contrition, however sincere and prolonged, is adequate to our sinnership. God alone knows our heart. In thinking that we are able to take the measure of our own sin and purge ourselves by our act of contrition, we persist in contradicting grace and in falsifying ourselves.

Interestingly, however, the first part of Thesis 40 reads: "A Christian who is truly contrite seeks and loves to pay penalties for his sins." What does Luther mean by this? He does not mean paying penalties for sin in the sense of compensating or atoning for our sin or achieving our justification. Rather, he means that the Christian who is contrite—and we must keep Thesis 30 in mind here, so as not to make an issue of the intensity of our contrition, as if it could ever be adequate or as if we earned something thereby—recognizes the Father's discipline. Luther is thinking of the passage in Hebrews, "Those whom the Lord loves, he chastens" (Hebrews 12:6). The Christian who has acknowledged his sin

---

2, pp. 178, 320, 566; Vol. 3, p. 132.

for what it is recognizes the value of fatherly discipline at God's hands, and for that reason loves it rather than dreading or fearing it.

In Thesis 62, Luther writes, "The true treasure of the church is the most holy gospel of the glory and grace of God." Two things can be said about this. First, the gospel as the true treasure of the church is also constitutive of the church; that is, the gospel determines the parameters of the church, and not the other way around. Where the gospel is heard and upheld and cherished, the church exists; without the gospel, the church is nothing. The institution has no power over the gospel and does not contain the gospel. Rather, the gospel contains and establishes it.

Second, Luther was making a veiled reference to the medieval notion of the "treasury of merit". This was the idea that there was a storehouse of accumulated merit vested in the church, consisting of the superfluous good works of the saints, on which people could draw for their own salvific good. This was the treasure of the church. Luther repudiates this notion here, because with God there is no question of merit at all apart from the merit of Jesus Christ. Moreover, how can merit be quantified? How could there ever be an excess of it? It is not a "thing" to be measured. And in any case, what would be the nature of the grace to which this merit is related? Luther resists any notion that grace can be reified and depersonalized—reduced to something detached from the person of Jesus Christ. Grace, he maintains, is simply the action of Jesus Christ moving upon and within us in the power of the Holy Spirit.

In addition to making superfluous merit available, the church offered indulgences. Thesis 76 reads, "We say on the contrary that papal indulgences cannot remove the very least of venial sins as far as guilt is concerned." Guilt has to do with our distorted relationship with God. As we noted before, when the psalmist says, "Against you only have I sinned," (Psalm 51:4) he is not denying that his sin against God also violates others. Rather he is affirming that sin is defined by reference to God and our right relationship with him. This being the case, only God can determine the violator's fate. If the church imposes its own penalty, then of course it can also rescind it by means of a papal indulgence, but it has no power with respect to the sinner's guilt or fate before the holy God. Only the gospel can deal with that.

These remarks about the church's authority re-introduce a point raised earlier in the seventh thesis. "God remits guilt to no one unless at the same time he humbles him in all things and makes him submissive to his vicar, the priest." This statement may sound as if the sinner's justification is conditional on obedience to the priest, but we know from his other writings that Luther does not intend this. He is not saying that believers must conform to institutional authority; in fact, that is precisely what he decries, since institutional authority is often at odds with the gospel it is supposed to reflect. The thesis is really about the earthly promulgation of the gospel of forgiveness. Luther is recognizing that the gospel cannot be intuited—indeed, it is inherently counter-intuitive— but must be rendered audible through human instrumentality, as it is declared and expounded by a human messenger. And this responsibility has been entrusted first of all to the clergy.

Calvin makes the same point more explicitly in his ecclesiology. God has given clergy authority in the church, he states, but that authority is exercised by pointing away from oneself to the authority of Jesus Christ. As soon as the pastor claims an inherent authority, he has contradicted the legitimate authority vested in him by God.[8] Luther has not fully developed his ecclesiology at this point, but we can understand the thesis if we bring his entire corpus to bear on it. In connecting the remission of guilt to submission to the vicar, Luther is claiming that there is no remission of guilt apart from our hearing and apprehending the gospel, and that this gospel cannot be heard unless declared by someone whom God has called, equipped, and commissioned to do so.

Finally, a comment needs to be made on the last two theses, 94 and 95, which actually form one sentence: "Christians should be exhorted to be diligent in following Christ, their head, through penalties, death, and hell; [a]nd thus be confident of entering into heaven through many

---

8.   See Calvin, *Institutes*, 4.4.3.

tribulations rather than through the false security of peace."[9] Luther is insisting, first of all, that Jesus Christ, raised from the dead, is our only true security. In the security that is Jesus Christ, believers may and must abandon all attempts to fashion their own security and simply follow Christ to hell and back—that is, through thick and thin, through everything that collapses upon them and threatens to crumble them. In other words, it is because Jesus Christ is our security that we can abandon ourselves to following him; knowing the source and nature of our security, we have the freedom to do nothing but follow. Conversely, those who do not know the source and nature of their security are always looking for it, always preoccupied with it and always trying to establish it—with the result that they are in bondage to themselves, forever lacking the freedom to follow.

It is only 1517; Luther has not yet worked out all the nuances of his theology of the cross, but he is anticipating that theology here. It would be presumptuous to think we could bear Christ's cross, the cross that atones and redeems. He alone can bear that cross, but because he does, he appoints us to bearing ours. We cannot bear his; he will not bear ours. Only a crucified disciple can follow a crucified Lord;[10] for this reason there can be no discipleship without cross-bearing. Disciple and Lord are both crucified, Luther would say, but for different purposes: Christ is crucified as Savior of the world, and we are crucified as servants of the Savior and those he names our neighbors. In short, Luther knew that the two poles of sin were attempting to bear Christ's cross (that is, to justify ourselves before God) and refusing to bear our own cross (that is, to disdain the service of the suffering neighbor.)

What is the "false security of peace" to which Luther refers? He has in mind here the medieval penitential system, which gave peace to the

---

9.   This is a reference to Acts 14:22b: "Through many tribulations we must enter the kingdom of God" (ESV).

10.   Mark 8:34, "And he called to him the crowd with his disciples and said to them, 'If anyone would come after me, let him deny himself and take up his cross and follow me'" (ESV).

conscience, but a peace too easily attained. He found that the medieval scholastics were entirely too successful, in that the people in whom they inculcated peace were genuinely at peace, for entirely wrong reasons. That was the problem. There is a self-renunciation required for discipleship which is cross-bearing. It is cheerful and willing, for following must be willing or it is not following at all, yet nonetheless it always involves the abandonment of our own agenda. Like repentance—and here we come full circle, back to the first thesis—abandonment of our own agenda must be a lifelong practice.

On October 31, Luther nailed these ninety-five theses to the door of the castle church in Wittenberg. What he wanted to do was promote debate; it was the kind of thing scholars in his era customarily did. Little did he know that by this act he had set something in motion that would convulse much of Europe.

PREFACE TO THE WITTENBERG EDITION OF LUTHER'S WRITINGS

We leap here from 1517 to 1539, and Luther is a much older man, a man of 56, with a much more developed understanding.

There are several salient points to note in the *Preface,* one of which is the primacy Luther gives Scripture. He says, "For all other writing is to lead the way into and point toward the Scriptures, as John the Baptist did toward Christ, saying, 'He must increase, but I must decrease.'"[11] By "all other writing," Luther means theological writing. Its whole purpose is to facilitate our grasp of Scripture, not merely in terms of familiarity with chapter and verse, but our grasp of the nature, logic, and substance of Scripture.

Calvin took the same view when writing his *Institutes.* One objective of that document was to assure the king, Francis I, that Reformed Christians were not seditious. Calvin's main purpose, however, was to provide a theological primer (2,000 pages long) to orient first-year students

---

11.   Lull, *Martin Luther's Basic Theological Writings,* p. 64.

in theology and help them understand Scripture—not that Calvin presented his book as the lens through which students were to read the Bible, or as a grid to be superimposed on it, for that would deny the Bible's integrity. Still he was aware that when they came to do their elementary work in theology, they would be helped to grasp the subtlety and logic of Scripture more readily if they were given an overview of the canonical collection and its self-consistent theological witness.

Luther writes, "Herein I follow the example of St. Augustine, who was, among other things, the first and almost the only one who determined to be subject to the Holy Scriptures alone, and independent of the books of all the fathers and saints." We must be careful how we understand those words, "subject to the Holy Scriptures alone." Perhaps the best way is by comparison with Wesley two centuries later, who called himself *homo unius libri*—a man of one book. He did not mean that any preacher could succeed in his task by reading only the Bible to the exclusion of all other books; Wesley had a five-hour daily study program for his lay preachers, and it included many other books besides the Bible. He meant that of all books, only one—the Bible—was authoritative or normative. Anyone who read nothing but the Bible, however, he called an "enthusiast", eighteenth-century parlance for a fanatic. And his definition of a fanatic was someone who elevates his experience above all else.

Notice how Luther's understanding assumes the necessity of interpretation. None of us can read Scripture unaffected by the perspective which our own experience provides. Both Wesley and Luther carefully make the point that to read Scripture only is to elevate our experience above Scripture, because we will have no other perspective from which to understand it but our own. In precisely the same way, Augustine, while he was "independent of all other books" in that he considered one Book alone to be normative, at the same time distanced himself from the Circumcellions who claimed a charismatic endowment rendering study superfluous if not deleterious. The example that Luther follows in Augustine, therefore, is not the exclusion of all other books but the recognition of Scripture alone as authoritative. Ultimately, the point of *sola Scriptura*—Scripture alone—is *solus Christus*—Christ alone, for Christ is the substance of Scripture and simultaneously Lord of the prophetic/apostolic testimony to him.

Moreover, Luther sees that the failure to recognize Scripture's normativity is the fount of all theological error. If we refuse to recognize Scripture as normative, our theology is skewed from the start. No matter how much we profit from theological books, says Luther, the Bible must remain on the pulpit: "And if the example of St. Augustine had been followed, the pope would not have become Antichrist, and that countless mass of books which is like a crawling swarm of vermin,"—Luther was always graphic—"would not have found its way into the church, and the Bible would have remained on the pulpit."[12]

What is the relationship between theology and exegesis? On the one hand, the Bible is to be preached. If that is the case, why bother with theology at all? There are many reasons, one of which is that theology allows us to see the truths of Scripture in their interrelatedness and wholeness. Another is that theology serves as a salutary caution concerning our exegesis. This is not to say that theology sits in judgment over Scripture, but that there is always a conversation between our work as theologians and our work as exegetes.

Luther's reminder safeguards the church against a facile identification of the gospel with any one part or passage of Scripture. Such an identification can only be erroneous, since it lacks the context of the whole of Scripture and must therefore forfeit the tenor of Scripture. Facile identifications abound, a common one being the notion that the gospel can be reduced without remainder to the parable of the Prodigal Son. The son becomes annoyed with his father, defiantly storms off into the "far country," comes back, is received joyfully by his father, and the two are reconciled: the gospel in a nutshell. At this point the comment is characteristically made, "You'll notice that in the parable of the Prodigal

---

12.   Given the paucity of visual symbolism in most Protestant worship, the symbols we do have are all the more important. One of these is the placing of the Bible on the pulpit at the beginning of the liturgy in some Protestant traditions.

Son, there's no mention of anything that corresponds to the cross. Who needs the cross? God calls us home to him; we come out of the far country and go home. Who needs the cross?" Overlooked, of course, is that according to Luke (not to mention Scripture as a whole), the cross is the only reason the penitent son can go home to his father. To omit the cross is to falsify the gospel. And this is the point about the dialogue between theology and exegesis: our theology, duly informed by the whole of Scripture, in turn protects us from distortion based on any isolated fragment of Scripture.

Luther writes theology, then, not because theology tells us what Scripture is allowed to say, but rather because theology raises the caution flag for us concerning our reading of Scripture. When we come to exegete a passage of Scripture, our theology ought to be whispering in our ear, "But have you got the balance right? Have you left out some important consideration, or falsified a major statement in the Christian understanding?" Luther, like the other magisterial Reformers, was exegete and theologian simultaneously, always recognizing the need for each to listen to each other if the gospel was not to be distorted.

A little further on in the *Preface*, Luther writes, "First, you should know that the Holy Scriptures constitute a book which turns the wisdom of all other books into foolishness, because not one teaches about eternal life except this one alone. Therefore you should straightway despair of your reason and understanding." Again, we must not misread Luther on this point. He is not counselling stupidity or irrationality. As noted earlier, by "reason" he means not thoughtfulness but philosophical speculation. Luther attached enough importance to cogent thinking that he accused the radicals of fanaticism for what he considered to be their undervaluation of intellectual rigor. His point, therefore, is not against the exactitude of reason, but against putting any confidence in philosophical speculation. Only Scripture informs us of the gospel and acquaints us with the truth and reality of God; no intellectual endeavor can do so.

But how do we understand Scripture? Luther goes on to say about King David: "Thus you see how David keeps praying in the above-mentioned Psalm...'Teach me, Lord, instruct me, lead me, show me,' and many more words like these. Although he well knew and daily heard and read the text of Moses and other books besides, still he wants to lay hold of the real teacher of the Scriptures himself, so that he may not seize upon them pell-mell with his reason and become his own teacher."[13] Who is "the real teacher of the Scriptures"? It is the exalted Lord, in the power of the Holy Spirit. Spirit and Word and Christ are never divorced in Reformation thought. Luther is saying that Scripture is never naturally intelligible; we apprehend its truth only as we are apprehended by the Lord of Scripture. Scripture is the occasion of our hearing and apprehending the one who has first apprehended us. Unless Jesus Christ moves among us as the teacher of Scripture, says Luther, what we find in Scripture will be only ourselves, our own opinions and aspirations and misunderstandings concerning God, ourselves, and the world.

The Emmaus road episode illustrates this. As the risen Lord falls in with the men on the road, he interprets to them the things about himself in the Scriptures, beginning with Moses and all the prophets (Luke 24:27). Jesus Christ, to whom all Scripture is transparent in the power of the Spirit, is preeminently the teacher of Scripture, and it is only as he apprehends us in our reading of Scripture that we apprehend him as the substance of Scripture.

Luther mentions three things needed to become a theologian: *oratio, meditatio, tentatio*: prayer, meditation, and trial (*Anfechtung* in German). Meditation meant something different for Luther from what it has come to mean for modernity; the image frequently conjured up nowadays is one of private reflection (often highly sentimentalized) that tries to find "spiritual values" in the text. But meditation for Luther means indwelling a passage of Scripture, absorbing it, walking around it so as to view it from different angles as the psalmist in Psalm 48 "walked about Zion," considering all its features in order to be able to "tell the next generation that this is God, our God, forever and ever." What Luther meant

---

13. Lull, p. 66.

by *meditatio* was not religious fantasy but protracted reflection on the subtlety and substance and depth of the text. *Meditatio* meant living with a text until its substance "osmosed" into the reader to the point of transmogrifying her. This is essential, says Luther, to becoming a serious Christian and a serious theologian.

Yet even the most rigorous examination of Scripture must be done in faith. Study is an aspect of faith, and for profitability requires the work of the Holy Spirit. It is a reformational conviction that Spirit and Word are always conjoined. Luther continues in this section, "For God will not give you his Spirit without the external Word; so take your cue from that." Attempts to isolate the Spirit from the Word lead to religious frenzy on the one hand or rationalism on the other—sheer subjectivism or frigid ideation. Word and Spirit together give access to the living, lordly person of Jesus Christ. For this reason all attempts at theology must be steeped in prayer.

The third thing we need, Luther says, is *tentatio*, or *Anfechtung* in German. *Anfechtung* is assault, trial, radical affliction, apparent for-sakenness—the temptation to despair. Luther would say that whatever face temptation might wear on a given occasion, underlying the specific temptation is the arch-temptation to despair: to decide that there is no God, or to tell ourselves that we have yielded to this temptation so many times in the past that our situation is hopeless and we will yield to it again, or, finding ourselves yielding to it again, to conclude that we have forfeited any possibility of forgiveness. Those are all forms of despair. The real temptation is a spiritual assault so intense that God is momentarily eclipsed by its force, leaving us in despair.

What is the antidote? We must cling to the promise of the gospel, says Luther, hang on to that promise by sheer determination, because when the assault is so intense as to eclipse God for us, all we are going to be able to feel is wretchedness. We are going to feel as if we are being disemboweled. We will doubt God's presence and faithfulness, and therefore his mercy. All we can do is hang on by our fingernails to the promise, "I will never fail you nor forsake you" (Joshua 1:5, cited in Hebrews 13:5), and that will eventually prove to be enough. Until we have confronted the worst, are driven to cling to God's promise in Christ, and find ourselves carried and upheld by him, we are not fit to engage in theology. We will not know what we are talking about.

Because of the terrible assaults on him in Germany, Luther knew whereof he spoke. He was misunderstood by the left and the right. The gnesio-Lutherans were after him, and so were the Philippists (the followers of Philip Melanchthon). The Roman Catholics put a price on his head and the Holy Roman Emperor was out to get him. Even the radicals despised him. He was attacked from all sides, and out of that experience he tells us that our only recourse, in those moments of terrible isolation and abandonment, is to cling to the promise.

Nobody had as vivid a sense as Luther of the Christian life unfolding in the theater of spiritual conflict. He believed that he was assaulted by the devil, and when he was, he never hesitated to address the devil in the second person. "You! Get behind me!" he would exclaim. There is a story, now regarded by most as apocryphal, that during one particularly horrible assault Luther threw his bottle of ink at the devil, and it hit the wall.[14] That is how vivid the conflict was for him, and this was largely because he knew something that many of us have lost sight of in the church today: that sin is repulsive to God and ought to be repulsive to us. Luther regarded temptation as the approach of Satan, covered in his own excrement.[15] In the day of no flush toilet, nothing could be more repulsive or nauseating than a pile of fresh human excrement. Sin is similarly repulsive to God, according to Luther. If in the approach of temptation we can view sin as less nauseating than that, we are done for. As soon as the sin with which we are tempted strikes us as attractive

---

14.   There is a stain on the wall of the Wartburg castle in Eisenach associated with this story.

15.   He wrote, of the devil, "*Sehet, wie hat der sich beschißen.*" (See how he has soiled himself.) His only recourse, when the devil tried to make sin appear less repugnant, was to shout, "*Das fressest Du!*" (Eat it yourself!) See H.A. Oberman, "*Teufelsdreck:* Eschatology and Scatology in the 'Old' Luther," in *The Impact of the Reformation* (Grand Rapids: Eerdmans, 1994).

or pleasant, and we begin turning it over in our mind, massaging it, capitulation is underway. In other words, sin is not merely an offense against God; it is loathsome to God. Not only does it break God's heart and provoke his anger; it arouses God's disgust. And if sin ceases to be similarly loathsome to us, we will find ourselves unable to resist its approach.

The point is that apart from these experiences, horrible as they are, a person is only dabbling as a Christian and can never become a theologian. *Anfechtung* is what drives us to Jesus Christ, the Victorious One. It is also what saves us from theological mediocrity. Our enemies force us to rearticulate our understanding of the gospel, if only to rebut them, and temptation saves us from theological shallowness.

One last point from the *Preface* has to do with Luther's oft-quoted parable about the donkey. Luther says that anyone who believes himself or herself to have "preached excellently" will find in the mirror "a beautiful pair of big, long, shaggy donkey ears." "See, See! There goes that clever beast, who can write such exquisite books and preach so remarkably well," he writes; and five lines later, "But in this book the honor is God's alone."[16] Since the substance of Scripture is Jesus Christ, all honor redounds to God. Whenever our preaching, writing, or lecturing leaves us preening ourselves, then no matter how much use we have made of Scripture, we have missed its substance. If anything in our theological activity leads us to congratulate ourselves, our theology is not about Jesus Christ.

We should be nervous, then, when we hear that somebody is a good preacher. What does that mean? That he is clever? That her illustrations are catchy? That he has a mellifluous voice? As James Denny said, "No man can give the impression, both that he is a great preacher, and that Christ is a great Savior." Anyone who thinks he can, according to Luther, is an ass.

---

16.   Lull, p. 68.

INDULGENCES: THE RESCINDING OF
TEMPORAL PUNISHMENT

It was the indulgence traffic that particularly provoked the ire of Martin Luther, as it had provoked that of Jan Hus before him. Indulgences had to do with the rescinding of temporal punishment only—what we would call today the consequences of sin. They never purported to affect eternal punishment. A "plenary" indulgence, which was the commodity sold by the indulgence trafficker, meant that all temporal punishment was rescinded.

The logic was as follows. We sin, repent before God, and are forgiven, but we need to make reparation and receive temporal punishment for our sin—whereupon the church, through the agency of its clergy, prescribes penance. There is a problem, though, in that we can be left at life's end wondering whether our penance exactly counterbalances the sins of our lifetime. Temporal punishment for sin may still be owing, and if it is, the remaining debt must be paid in purgatory after death. What is at issue here is not damnation, but the amount of temporal punishment owing for sin. Having received the sacrament of penance, we are released from temporal punishment if our penance is exactly commensurate with the punishment due us. But what if it is not? An indulgence releases penitents from the rigors of purgatory, and can be procured through the performance of good works or through a cash payment.

All of this was deemed to fall under "the power of the keys" vested in the church; that is, the authority and power Christ gave the church either to remit temporal punishment or to retain it. Needless to say, "the power of the keys" was thought of differently by the Reformers. For them it was simply the preaching of the gospel.

Earlier in this chapter we touched on the "treasury of merits": the merit gained by Jesus Christ and the saints in excess of the minimum needed to avoid damnation and gain heaven, calculated and "deposited" in a merit-book. Although the treasury of merits was not essential to the theory of indulgences, it helped people psychologically by offering the notion that they were purchasing some of this accumulated surplus merit. "Good works" indulgences could be prescribed that allowed people to "work off" temporal punishment and thereby be rid of any remaining purgatorial rigors. Eventually, the notion overtook the church that by cash payment one could out-and-out purchase release from purgatory.

What were Luther's objections to this practice? First there was the crass materialism of it all, the reification of the gospel and of the Christian life—as if we were dealing with bookkeeping entries in a ledger; as if merit and punishment were quantifiable and could be traded against currency. This subpersonal, mechanical notion of merit and merit-book contradicted the radical personalism of God and of the gospel.

Luther also objected to what he saw as the sheer effrontery of indulgences, the fact that the church was usurping God's prerogative with respect to temporal punishment. Nor could he countenance the role given to the saints as co-redeemers. Both of these objections are ultimately related to what Luther considered to be Rome's overall misunderstanding of the nature of the church. According to this misunderstanding, the "power of the keys" meant that the church exercised control, on behalf of God, over God's dealings with his creatures. As pointed out above, however, Luther and the other Reformers saw the "power of the keys" as simply the efficacy of the Word preached; the Word, for the Reformers, always means the Word preached. The church attests the Word, and the authority exercised by the church with respect to the forgiveness of sins is to point away from itself to him who is uniquely authoritative, Jesus Christ.[17] Luther insisted that God never hands his divine authority over to somebody or something else; God never relegates his authority or delegates it, never deputizes anyone. Moreover, the God-ordained authority proper to the church is not an authority to rule or to control, but to serve. The church has been

---

17. For a detailed exposition of Calvin's understanding of the "power of the keys" see Victor Shepherd, *The Nature and Function of Faith in the Theology of John Calvin* (Vancouver: Regent College Publishing, 2004), chapter 7.

given the office of servant of the gospel, and one aspect of this service is proclamation.

Luther feared that Jesus Christ was thought at that time to inhere the church. If this were the case, Christ would cease to transcend the church as its Lord. Christ is indeed to be found through the ministry of the church, and it is the church's role to acquaint people with him. Then is the church's Lord in the church's hand? Is Christ someone the church can either grant or withhold? Even as Christ appoints himself to be visited upon people through the instrumentality of the church, he ever remains Lord over the church.

Thirdly, Luther rejected the whole logic of indulgences, which turns on a confusion between the penalty for sin and the consequences of sin (a confusion that persists, let it be noted, in church life today). The penalty for sin is alienation from God; the consequences of our sins are their "after-shocks" reverberating through sinners' lives and through all whom their lives touch. The consequences of driving while impaired, for example, are that somebody else is dead; a child has been rendered fatherless and a wife rendered a widow. These consequences remain even though the penalty—estrangement from God—is rescinded as the penitent sinner owns the mercy of God.

By the mercy of the gospel, then, the penalty for sin is dealt with as the sinner is reconciled to God. The consequences of sin, on the other hand, continue spreading like ripples from a stone dropped into water. John Newton praised God for his salvation, but for the rest of his life he deplored the evil he had unleashed through the slave trade. He could do nothing about it. Luther recognized that none of us can obviate the temporal consequences of our sin, and neither can the church through a system of indulgences.

Contemporary Protestantism does not have an indulgence system as elaborately worked out as that of the medieval church, but there often appears to be something akin to it at a more popular, less explicit, and less formal level. It needs to be identified so that how and where and why it operates can be dealt with as the gospel is trained upon it. The gospel must be held up constantly, always reasserted as that which renders any indulgence system not only superfluous but iniquitous. If Luther is heard and heeded, all informal, psychoreligious indulgence systems will be eschewed as a denial of the truth and efficacy of the gospel; that is, as an affront to God.

5

The Righteousness of God

Although he wrote no systematic theology, Luther produced numerous occasional writings that addressed developments in theology, church, the state, domestic matters, the Christian life—in short, anything and everything to which the gospel spoke. In so doing he returned to the same subjects again and again in different contexts, making it difficult for students of Luther to locate readily all the material he wrote on any single topic. Instead of attempting to cull Luther's corpus concerning the rigthteousness of God, we shall probe two representative tracts written in 1519: "Two Kinds of Righteousness" and "A Meditation on Christ's Passion."

TWO KINDS OF RIGHTEOUSNESS

"There are two kinds of Christian righteousness, just as man's sin is of two kinds," writes Luther.[1] The two kinds of sin he has in mind are those already distinguished in this book as *Sin* and *sins*—the former being the human condition or our systemic sinnership, analogous to

---

1.   Lull, *Martin Luther's Basic Theological Writings*, p. 155.

blood poisoning, and the latter being the wrong deeds that are the outcropping of this systemic condition. Each of these, Sin and sins, is addressed by a different kind of righteousness.

The righteousness of Christ is the remedy for our original sin, and Luther calls it "alien righteousness" because it comes from outside us and is simply given to us. "Proper righteousness," on the other hand, is our own righteousness, though it is still not our achievement; it is the mortification of the 'old man', the repudiation of the arrears of sin in us, by grace. This proper righteousness is possible only on account of the alien righteousness, which remains foundational: "This is the righteousness of Christ by which he justifies through faith, as it is written in I Corinthians 1," writes Luther; he is referring to verse 30 of that chapter, where Jesus Christ is called our wisdom and righteousness, sanctification and redemption.[2] The heart of the gospel, overturning every aspect of medieval meritocracy, is that Christ is our righteousness; we are not our own righteousness. To think of retaining even a smidgen of inherent righteousness before God is to contravene the righteousness of Christ as pure gift.

"This righteousness, then, is given to men in baptism and whenever they are truly repentant," Luther asserts. There is a certain ambiguity here around the issue of baptism. On the one hand Luther upheld infant baptism, but on the other hand he insisted on the necessity of repentance and faith. One reason for this tension was Luther's desire to distance himself from the theology of the Anabaptists, a major aspect of which was their eponymous repudiation of infant baptism and their espousal of believers'. He seemed to think that to surrender infant baptism was to identify oneself publicly with everything the radical Reformation endorsed. But the magisterial Reformers' magnification of faith, together with their insistence that faith occurs only where *something* of the gospel is understood (however rudimentarily), and

---

2. This was, incidentally, John Calvin's favorite text, to which he returns endlessly in his writings because it enshrined for him the totality of the gospel. It is also one of the texts most frequently quoted by John Wesley.

their insistence that assurance of faith is an aspect of faith, would seem to point to a doctrine of believers' baptism. Only two decades after the appearance of the Luther texts under examination, Calvin would write, "What is a sacrament received apart from faith but the most certain ruin of the church?"[3]—raising at once the question, in the case of infant baptism, of *whose* faith is operative. Aware, however, that every theological statement has political and psychological overtones, the Reformers were afraid that if they ceded anything to the Anabaptists on the question of baptism, they would be seen as supporting the socio-political and economic dimensions of the radical reformation. (The radical reformation was, among other things, anti-entrepreneurial, anti-capital, anti-trading, and pacifist.) Luther maintained, in the face of Anabaptist criticism, that infant baptism—where something is done to a sinful creature incapable of doing anything for herself—highlighted the truth of justification, wherein the righteousness of Christ becomes ours apart from anything we helpless sinners can do for ourselves.

Baptism, then, is invoked to underline the truth that the righteousness we need for justification is not ours, but is another's and must be given to us. This affirmation is followed by a crucial point: "Through faith in Christ, therefore, Christ's righteousness becomes our righteousness and all that he has becomes ours; rather, *he himself becomes ours.* [emphasis mine]"[4] In any discussion of justification—that is, of the alien righteousness of Christ—we must understand that we do not receive a property or quality of Christ without receiving Christ himself. Luther does not fall into a mechanistic or subpersonal approach to justification, an approach seemingly taken by the Lutheran scholastics who came after him. Losing sight of the Righteous One himself, they spoke of the transfer of a quality: the quality of righteousness. Luther says that Christ's righteousness becomes ours only as we are united

---

3.   Calvin, *Institutes,* 4.14.14.
4.   Lull., p. 156.

with Christ the Righteous One in faith. We embrace or "put on" Christ himself, as Paul declares in Galatians 2:20.

This raises a question much discussed recently by N. T. Wright[5] and others. All in the evangelical tradition agree that this alien righteousness is related to faith, but whose faith is being referred to in Galatians 2:20? Is it our faith in Christ, or is it the faith *of* Christ, Christ's faithfulness? The genitive case found in the Greek text suggests that Paul is talking about the faith *of* Christ. God created humankind for faithful covenant partnership with himself, but did not find such faithfulness anywhere except in Jesus Christ. The covenant-keeping faithfulness of Christ, unique among humans, is the presupposition of our faith in him.[6] In other words, faith in Christ, the *sine qua non* of justification, is ultimately faith in the faithfulness of Christ.

Amplifying the notion of alien righteousness, Luther writes, "This is an infinite righteousness, and one that swallows up all sins in a moment, for it is impossible that sin should exist in Christ." In other words, while sanctification is a lifelong progress and pursuit, the justification accomplished by Christ's alien righteousness is instantaneous. Either we are forgiven and acquitted, or we are not. There can be no degrees of acquittal, any more than there can be degrees of pregnancy. The righteousness of Christ "swallows up our sins in a moment." To say the same thing differently: as soon as we put on Christ, he is the determination of our existence. The Christian continues to live under two determinations, that of Christ and his righteousness and that of the old creature of sin which still clings to us, but these are not weighted equally so as to leave us on a teeter-totter with the outcome of our identity utterly at risk. Our determination in Christ is always greater,

---

5. N. T. Wright, *Paul* (Minneapolis: Fortress Press, 2005), p. 47.

6. The literature on this subject has helped restore to the modern church an appreciation of the significance, for our humanity, of the human faithfulness of Jesus Christ. We have stressed the descent and condescension of God in the Incarnation and in the atonement, but have undervalued the ascent and exaltation of humanity in the obedient life of Christ. Luther recognized this centuries ago.

for the simple reason that Christ rules in his people. The old creature resides, but Christ alone presides.[7]

In the next sentence of this tract Luther exclaims, "On the contrary, he who trusts in Christ exists in Christ; he is one with Christ, having the same righteousness as he." As Christians we do not exist in our own selves, or forge our own identity. We are given our identity *in Christ.* Even more than Romans 1:17, "The just shall live by faith," Luther loved Colossians 3:3: "Your life is hid with Christ in God." Our identity before God is found in Christ, known to the Father, and reflected back to us; he sees us in our being of righteousness only as we are found *in Christ.* This is of immense significance theologically, and hence also psychologically: the old creature of sin continues to haunt us, with the result that all we can do is cling to our identity in Christ in accord with God's promise and pronouncement, even though self-examination finds us with lamentably little evidence of our newness in Christ.[8] Obviously we must persist in declaring that our identity in Christ is vouchsafed to all of us who are his, however much we appear to contradict it. Needless to say, what we want others in the Christian community to acknowledge concerning us we must be prepared to acknowledge in them.

We have "the same righteousness as he," the same righteousness as the Son with whom the Father is well pleased. Jesus is ever that Son, even and especially in the dereliction, when he not only feels God-forsaken but is, in fact, God-forsaken. In that moment he remains the Son with whom the Father is well pleased, for the very reason that his

---

7.   Luther was always suspicious of a perfectionistic Christian faith which denies the arrears of sin in the old man or woman. The radicals upheld the notion that one's sanctity admitted one to the church and kept one there. The magisterial Reformers believed that God's forgiveness admits one to the church and keeps one there. Believers know the forgiveness of God and *aspire* after sanctity.

8.   Though related, theology and psychology must not be confused. From the standpoint of psychological maturation, we do need to form our own identity; none of us is to be a clone of anybody else. But theologically, the identity of each of us is that of the Son with whom the Father is well pleased. If that were not our identity, we would have no standing before God at all.

obedience did not stop short of dereliction. Because of his forsaken-
ness, we are never God-forsaken; we may have terrible moments when
we feel we are forsaken by God, but what is determinative at all such
moments is the truth of God deeper than the actuality of our distress,
that we are still, thanks to our identity in Christ, that son or daughter
with whom the Father is well pleased. Because the Father is pleased
with the Son, he cannot fail to be pleased with us in the Son, and indeed
that is the only way he can be pleased with us.[9]

A little further on, however, Luther seems almost to contradict
what he has said about Christ's righteousness swallowing up all sins
in a moment. "Christ daily drives out the old Adam more and more
in accordance with the extent to which faith and knowledge of Christ
grow. For alien righteousness is not instilled all at once, but it begins,
makes progress, and is finally perfected at the end through death."
The crucial concept here is 'instilled'. Christ's alien righteousness is
imputed instantaneously, and *does* blot out or swallow up all our sin in
a moment; that is what is meant by "justification". But this same alien
righteousness, which gives rise to proper righteousness, is *instilled*
gradually, and that is sanctification. Luther discusses this in the next
sentence: "The second kind of righteousness is our proper righteousness, not because we alone work it, but because we work with that first
and alien righteousness." The proper righteousness arising from alien
righteousness is our putting the old creature to death each day. It does
not die without a struggle; the corpse continues to twitch. This is the
undeniable paradox in Paul's understanding of the gospel; namely, that
the event of our putting on Christ slays the old man (Romans 6:4) and
yet we are exhorted to keep putting him to death. *How* can we, *why*
must we, put to death what is already slain? Paradoxically, we *can* put
the old man to death in Christ only because Christ has already slain
him. We *must* put him to death, or else we are indulging sin. Of course,

---

9.   It is clear from the foregoing how thoroughly Christology shapes the theology
of the Reformers.

we will want to put the old man to death only as we are aware of his continued twitching. Only as we are aware of the arrears of sin in us can we repudiate sin. There is a realism here that Luther upholds consistently (and that the church today has largely lost).

In that same passage, Luther introduces the Pauline concept of flesh, in the context of slaying the flesh. We need to be clear that *flesh* for Paul means 'sinful human nature.' It does not mean body, or bodiliness, or normal physical appetites; it means human existence with no vertical dimension. Flesh is not a *part* of our being; it is our whole being oriented away from God: our physical, mental, emotional, and spiritual self in flight from God. That is why, in discussing the works of the flesh in Galatians 5, Paul includes such things as bickering, strife, and envy. These are not what people commonly call sins of the flesh, but Paul calls them by that name because they are outcroppings of our human nature oriented away from God.

"This righteousness," continues Luther, "goes on to complete the first, for it ever strives to do away with the old Adam and to destroy the body of sin." He does not mean that Christ's righteousness is incomplete or insufficient in any sense; in fact, it is so thoroughly sufficient that it grounds and empowers our proper righteousness. In other words, while the alien righteousness of Christ is sheer gift, it is a gift we must exercise, and the exercising of it is proper righteousness. The alien righteousness of Christ is not a legal fiction, then, or a coat of whitewash applied to us without changing us; rather, it occasions and is fulfilled by proper righteousness in us. Nevertheless, our proper righteousness, our repudiation of the old man or woman, is never sufficient to ground our standing before God. Christ's alien righteousness remains the sole ground of our justification, the stable basis of all else in the Christian life, and our final refuge.

Pursuing the paradox of slaying what has already been slain, we should understand as well that only believers are ever urged to put off the old man, for the simple reason that unbelievers cannot: the old man is all that they are, their sole determination. Moreover, it is only in the strength of the new man that anyone can repudiate the old. Every effort at proper righteousness outside the alien righteousness of Christ is vain, since it renders us simply that much more firmly entrenched in our sinnership.

A particularly moving part of the tract follows: "Therefore through the first righteousness arises the voice of the bridegroom who says to the soul, 'I am yours,' but through the second comes the voice of the bride who answers, 'I am yours.'" Sometimes in the church we discuss justification in a cold, courtroom way. As Luther points out, we are the beneficiaries of Christ's righteousness only as we put him on, but Christ encourages us to put him on and confirms us in the truth, the determination, that he is for us. Simultaneously he speaks to us, saying, "I am yours," moving us to reply, "And I am yours." Without the warmth and intimacy of mutual embrace and mutual pledge, justification remains only a forensic category. To be sure, the law court is one metaphor used in Scripture to describe our new life in Christ, but it is not the only one. It must always be balanced by other, more personal and relational ones—such as reconciliation and marriage—lest our life in Christ be depersonalized.

The foregoing is underlined in an earlier passage where Luther writes, "So, too, it is not yet knowledge of the gospel when you know these doctrines and commandments, but only when the voice comes that says, 'Christ is your own, with his life, teaching, works, death, resurrection, and all that he is, has, does, and can do.'" Notice the words "But only when the voice comes ...": here again we find Luther's emphasis on the personal address of Christ to our heart, an emphasis that tended to fade in scholastic Lutheranism under the weight of endless refinement of doctrine not balanced by a comparable emphasis on faith as living engagement with its living Lord. As doctrinal subtlety is pursued (and it has to be pursued), the person of Christ is in danger of receding, leaving no more than impersonal abstraction. At that point his voice addressing our hearts is neither heard nor listened for; all that is thought to matter is having correct doctrine firmly established in our heads. But the subtlest cerebralism will not save, says Luther. The biblical God is characteristically a speaking God. Christ embraces us in grace and in that act speaks to us, or else we would never be aware of his embrace and its meaning.

For Luther, knowledge of Christ is intimacy with Christ, and can never be reduced to the apprehension of "doctrines and commandments". Neither can it be reduced to "his life, teaching, works, death, and resurrection,"[10] though it necessarily includes these things. The life of Jesus is the obedience he gives to God that all other humans fail to give, and his teaching is the direction he imparts to our discipleship. His works are the incursion of God into this world and our lives. His death is his bearing our sin and bearing it away, while his resurrection is his victory on our behalf. We can apprehend all of this and endorse it, but it is only as we are intimately acquainted with the living person of Jesus Christ himself, who brings these things to us, that we "know" the gospel. Saving faith arises only as we engage *him*—aware that he always comes to us *with* his "life, teaching, works, death and resurrection"—hear him speak, and speak to him in heartfelt response.

Returning now to the discussion of Christ's alien righteousness, we read, "The soul no longer seeks to be righteous in and for itself, but it has Christ as its righteousness and therefore seeks only the welfare of others." Luther is saying that union with Christ frees us from pursuit of self-justification and from anxiety concerning our righteousness, leaving us able to serve our neighbor. This one sentence anticipates his entire seventy-five-page tract, *The Freedom of a Christian*. In Christ, we are spared anxiety over our spiritual condition. While we ought always to be vigilant about putting the old man to death lest he overtake us, we are not to be worried about him, because Christ is our righteousness; freed from anxiety over that, we can attend to serving our neighbor. (Pastoral experience bears this out. The people who are most self-giving in the service of their neighbor are those who are most secure in their assurance of Jesus Christ, because they are not preoccupied with their own religiosity in hopes of being justified by it.)

---

10.   Lull, p. 158.

Luther expands on this theme of self-forgetfulness in a reference to Paul. "Paul's meaning is that when each person has forgotten himself and emptied himself of God's gifts, he should conduct himself as if his neighbor's weakness, sin, and foolishness were his very own. He should not boast or get puffed up. Nor should he despise or triumph over his neighbor as if he were his god or equal to God."[11] The alien righteousness of Christ, which is ours as we embrace Christ, issues first of all in self-forgetfulness—which is, incidentally, the only true humility there is. It should not be confused with self-belittlement or self-rejection, for they merely keep the self at the forefront of our consciousness and agenda and are not humility at all.

The second outcome of this alien righteousness is our emptying ourselves of God's gifts, in the sense that our talents become the occasion of service rather than of our own pleasure, advancement, or self-adulation. Third, says Luther, to possess the righteousness of Christ means that we take on our neighbor's sin and shame the way that Jesus Christ has taken on ours; that is how we love our neighbor. The Christian never lives in herself—a point to which Luther returns again and again in *The Freedom of a Christian*—and it is fatal to try to do so. We are most profoundly ourselves, with the strongest identity we will ever need, as we live in another. We live in two others, in fact: in Christ by faith, and in our neighbor through love, and in this way are given ourselves.

According to Luther, there are various "degrees", as it were, of living in the neighbor through love. The first is sharing our neighbor's *need*. This is not especially difficult, particularly for middle-class types who have a surplus of goods; we see the needy neighbor and give out of our abundance, at little cost to ourselves. If we notch it up a degree, though, we share in the neighbor's *suffering*. That is a good deal more difficult, since it entails pain for us, but at least it also brings social recognition; it is publicly commended and sometimes even rewarded. The real cost,

---

11.   Lull, p. 160.

however, comes when we live in our neighbor by sharing her *shame*, because then we will be spattered by the contempt and condemnation visited upon her. Voices around us will say, "You can tell a person by the company he keeps. If you lie down with the dogs, you get up with the fleas." We will know ostracism and contempt. But what is this but to cling in faith to the Crucified, who was numbered among the transgressors and shared our disgrace so as to give us a future with God?

Luther was aware that when Hosea went down to the marketplace and retrieved his wife, Gomer, for fifteen shekels—half the price of a slave, proving the degradation to which she had sunk—he would have had to do so in front of other men. They would have taunted and ridiculed him. "Ah, Hosea, so you're taking your wife home? Worth half the price of a slave, is she?" Hosea identified with his wife's disgrace in a way that is scarcely imaginable for us. Our Lord likewise identified with our disgrace for our sakes, and the consequence was the horror of the dereliction, beyond our imagining. The good news of the gospel, Luther maintained, is that Christ has declared his love for us and enacted it precisely by sharing our shame. Can we do less for our neighbor (including the disgraced family member who is also "neighbor") if we claim to love the neighbor?

Notice also the words, "Nor should he despise or triumph over his neighbor as if he were his god or equal to God." The essence of the Fall and of our sinful nature is that we want to be our own lord, and not only our own but our neighbor's as well. Having subordinated God to ourselves, we seek to establish our superiority over our neighbor, because if we are not superior to another in *some* respect, we feel we are nobody.[12] Luther reminds us that our identity before God is given to us in Christ when we put him on. Knowing this, established and

---

12. Hegel writes profoundly on this in his discussion of "Master and Slave" in *The Phenomenology of Mind* (New York: Cosimo Publications, 2006), setting out the following dialectic: my identity is tied up in my superiority to my neighbor; I need his recognition of my lordship in order to be who I am. However, this is something that

dignified by this Christ-forged identity, we do not need to lord it over our neighbor. We are free simply to serve him.

"For you are powerful," continues Luther, "not that you may make the weak weaker by oppression, but that you may make them powerful by raising them up and defending them. You are wise, not in order to laugh at the foolish and thereby make them more foolish, but that you may undertake to teach them as you yourself would wish to be taught. You are righteous that you may vindicate and pardon the unrighteous, not that you may only condemn, disparage, judge, and punish." Just as God exalts the humble and the weak, so does the Christian. Christ forgives and defends and exalts us; when the world accuses us of being nothing but sinners, or we accuse ourselves of being as much, Jesus Christ claims us, presses himself upon us, and clothes us in the truth and assurance of his pardon, all the while announcing loudly that contrary to what anyone else thinks, our true life is hid in him. In the same way we must do all of this on behalf of our neighbor, defending and forgiving her when she is overtaken by sin or slandered or ridiculed. If we are powerful, wise, and righteous, then the fact that we are "in Christ" means that our power is to empower the neighbor (not leave her weak, helpless, vulnerable); our wisdom is to make her wise (not humiliate her through our vaunted superiority); our righteousness is to do what is right by her.

One final point to note here is that the exercise of proper righteousness requires spiritual discernment. Luther writes, "In the third class are those who in persuasion are like the second type just mentioned, but are not like them in practice. They are the ones who demand back their own property or seek punishment to be meted out . . . These are called 'zealots' and the Scriptures praise them. But no one ought to attempt this unless he is mature and highly experienced in the second class just mentioned, lest he mistake wrath for zeal and be convicted

---

he might withhold. If he withholds it, I want to kill him, but if I kill him, he will not be there to recognize me. This is a dialectic only the gospel can deal with.

of doing from anger and impatience that which he believes he is doing from love of justice. For anger is like zeal,"—that is, they have a certain phenomenological similarity—"and impatience is like love of justice so that they cannot be sufficiently distinguished except by the most spiritual."[13]

The important point here is that our own sin, if we are not careful, can masquerade as the action of proper righteousness. We ought to pursue justice, but not to use it as cloak for our own rapaciousness, cruelty, impatience, or superiority. We ought to be zealous, particularly in our commendation of the gospel amidst unbelief, but we ought not to lose our temper with people who reject our commendation of the gospel and therein reject our Lord. Luther is pressing here the difference between vindictiveness and vindication, an important biblical distinction and one seen later in his attitude to the peasants' revolt of 1524. When the peasants revolted against their overlords and the state, Luther initially sympathized with them, because their cause was just: they were genuinely oppressed and had been treated shabbily. But when their pursuit of justice boiled over into wanton cruelty visited upon their tormentors, he withdrew his support for the peasants, accusing them of having become as bad as the people against whom they were rightly protesting. A redress of dehumanizing injustice cannot be achieved by dehumanizing one's oppressor in turn.[14]

---

13. Lull, p. 164.

14. In understanding Luther's response to the actions of the peasants, it is also important to remember the very real threat of social chaos that loomed constantly in the sixteenth century. Mention has already been made in an earlier chapter of the fear of attack by the Turks. People were also very afraid of social revolution which would plunge everybody, including the revolutionaries themselves, into unlivable chaos. It is in view of this fact, as well as the theological objections outlined above, that Luther opposed the peasant revolt in his tract, *Against the Robbing and Murdering Hordes of Peasants*. The peasants were in fact murderous; the Münster Rebellion, during which seditious Anabaptist radicals uncharacteristically took up arms against troops sent by the bishop to restore order, was a case in point.

The finest of lines separates the exercise of our proper righteousness from an excuse for our lingering depravity, and the distinction requires spiritual discernment. If criminality occurs, there must be a social response: someone must be arrested, tried, convicted, punished. But we must ask ourselves whether our pursuit of this is motivated finally by our desire to see public order maintained or by our desire for personal gratification; that is, by our desire to see the perpetrator receive his comeuppance as well as to remind ourselves that we are not a criminal like him. It is easy to say that our motivation is the first when secretly (or not so secretly to others) it is the second. If our pursuit of justice obliterates our willingness to share our neighbor's suffering and shame, it is not an exercise of proper righteousness.

In view of Luther's insistence that alien righteousness issues in such concern for our neighbor, it might come as a surprise that he was later criticized for advocating political quietism or social indifference.[15] This criticism results partly from misreading Luther's writings on church and state and isolating them from his other writings, especially on the service of one's neighbor. Luther did say that God rules the church by the gospel and the state by the political authorities or the law, but that does not give *carte blanche* to every kind of state activity. It means only that the state has the right to coerce malefactors—a right which few people would deny. It would be absurd to conclude from the totality of Luther's writing that political authority, though God-ordained, could overturn the exhortation to defend and serve our neighbor. If that were true, he would never have sympathized with the peasant revolt at all,

---

15.   William Shirer, for example, in *The Rise and Fall of the Third Reich* (New York: Simon and Schuster, 1990), spends many pages analysing the mindset of the German people that gave rise to the Nazi era. It was a mindset of political acquiescence, for which Shirer faults Luther's theology. However, in a conversation with a Luther scholar a few years ago, Shirer admitted that he had read virtually none of Luther's writings. It appears that his criticism was merely the repetition of commonplace.

even in the beginning. All his life Luther's heart, as huge as a house, could be broken by beholding suffering of any sort.

A MEDITATION ON CHRIST'S PASSION

A primary focus of this tract is the personal character of faith. The latter is everywhere an important aspect of Luther's theology, and he broaches it almost at once in the *Meditation*: "Of what help is it to you that God is God, if he is not God to you?"[16]

Doctrine describes the truth of Christ, but no description of the truth is of the same order as "Truth" or reality, the living Person, presence, and voice of Christ. In recognition of this fact, Luther insists that faith—as contrasted with mere "belief"—is the engagement of the Christian's total person with the Person of Jesus Christ.

As mentioned already, the personal note sounded by Luther was somewhat obscured by the Lutheran scholastics who followed him. One way they did this was by one-sidedly emphasizing the forensic dimension of justification as a legal transaction whose benefit is applied to us in the absence of any intimacy with Christ our Justifier. They also appeared to misinterpret the *extra nos* aspect of the gospel. *Extra nos* means 'outside of us': Christ must do something outside us if he is to do anything salvific *for us*; and what he has done *for us* must come to be done *in us*. The *extra nos*, then, grounds the *for us* and *in us*, thus providing the foundation of our discipleship. But while it is always necessary, it is never sufficient; that is, it is never a substitute for *in nobis*. There are times when we are confronted with our residual depravity and are driven to wonder what exactly Christ has done in us. And on those occasions, the *extra nos* dimension in Luther provides the requisite anchor. If regarded mechanically or impersonally, however, it can be used as a cavalier cover-up for sin, fostering only spiritual indifference. Luther maintains that while Christ has done all that is needed, *extra nos*, to ground our justification, it remains the case

16. Lull, *op. cit.*, p. 166.

that we are justified by faith only as we embrace, put on, live in and love the Justifier himself.

Faith, for Luther, has the three ingredients of understanding, assent, and trust (*notitia, assensus, fiducia*), but it is *fiducia* or trust that is properly definitive, and its object is always a person. Assent can be assent to an abstract truth; assent to the truth of the gospel is presupposed in trust, yet there is no faith, properly speaking, without trust in a person. "Faith resides in the personal pronouns," Luther never tired of saying. By this he meant that faith is not credence given to the tenets promulgated by a church or set forth by a theology. Faith arises not when we understand that Jesus Christ is Savior, even Savior of the world; it arises, said Luther, when I am constrained to own him as *my* Savior, *my* Lord. Luther was forever moved at Paul's exclamation, "He loved *me*, and gave himself—*for me*" (Gal. 2:20).

This insistence on the cruciality of the personal pronouns means that there courses through Luther's theology a profound piety.[17] Today piety has a decidedly negative connotation, or at least piet*ism* has. Piet*ism* brings to mind something subjective, uncritically emotional, romantic, individualistic, sentimental; it suggests anti-intellectualism and retreat from the transformation of culture. Pietism is manifestly foreign to Luther. However, true piety, "the Word in the heart," is something the Wittenberger cherished. He would have found cloying the piet*ism* of Lutheranism seventy-five years later, yet appears closer to the ethos of those labeled Lutheran Pietists—such as Philipp Jakob Spener (1635-1705), August Gottlieb Spangenberg (1704-1792), and August Hermann Francke (1663-1727)—than to the scholastic orthodoxy of yet another branch of the Lutheran family. His hymn-writing is one expression of his piety, and his Christ-formed, Christ-informed and Christ-normed mysticism is another. His aphorism *simul peccator, simul iustus*—"simultaneously both sinful and justified"—may be better

---

17.   Piety is a major aspect of Calvin's theology. He speaks of it as "...that reverence joined with love of God which the knowledge of his benefits induces" (*Institutes* 1.2.1).

known than his *simul gemitus, simul raptus*—"at once groaning and thrilled"—but it is the latter that captures the simultaneous anguish and ecstasy of the life of a Christian. Believers are always aware of the arrears of sin within that cause them to cry out for deliverance, and are always assaulted by the world as well, yet are never without the deeper, more telling joy of their union with Christ. Because Luther's theology came to birth at a time of doctrinal controversy, we are inclined to be dazzled by his ability to forge and articulate doctrine, overlooking the fact that it always subserved the reality of our throbbing joy in Jesus Christ. (Dietrich Bonhoeffer, a Lutheran, did not fail to own this aspect of Luther's faith. Bonhoeffer's writings, especially his prison correspondence, exhale Luther's *simul gemitus, simul raptus* throughout.)

It is against this background of personal faith, then, that Luther goes on to talk about the contemplation of Christ's passion. "They contemplate Christ's passion aright who view it with a terror-stricken heart and a despairing conscience," he writes. The proper viewing of Christ's passion, in the first place, is not to analyze it intellectually in the sense of determining what exactly the place of the cross is in the plan of salvation. We view it properly only when we are devastated by it.

On the one hand, Luther is picking up on a medieval motif here: the medievalists were wont to talk a great deal about contemplating Christ's passion. On the other hand, Luther's understanding of this spiritual exercise is different. While the medieval tradition aimed at magnifying our pity for Christ's suffering, Luther recognizes that element as foreign to the apostolic church. The point is not the physical agony Christ suffered, since he suffered no more than the two criminals crucified alongside him and less than many people have suffered since. The apostolic emphasis falls instead on the nature and efficacy of his spiritual torment. The heart of Christ's passion is the dereliction, the agony of Godforsakenness in the midst of which the Son drinks to the bitterest dregs the cup of the Father's just judgment on sin. The result of such suffering is that our sin is borne and borne away. Luther wants us to contemplate Christ's suffering not so that we will be moved to pity for our Lord (this he regards as spiritually useless if not deleterious), but so that we will be horrified at our sinnership:

> It must be an inexpressible and unbearable earnestness that forces such a great and infinite person to suffer and die to appease it. And if you seriously consider that it is God's very own Son, the eternal wisdom of the Father, who suffers, you will be terrified indeed…We must give ourselves wholly to this matter, for the main benefit of Christ's passion is that man sees into his own true self and that he be terrified and crushed by this.[18]

Three important truths are uttered here. First, the cross is an act of revelation. Luther does not mean by "man sees into his own true self" that the purpose of the cross is to facilitate self-awareness. The purpose of the cross is to make sinners "at one" with God. Nevertheless, one major benefit arising from the finished work of Calvary is an apprehension of how sinful we are. It is only in light of our redemption that sin is revealed and discerned.

By implication, then, there is no natural knowledge of sin. There can be natural awareness of guilt, insecurity, moral failure, vice, psychological distress, and finitude, and these have frequently been magnified in the church's preaching because the gospel is thought to gain credibility as human unease is inflamed. None of this, however, is the same as awareness of sin. Sin is a violation of God. Violation of God can be known only as God is known, and God is known only as we are made the beneficiaries of God's reconciliation of violators. Only the cure discloses the disease. Only the gospel (discerned in faith, since it is not naturally intelligible) acquaints people with the fact, nature, and scope of sin. Any claim for a natural knowledge of sin moralizes both sin and the gospel, denaturing the entire Christian economy of salvation.

Second, this arch-revelation of sin is the nadir of God. It takes nothing less to acquaint us with our sinnership than the self-alienation of God in the Son's dereliction. When Luther says that "it is God's very

---

18. Lull, p. 167.

own Son... who suffers," he does not mean that it is only the Son who suffers while the Father does not. He did not believe the traditional notion that God cannot suffer, a view under which God is remote, one-sidedly transcendent and out of touch with the world. It is true that God is not subject to mood alterations and cannot be manipulated through pain, but this is no ground for saying that he does not suffer; the Older Testament indicates on every page that he does. Indeed, further on in his tract Luther refers explicitly to "God's sufferings", for he was far too good a Hebraist to deny God's anguish. What the Father tasted in the Son's dereliction can be no less than what the Son tasted, or the identity of substance between the Father and the Son collapses, and with it the doctrines of Incarnation and Trinity. Simply put, it costs God greater anguish to acquaint us with the nature of our sin than it costs us to become acquainted with it.

Third, the outcome of such revelation is that we are "terrified and crushed." While the psychological dimension of being "terrified" is undeniable, Luther's ultimate concern is theological rather than psychological. The despair of the conscience-stricken ("crushed") is despair of our own righteousness before God. Yet the outcome, as Luther goes on to say, is new standing before God, a standing rooted not in ourselves but in Jesus Christ (justification), and a new nature at God's hand (sanctification).[19]

> [H]e who contemplates God's sufferings for a day, an hour, yes, only a quarter of an hour, does better than to fast a whole year, pray a psalm daily, yes, better than to hear a hundred masses. This meditation changes man's being and, almost like baptism [note the qualification] gives him a new birth. Here the passion of Christ performs its natural and noble work, strangling the old Adam and banishing all joy, delight, and confidence which man could derive from other creatures, even as Christ was forsaken by all, even by God.[20]

---

19.   Just how Law-induced terror gives rise to to gospel-induced assurance will be made plain in the chapter, "Law and Gospel."

20.   Lull, p. 169.

The meditation that Luther has in mind here is not sentimental musing on a text, but indwelling the text and absorbing its message until Jesus Christ emerges from within it and seizes us, strangling the old Adam in us. Such slaying (and subsequent quickening), it must always be remembered, banishes any hint of confidence in our own righteousness.

Amplifying the foregoing, Luther adds:

> Until now we have sojourned in Passion Week and rightly celebrated Good Friday. Now we come to the resurrection of Christ, to the day of Easter. After man has thus become aware of his sin, and is terrified in his heart, he must watch that sin does not remain in his conscience, for this would lead to sheer despair. Just as our knowledge of sin flowed from Christ and was acknowledged by us, so we must pour this sin back on him and free our conscience of it.[21]

The order is crucial. Jesus Christ (alone) reveals our sinnership, but if this is all that happens, our situation is worse than ever. Rather, together with this newly-granted knowledge of our sinnership, we need the knowledge that our sin is borne by Christ, and borne away. In fact, it is precisely in the course of appearing to us as sin-bearer that Christ acquaints us with our sin. Therefore, if sin lingers in our conscience, it is not Christ who has acquainted us with it.[22]

Pressing the point made above Luther continues, "If we allow sin to remain in our conscience and try to deal with it there, or if we look at sin in our heart, it will be much too strong for us and will live on forever. But if we behold it resting on Christ and overcome by his resurrection, and then boldly believe this, even it is dead and nullified."[23] It is the fact of Jesus Christ, and specifically the cross, which properly arouses our conscience only to pacify it again.

---

21. Lull, p. 170.

22. The same thought is expressed by Calvin's statement that to contemplate Christ aright is always to contemplate oneself in him, that if we see Jesus Christ over there and ourselves over here, what we are looking at is not Christ. The reality of Christ is Christ with his people in him (*Institutes*, 3.2.24).

23. Lull, p. 170.

Then Luther adduces the support of the apostle: "St. Paul says, 'God has made him a sinner for us, so that through him we would be made just.' You must stake everything on these and similar verses." What is described in that passage in 2 Corinthians 5:21 is known as "The Great Exchange," in which Christ takes on our sinnership and gives us his righteousness instead. For Luther, this is the core and substance of the gospel, indicating once again that the gospel is not a message *about* something (if it were, the gospel would essentially be instruction), but rather the truth and reality of Jesus Christ himself, the *power* of God saving us at this moment (Romans 1:16).

But notice that Luther, appearing to be quoting 2 Corinthians 5:21, writes, "God has made him a sinner for us," where the biblical text actually says, "He who knew no sin was made to be sin for us." Paul says "sin," but Luther, deliberately and significantly, changes it to "sinner." Remember that he was criticized for introducing the word *allein*, or "alone," in his translation of Romans 3:28: "Man is justified by faith alone, apart from works of the law." He knew, of course, that there was no equivalent of the word *allein* in the Greek text of that verse, but he defended himself on the grounds that the *meaning* of justification by faith everywhere in Paul was faith *alone*. We must conclude that Luther's retranslation of the text in 2 Corinthians 5:21 was similarly motivated by a respect for what he considered the intent of the author, and ask ourselves what it meant for Paul to say that Christ was made sin.

Many commentaries distinguish carefully between sin and sinner in interpreting this passage, but this distinction relies on a reification of sin. The fact is, there is no such thing or entity or substance as sin; there are only persons who sin, just as there is no love apart from persons who love. Strictly speaking sin does not exist; only sinners do. When we speak of the forgiveness of sins, then, what we really mean is the forgiveness of sinners. It is sinners who are pardoned, not sin.

Was Christ made *sin* for us, then, or was he made *sinner*? On the one hand, he is not a sinner in the sense that we are, or far from making atonement for us he would need to be atoned for himself. Nevertheless, to be "numbered among the transgressors", as he was, is to be *identified* with sinners. In a sense that we can glimpse but not fully comprehend, Jesus Christ is for our sakes made to be sinner. He not only substitutes for us—that is, takes our place instead of us—but represents us: he stands for us, stands with us, gathers us up in himself. God was punishing not sin but sinners, because sin has no existence apart from sinners; Christ assumed that sinnership, and hence bore the punishment.

Notice how Luther's "became sinner" emphasizes again the personal character and content of the gospel as opposed to reducing it to mere ideation or abstract statements. When we speak of the love of God, what we really mean is not a quality, "love," that God possesses and now presses upon us. The love of God, rather, is the activity of God himself loving us at this moment. As Calvin would shortly say, the person of God is found in all the acts of God.[24] God's judgment is God judging us, and God's love is God himself loving us. In the same way, when Christ is "made sin", it is not that our sin, in the abstract, is placed on Christ. Rather, Christ himself takes on the identity of *us who sin*, the identity of sinners, and for that reason receives our punishment. This is what keeps the exchange from being a legal fiction or an external transaction. We always live in the realm of the person and personhood; the person of the sinner and the person of God are concrete, and it is at the level of the concrete that redemption must occur.[25]

---

24. Calvin, *Institutes*, 1.7.4.

25. This discussion also calls into question the Christian aphorism "Love the sinner but hate the sin". The advice backfires by encouraging us to lose sight of what we are dealing with at all times: not adultery, not child abuse, but *persons* who do these things. If sin has no existence apart from sinners, it is logically impossible to love the sinner and hate the sin; we can only love and hate the sinner herself at the same time. It is extremely dangerous to say this, of course, lest we legitimate the church's cruel rejection and condemnation of sinners; the hatred of sinners is not safe in our hands. It is safe in the hands of God, however, whose hatred is always a manifestation of his love, always acting passionately to bring the sinner to the end of herself. Our hatred, on the other hand, always risks being nothing more than unqualified hatred and rejection, an expression of our depravity.

We then come to a rather unusual passage in the tract: "If, as was said before, you cannot believe, you must entreat God for faith. This too rests entirely in the hands of God...[S]ometimes faith is granted openly, sometimes in secret."[26] This reference to the granting of faith "in secret" is Luther's twofold reminder: one, we are not the author or the measure of our faith; two, we can possess faith even when we lack assurance of faith.

Luther's accommodation here contrasts with Calvin's unqualified insistence, in his *Institutes*, that assurance is an essential aspect of faith. Where there is no assurance of faith, says Calvin, there is no faith. Yet even he, when working closer to the text, sees what Luther sees. In his magnificent commentary on John 20, Calvin notes that the women go to the tomb on Easter morning to anoint a corpse; in other words, they are not anticipating the resurrection, and their non-expectation would seem to be an instance of unbelief. However, says Calvin, "some seed of faith remained in their hearts, but smothered for a time, so that they were not aware of possessing what they did possess," namely, faith in Jesus Christ, which includes his resurrection. Calvin continues, "Although this feeling of piety which they had was confused and mingled with much superstition, yet I call it, though imprecisely, faith, because it was conceived only by the teaching of the gospel, and had Christ alone as its object."[27] For Calvin there are people who possess genuine faith in our Lord without being fully aware of it, and there are those whose faith is mixed up with all kinds of extraneous matter, even superstition. Still, in the midst of it all, there is that iota, at least, of justifying faith.

John Updike's novel *In the Beauty of the Lilies* features a Presbyterian minister living in New Jersey in 1910. In one scene we see the minister searching his heart in agony for the faith that has somehow eroded, and he cannot find it. With biting irony, the narrator says, "Imagine the

---

26. Lull, p. 171.
27. Calvin, *Commentary on John* (Grand Rapids: Eerdmans, 1994), p. 193.

cruelty of a theology that leaves you ransacking your nervous system for a passage to heaven, or even the shred of a ticket."[28] The cruelty is the result of insisting that there is no faith without assurance; it plunges us into the fruitless torture of introspection, "ransacking our nervous system for a passage to heaven." The reality, by contrast, is that assurance steals over us as we are not looking for it but are looking instead away from ourselves to Jesus Christ. Here once again is the Christological emphasis of the Reformation, and of Luther in particular. We never look into our hearts for truth, because Jesus Christ, who exists for us outside of us *before* he dwells within us, is the truth. As we keep looking away from ourselves to *him*, the truth does steal in upon our heart, overtake us, and flood us with the assurance we would never gain by intrapsychic investigation.

Bonhoeffer, a theological genius to be sure, nonetheless everywhere exudes his debt to his theological parent. Always mindful of the cruciality of community in matters of faith and assurance, he adds something else to the admonition to look away from ourselves to Christ: he insists that the Christ we see in the face of our sister or brother is stronger than the Christ we find in our own heart.[29] When we become aware of our compromised discipleship and wonder if we are Christ's at all, or when the vicissitudes of life have robbed us of the confidence of faith, we can look at our fellow Christian and find our assurance strengthened by the Christ he reflects to us. The Christ that we see outside of us restores our assurance of the Christ within us. That is why we must continue to mirror Christ to one another, especially in times of distress, and so confirm one another in the truth that Christ has never forsaken any of us. Insofar as we do this, the assurance we need for pursuing the Christian life is restored to us amidst all assaults from without and all upheavals within.

---

28. John Updike, *In the Beauty of the Lilies* (New York: Knopf, 1996), p. 44.

29. This theme occurs repeatedly in Dietrich Bonhoeffer, *Life Together* (London: SCM, 1972), but especially in chapters I and IV.

6

Freedom in Christ

THE FREEDOM OF A CHRISTIAN

Written in 1520, *The Freedom of a Christian* is one of Luther's major tracts and probably his best known. Its importance lies perhaps in its comprehensiveness; Luther said of this piece of writing, "Unless I am mistaken, . . . it contains the whole of Christian life in a brief form."[1]

The introduction to the tract is a reminder of the context in which the Christian's freedom is operative, namely the ongoing conflict between the gospel and its enemies. "Unfortunately," Luther writes, "there are many people, especially those who are proud of their titles, who oppose the truth with all their power and cunning."[2] Luther is aware that the gospel faces unremitting opposition—that the venue and theatre in which we live and proclaim the gospel is a maelstrom of spiritual forces.[3] And in this he is always conscious of the apocalyp-

---

1. Lull, *Martin Luther's Basic Theological Writings*, p. 595.
2. Ibid., p 585.
3. Heiko Oberman's biography of Luther, *Luther: Man Between God and the Devil* (New Haven: Yale University Press, 1982), brings this out clearly.

tic dimension of eschatology—that is, the intensification of spiritual conflict that must precede the ultimate resolution, in God's Kingdom, of all that contradicts him and his way now.

Luther is aware, moreover, that it is as truth in the sense of "reality" that the gospel is opposed. To oppose the gospel, therefore, is not to disagree with a statement or even message; it is to oppose the living Lord Jesus Christ himself. He is the real object of resistance on the part of spiritual antagonists.

Who are these antagonists? Luther identifies them as "those who are proud of their titles", that is, the socially prominent. The simple reason is that the gospel levels humankind, and such people prefer their social self-elevation to exaltation at God's hand.

Addressing Pope Leo X, Luther writes:

> There is one thing, however, which I cannot ignore and which is the cause of my writing once more to Your Blessedness. It has come to my attention that I am accused of great indiscretion, said to be my great fault, in which, it is said, I have not spared even your person. I freely vow that I have, to my knowledge, spoken only good and honorable words concerning you whenever I have thought of you.[4]

In other words, Luther has no personal animosity towards Pope Leo X. What is at issue, as far as he is concerned, is the truth of the gospel. On this issue he remains adamant: "In all other matters I will yield to any man whatsoever; but I have neither the power nor the will to deny the Word of God."[5] He means that he would prefer to avoid the public conflict in which he finds himself, but at the same time, personal niceties must never be allowed to obscure the Word of God. The risk of being misunderstood, of appearing to be involved in a personal vendetta when in fact he is upholding the gospel, is something he must live with for now.

---

4.   Lull, p. 586.
5.   Ibid., p. 587.

Luther goes on to criticize the Roman see and the church as a whole while sparing the pope himself:

> I have truly despised your see, the Roman Curia, which, however, neither you nor anyone else can deny is more corrupt than any Babylon or Sodom ever was, and which, as far as I can see, is characterized by a completely depraved, hopeless, and notorious godlessness...[T]he Roman church, once the holiest of all, has become the most licentious den of thieves, the most shameless of all brothels, the kingdom of sin, death, and hell. It is so bad that even Antichrist himself, if he should come, could think of nothing to add to its wickedness...Meanwhile you, Leo, sit as a lamb in the midst of wolves and like Daniel in the midst of lions. With Ezekiel you live among scorpions.[6]

Luther is using the word "brothel" both metaphorically, as it is used in the book of Revelation, and also literally to allude to the sexual malfeasance of the clergy. We have already spoken about the frequent practice of priests taking mistresses, despite vows of celibacy, and the contempt with which these mistresses and their children were regarded in society. Having drawn attention to the sexual abuses in the church, Luther would say that even if the church of Rome were rid of all abuses, its theology would still obscure the gospel, and as long as the gospel is obscured, ungodliness will thrive. Meanwhile, his references to Daniel and Ezekiel, the two Old Testament books most frequently quoted in Revelation, are examples of his use of apocalyptic idiom. He is always aware of the "end-time" pressure visited upon the world as Jesus Christ, who is always coming to his people, collides with the spiritual forces that oppose him.

Luther then extends his remarks to any denominational bureaucracy in any era: it fears reformation. "The Roman Curia is already lost," he continues, "for God's wrath has relentlessly fallen upon it. It detests church councils, it fears reformation, it cannot allay its own

---

6.　Ibid., p. 588.

INTERPRETING MARTIN LUTHER

corruption."[7] To defend, cloak, deny, and exploit their own corruption is simply the nature of religious bureaucracies. That is why Luther says, "I never intended to attack the Roman Curia or to raise any controversy concerning it. But when I saw all efforts to save it were hopeless, I despised it, gave it a bill of divorce, and said, 'Let the evildoer still do evil, and the filthy still be filthy'." In other words, it is not the vocation of believers to try to cure institutional corruption. We deal with it only tangentially in the pursuit of our real vocation, which must always be the gospel, the work of attesting Jesus Christ, the task of lending visibility to the Kingdom that Christ the King has brought with him.

Luther spends considerable time on one particularly notorious opponent of this gospel, Johann Eck. "Satan opened his eyes and then filled his servant Johann Eck, a notable enemy of Christ, with an insatiable lust for glory."[8] By "insatiable lust for glory," Luther does not mean primarily that Eck seeks aggrandizement, but rather that Eck embraces a theology of glory in conflict with the theology of the cross. One feature of this theology of glory is triumphalism—not confidence in the triumph or efficacy of the gospel, but the triumphalism of the church—and Eck's unwillingness to acknowledge openly the failure of church leadership is evidence of this triumphalist theology. "From his example alone we can learn that no enemy is more pernicious than a flatterer," says Luther. Eck flatters the pope, and since such flattery suppresses the truth of the gospel, it is more harmful than outright hostility. In fact, it makes Eck an enemy not only of the pope, but ultimately of humankind: if the gospel is God's saving activity, then to suppress it is to impede the one thing that people need more than anything else.

Finally, in a statement expressing one of the great breakthroughs of the Reformation, Luther writes, "I acknowledge no fixed rules for the interpretation of the Word of God, since the Word of God, which

---

7. Ibid., p. 588.
8. Ibid., p. 590.

teaches freedom in all other matters, must not be bound." To say that there are no fixed rules is to say that Scripture possesses its own logic, militancy, and integrity and therefore does not need any interpretive grid imposed upon it. Previously there had been a fourfold method for interpreting Scripture, yielding its literal, allegorical, tropological, and anagogical meanings; the tropological interpretation was the moral one, and the anagogical an ultimate spiritual or mystical meaning beyond the others. Luther rejects this. Scripture must be allowed to convince and convict readers of the truth of its plain sense.

The church has always had difficulty understanding the logic, militancy, and integrity of the gospel and therefore of Scripture. Once we lose confidence in Scripture's coherence and inherent efficacy, we are obliged to bring an interpretive tool to it, such as existential philosophy, Kantianism, Hegelianism, or simply the *Zeitgeist*, the spirit of the age. In a 1955 novel, *The Man in the Gray Flannel Suit*, Sloan Wilson applies to Scripture the grid consisting of business principles, and thus retells the story of Jesus as the entrepreneur who is truly wise and ahead of his time. More recently, the Jesus Seminar has attempted to establish external criteria for determining which sayings of Jesus reported in the gospels can be affirmed as his, which ones might be his (with varying degrees of likelihood), and which ones could never be his but are simply the invention of the primitive church. Luther, however, reflecting the Christological heart of the Reformation, declares that no philosophical foundation or buttress or interpretive key is needed to apprehend Jesus Christ; Christ does not merely illustrate or implement a truth lying behind him, but is himself the truth and reality which confronts us as the gospel is proclaimed. When he surges upon us in the power of the Spirit, he does not dovetail with the categories we possess already and by which we deem him "relevant"; instead he forges within us the categories needed to apprehend him and the vocabulary by which we can speak of him.

This Christological sufficiency, integrity, militancy, and efficacy, reflected in the integrity of Scripture, lies at the heart of the Protestant Reformation. Not long afterwards, both Lutheran and Calvinist brands of scholasticism lost sight of it, reverting to an Aristotelian philosophical foundation in which they nestled their theology. According to Luther, any such combination denatures the gospel and constitutes opposition to it.

CHRISTIAN FAITH AND THE WORD OF GOD

Luther begins the main text of the tract with a caution against misunderstanding the faith that characterizes a Christian: "Many people have considered Christian faith an easy thing, and not a few have given it a place among the virtues. They do this because they have not experienced it and have never tasted the great strength there is in faith."[9]

There are at least three points here that are germane to the discussion of Christian freedom. The first is that faith is not easy; we have to wrestle for it, and having done so, we are committed by that faith to contending in the world. In other words, faith always finds the Christian contending. Second, faith is not a virtue. In the ancient world, faith, hope, and love were considered the three theological virtues. As soon as we speak of faith as a virtue, however, our focus ceases to be Christological and becomes moralistic; we tend to view faith as a quality in us that we have developed, like temperance or courage, when it is rather a matter of embracing Jesus Christ in the strength and desire arising from his prior embracing of us. This is qualitatively different from virtue or vice. Third, it is in this faith, this clinging to Christ, that strength resides—the strength needed for the very contention to which the same faith commits us. Luther speaks a little later on of "the courage which faith gives a man when trials oppress him." Trials oppress the Christian because, as we saw in the tract's introduction, the gospel relentlessly arouses antagonism to itself. Insofar as the Christian is identified with the gospel, she is targeted by this antagonism in the form of assaults, trials, and testing—the *Anfechtungen* discussed previously. Indeed, our experience of these things is evidence that we are

---

9.   Ibid., p. 595.

on the leading edge of Christ's engagement with the principalities and powers. In clinging to him, however, we are given courage to withstand these trials.

Luther then sets out the thesis of the tract:

> A Christian is a perfectly free lord of all, subject to none.
> A Christian is a perfectly dutiful servant of all, subject to all.[10]

The outcome of this, to which everything in the ensuing pages directs us, is later stated as follows:

> We conclude therefore, that a Christian lives not in himself, but in Christ and in his neighbor. Otherwise he is not a Christian. He lives in Christ through faith, in his neighbor through love. By faith he is caught up beyond himself into God. By love he descends beneath himself into his neighbor.[11]

In other words, we find in the end that our freedom takes the form not of living in ourselves but of living in Christ and our neighbor, in contrast to what the world understands by freedom.

What the world customarily understands by "freedom" is mere indeterminism: the absence of anything external to us coercing the decision we make. Thus we are "free" to choose to sleep or study, purchase ice cream of whatever flavour, eat fish or meat. This cannot be defended as synonymous with freedom, however. Freedom is, more profoundly, the absence of any impediment to acting in accord with one's true nature. If a derailing switch is placed upon railway tracks, the train is prevented from traveling along the rails; when the switch is removed, the train is said to be free to run along the rails. If someone asks, "But is the train free to float like a boat?" the proper reply can only be, "But it is not a train's nature to float like a boat." When the apostle Paul reminds the Christians in Galatia, "For freedom Christ has set us free" (Gal. 5:1), he can only mean that Christ has set us free for obeying Christ. It is

---

10. Ibid., p. 596.
11. Ibid., p. 623.

preposterous to think that Christ has set us free to choose between obedience and disobedience. In other words, freedom is not freedom of choice, in the sense of selecting between alternatives, but freedom from choice.

Where does this Christian freedom come from? "One thing, and only one thing," writes Luther, "is necessary for Christian life, righteousness, and freedom. That one thing is the most holy Word of God, the gospel of Christ."[12] Notice the relation of these four terms: Word of God, gospel, righteousness, freedom. They characterize Luther's understanding, not surprisingly surfacing again and again. The Word of God is the content of the gospel in its inherent efficacy; the Word of God relates us rightly to God, and this right relationship is righteousness; once rightly related to God, we possess Christian freedom. The logical order is important: the Word of God, the essence of the gospel, gives rise to righteousness, which in turn fosters freedom. Only the gospel, then, frees humankind in the sense of removing any and all impediments to our acting in accord with our true nature as daughters and sons of God.

Throughout his discussion of Christian freedom Luther is preoccupied with our situation before God. He would never deny that a humanly-fashioned freeing can occur through psychotherapy, for instance, or that financial sufficiency provides a modicum of material freedom. But only the gospel frees us before God, releasing us from our bondage and undoing the ravages of sin in us. For this reason, he says, "the soul can do without anything except the Word of God and…where the Word of God is missing there is no help at all for the soul." Only the Word of God reconstitutes the person before God.

Reinforcing this point, Luther reminds us of the psalmist's yearning and sighing for the Word of God in Psalm 119, understanding the Word of God here not primarily as Scripture, but as the self-utterance and self-bestowal of God in our midst. This is important, as we will see

---

12. Ibid., p. 597.

later in this chapter; we are wont to interpret the many references to the precept, commandment, counsel, or way of God in Psalm 119 as law or duty, while ultimately the content of the Word of God is the gospel.

All of this brings us back to that Christological sufficiency cherished by the Reformers. The Word of God does not need to be supported, buttressed, propped up by apologetics, argued for philosophically, or grounded in a metaphysic. The Word of God is God himself so coming upon men and women and forging his way within them as to make himself known to them for who he is. It is not the case that, having encountered the Word of God, people are left saying, "What's happened?" God himself, in Christ, identifies for them the nature and significance of his action upon them and within them.

Luther says, with reference to the ministry of the Word:

> On the other hand, there is no more terrible disaster with which the wrath of God can afflict men than a famine of the hearing of his Word, as he says in Amos. Likewise there is no greater mercy than when he sends forth his Word, as we read in Psalm 107 [vs 20: 'He sent forth his word, and healed them, and delivered them from destruction.']. Nor was Christ sent into the world for any other ministry except that of the Word. Moreover, the entire spiritual estate—all the apostles, bishops, and priests—has been called and instituted only for the ministry of the Word.[13]

The last statement is not a one-sided shriveling of the function of clergy. It is a recognition that although pastoral ministry may take many forms, all of which are implicates of our life in Christ, none of them is a substitute for the ministry of the Word.

"The entire Scripture of God is divided into two parts: commandments and promises," continues Luther; "The commandments show us what we ought to do but do not give us the power to do it." The commandment of God exposes our spiritual impotence and pushes us to spiritual despair so that we are impelled to embrace Jesus Christ

---

13.   Ibid., p. 598.

in faith. We should not imagine, however, that the commandment or law corresponds to the Older Testament while the promise or gospel is confined to the New. Both testaments are Word of God, hence Law and gospel are found in both, and are subtly related; any one pronouncement in Scripture can be either law or gospel, depending on the context in which it is heard.[14]

THE POWERS OF FAITH

Throughout this discussion Luther is approaching what he calls the first power of faith, but he does not identify it at the outset. Rather, he circles around it, finally lands on it, and then announces that what he has just been talking about is the first power of faith. On his way there he writes:

> No good work can rely upon the Word of God or live in the soul, for faith alone and the Word of God rule in the soul. Just as the heated iron glows like fire because of the union of fire with it, so the Word imparts its qualities to the soul.[15]

He is perhaps a trifle careless with his illustration, because while fire imparts fire, the Word, as God, does not impart Godhood; it imparts godliness. That is, in receiving the Word himself, we are made not divine but righteous—and in that sense authentically human. In Luther's defence, some readers draw attention to the fact that he refers to the imparting of qualities, not properties, the Aristotelian distinction being that properties are definitive while qualities are not. It is unlikely that Luther had this kind of subtlety in mind at all. He simply meant that the God-ness of God confers godliness on God's people. And this conferral of godliness or righteousness is the first power of faith.

The second power of faith is that it honors God by vesting all our trust in him. To honor and trust God in this way is always to obey

---

14. See the later chapter on Law and Gospel for an amplification of this point.
15. Ibid., p. 601.

him; the law commands us, and the gospel invites us, to trust God to fulfill his promises within us. Obedience is obedience only where the goodness and truth of God are trusted, and trust in God is sincere and genuine only when those who say they trust God also obey him. In other words, trust in God and obedience to God always presuppose and imply each other.[16]

In the same section, Luther writes:

> Is not such a soul most obedient to God in all things by this faith? What commandment is there that such obedience has not completely fulfilled? What more complete fulfillment is there than obedience in all things? This obedience, however, is not rendered by works, but by faith alone.[17]

and later:

> You see that the First Commandment, which says, 'You shall worship one God,' is fulfilled by faith alone . . . Therefore it is a blind and dangerous doctrine which teaches that the commandments must be fulfilled by works. The commandments must be fulfilled before any works can be done, and the works proceed from the fulfillment of the commandments.[18]

Luther is insisting here that the command of God can be obeyed only in faith—a reference, once again, to "first-commandment righteousness," or the notion that only faith, as enjoined by the first commandment, makes us righteous before God. In other words, insofar as we have no other gods before God, meaning that we have abandoned ourselves to trust in him, we will keep all ten commandments. Apart from that trust or faith, on the other hand, the commandments become a moral code against which we measure ourselves, and our conformity

---

16. For an extended treatment of this point see the Lutheran thinker, Dietrich Bonhoeffer, *The Cost of Discipleship*.

17. Lull, p. 602.

18. Ibid., p. 605.

to them is not obedience at all but the establishment of ourselves as our own lord. As Luther puts it, "[I]f a man were not first a believer and a Christian, all his works would amount to nothing and would be truly wicked and damnable sins." This does not mean, of course, that our unbelieving neighbor's ethical aspiration is pointless—after all, we would rather live next to a neighbor who does not steal than one who does—but that it has no saving efficacy, for where there is no faith, people are not rightly related to Jesus Christ and their ethical aspiration is just another effort at self-salvation. By contrast, the Ten Commandments describe the life of a believer who has been rendered a child of faith by the gospel—for, as Luther never tired of pointing out, the preface to the Decalogue is pure gospel: "You were slaves in Egypt, you were helpless and hopeless, and I saved you with my outstretched arm."[19] It is the purpose of the gospel to engender faith, and faith in turn honors God with obedience.

It might seem that Luther invented this concept of first-commandment righteousness himself. He did not, of course; Paul says in Romans 14:23, "whatever does not proceed from faith is sin." If anything about us does not proceed from faith, it can only proceed from unbelief, and in that case it is sin no matter how morally virtuous it is. Unbelief—the refusal to take God at his Word (or promise) and entrust ourselves to him—remains the arch sin.

"The third incomparable benefit of faith is that it unites the soul with Christ as a bride is united with her bridegroom,"[20] says Luther. We have already encountered that biblical metaphor in his tract *Two Kinds of Righteousness.* He said there that it is not enough merely to understand the doctrine of justification or righteousness; we must hear in it the voice of Christ, saying to us like a groom to his bride, "I am yours,"— and must respond, like the bride, "And I am yours."

---

19.   Lutherans continue to regard this preface as part of the first commandment.

20.   Ibid., p. 603.

It is odd, however, that Luther cites this union with Christ as the third benefit of faith, when logically it is the first. It is only by virtue of that union, after all, that we receive anything, as we saw in the previous chapter: we have Christ's righteousness because we are identified with him and have our identity only in him. This conferral of righteousness would then be the second benefit of faith, and the third would be that we are rendered trustworthy servants of Jesus Christ. Since there is no benefit apart from our union with Christ, that union is logically the first benefit.

In fact, Luther returns to this fact a few sentences later:

> Accordingly the believing soul can boast of and glory in whatever Christ has as though it were its own, and whatever the soul has Christ claims as his own. Let us compare these and we shall see inestimable benefits. Christ is full of grace, life, and salvation. The soul is full of sins, death, and damnation.[21]

As Luther goes on to explore the significance of what he calls the third benefit of faith, namely union with Christ, he celebrates the fact that the risen Christ with whom we are united both teaches and intercedes: "Nor does he only pray and intercede for us but he teaches us inwardly through the living instruction of his Spirit, thus performing the two real functions of a priest, of which the prayers and the preaching of human priests are visible types."[22] Luther has in mind here, of course, the episode on the road to Emmaus, where the risen Christ interprets to his companions on the road everything in the Scriptures concerning himself. He does the same every day for the church as a whole, says Luther, teaching us in such a way that we see everything in the Scriptures as pertaining to him and to us who are found in him through faith.

In addition to conferring his righteousness on us, our union with Christ gives us a unique role in the world: "Hence all of us who believe

---

21.   Ibid., p. 603.
22.   Ibid., p. 606.

in Christ are priests and kings in Christ, as 1 Peter 2 says: 'You are a chosen race, God's own people, a royal priesthood.'" What Luther captures correctly here is that Christ's people exercise a priestly ministry by virtue of their union with Christ. One could argue, however, with his attribution of this role to Christians as individuals. In the New Testament it is never the individual believer who is said to be a priest, but the body of believers. The logical successor to the Old Testament priest is not the clergyperson or even the apostle, but Jesus Christ himself, and in him all those united with him as his body. The Old Testament priests were involved in the sacrificial system of the Temple; Jesus gathers up the truth and significance of the sacrificial system into himself. He *is* the sacrifice, as well as the one who offers it. In the wake of Christ's resurrection and ascension, the congregation in turn exercises a priestly ministry, *as a congregation*. Peter says, "You are . . . a royal priesthood," the collective noun translated *priesthood* necessarily referring to the whole people of God. Nowhere in the New Testament is the individual believer said to be a priest.[23]

Expounding the "royal" or kingly aspect of the church's priesthood, Luther writes:

> The nature of this priesthood and kingship is something like this: First, with respect to the kingship, every Christian is by faith so exalted above all things that, by virtue of a spiritual power, he is lord of all things without exception, so that nothing can do him any harm.[24]

The mention of harm takes us back to the notion of *Anfechtung,* assault. Nothing can do us any harm because our life is hid with Christ in God, but everything tries to. Any number of assaults can and will

---

23.   This puts the lie to C.S. Lewis' argument in his essay, "Priestesses in the Church," denying the legitimacy of women's ordination. Lewis says that the Christian clergyman is a successor to the Old Testament priest, all of whom were males. See C.S. Lewis, *God in the Dock* (Grand Rapids: Eerdmans, 1970).

24.   Lull, p. 606.

come upon Christians just because they are Christians. But in the midst of it all, says Luther, we are secure from devastation because of the kingly lordship granted us. "The power of which we speak is spiritual," he points out. "It rules in the midst of enemies and is powerful in the midst of oppression."

Few people can speak so movingly on this subject as Luther, who was himself under assault from every quarter, including from friends who misunderstood him. He knew what it was like to be sustained by the powerful, efficacious Word of God in the midst of terrible assault. That is why he is able to write, a few lines later, "I need nothing except faith exercising the power and dominion of its own liberty." In this marvellously compressed statement, Luther is saying that by faith we have a freedom that nothing antagonistic to God can dominate, since Christ alone is *Dominus,* Lord, and we are *domini,* lords, kings, in him. In short, faith frees, and frees effectually.

THE SPECIAL FUNCTION OF THE ORDAINED MINISTRY WITHIN THE ROYAL PRIESTHOOD

Luther manages to weave something into this tract from almost every theological topic. At this point he digresses to focus on the role of the ordained ministry. Taking up the notion of the priesthood of all believers, he is careful to distinguish between that priestly function and the special office of the ordained minister. "Although we are all equally priests," he writes, "we cannot all publicly minister and teach."[25] And a little further on, with reference to the Roman clergy, "That stewardship [of the mysteries of God] . . . has now been developed into so great a display of power and so terrible a tyranny that no heathen empire or other earthly power can be compared with it, just as if laymen were not also Christians."

Two points are made here: first of all, that the ministry of the clergy is to steward the gospel, to hold congregations to the apostolic confes-

25.   Ibid., p. 608.

sion of Jesus Christ. There may be others in the congregation who are as good or better at the art of preaching, but it is the responsibility of the ordained minister to see that the congregation does not deviate from the prophetic and apostolic confession of Jesus Christ—as it will, if left to itself. This responsibility to ensure that the gospel remains unobscured is not about control, however, and that is the second point. The ministry is never to tyrannize the congregation or the people of God spiritually; rather, it is to point to the One who, untrammeled, apprehends the congregation in his undelegated and unshared lordship.

More specifically, stewardship of the gospel means preaching Christ not only as a historical figure or teacher, but as the faith-quickening Word.

> [I]t has now become clear that it is not enough or in any sense Christian to preach the works, life, and words of Christ as historical facts, as if the knowledge of these would suffice for the conduct of life; yet this is the fashion among those who must today be regarded as our best preachers. Far less is it sufficient or Christian to say nothing at all about Christ and to teach instead the laws of men and the decrees of the fathers.[26]

Every quest for the "words of Christ as historical facts"—that is, every quest for the historical Jesus—reduces Jesus to a teacher; the saving significance of the cross is always lost, as are the mighty works of Jesus. And reducing Jesus to a teacher renders him superfluous, for once we learn the teaching, we no longer need the teacher. Once a high school student has learned from his math teacher how to solve an algebraic problem, he no longer needs her; he can do it himself. Liberal theologians, in a misguided effort to highlight and retain what it is of Jesus that faith grasps, nearly always collapse him into his office as teacher, not realizing that by doing so they have forfeited Jesus as living person. It is not sufficient, or even Christian, says Luther, to preach Christ as bare historical fact, his words and example, because the Christian life

---

26.　Ibid., p. 609.

is not a matter of naturalisic understanding and imitation. Christ must be preached as the faith-quickening Word: "Rather ought Christ to be preached to the end that faith in him may be established, that he may not only be Christ, but be Christ for you and me, and that what is said of him . . . may be effectual in us."[27]

THE INNER AND OUTER MAN

Luther now comes to a discussion of the inner man and the outer man. The inner man is that which God alone sees, while the outer man is subject to public scrutiny. The outer man, of course, can always be evaluated and criticized by those who observe it, but the inner man is our identity in Christ, to which no one but Christ has access and therefore which no one else may assess.

We have some access to the outer man of our fellow believer, and may know her to be somewhat petulant. We have some access to our own "outer man"; we know what our psychological makeup is, our personality type, and the situations in which we become nervous and insecure. This is not to say that we know ourselves as well as we might think we do; other people may have a much more accurate perspective on our "outer man" than we do. The point is, however, that both perspectives are inadequate, because the inner man—who we are ultimately—is hid with Christ in God (Col. 3:3). He has made us who we are, and reflects that truth and reality back to us. We are that son or daughter with

---

27.   We must remember Luther's famous saying, "Faith resides in the personal pronouns." It is not enough that Christ be Christ; he must be Christ *for me.* Note the relation of "for you and me" to the word "effectual." Christ becomes effectual within us when we own him in the personal pronouns: *for you, for me.* Luther always understood that the purpose of recovering the Christology of the apostolic confession was to foster personal intimacy with Christ himself. For him faith could never be reduced to belief (a misunderstanding that occurs relentlessly in the church). He had the warmest, personal, intimate acquaintance with the Lord Jesus. It was never sentimental or presumptuous, but it was intimate.

whom the Father is well pleased, just because we cling in faith to the Son with whom the Father is always well pleased.

With regard to the dialectic of inner and outer, Luther writes, "As long as we live in the flesh we only begin to make some progress in what shall be perfected in the future life."[28] We discussed this in the previous chapter with reference to the alien righteousness imputed to us and the proper righteousness to which we aspire in ourselves as a result. Alien righteousness is perfect and swallows up our sins in a moment; proper righteousness increases gradually as daily we aspire to its full manifestation. It is not perfected in this life and requires daily repentance.[29] Once again, Luther is heading off the perfectionist teaching of some of the radical Reformers; namely, that to be a Christian is to be sinless. He is acknowledging the residue of sin in us, so very unsightly, that must be dealt with as we repudiate the old man.

"While he [the believer] is doing this," Luther continues, "behold, he meets a contrary will in his own flesh which strives to serve the world and seeks its own advantage. This the spirit of faith cannot tolerate, but with joyful zeal it attempts to put the body under control and hold it in check, as Paul says in Romans 7." Clearly, then, Luther is reading Romans 7 as a description of the Christian rather than the pre-Christian. Calvin and the other Protestant Reformers agreed. It is only the person in Christ who becomes aware of his self-contradicted existence; the pre-Christian is not aware of any contradiction. The new man or woman in Christ is aware of being a new creature, but the old man or woman does not go away; as we saw before, it has been slain, but the corpse still twitches. It does not rule or determine our existence, however, because Christ rules as Lord. Sin continues to reside in Christians, but Christ presides.

Luther maintains that the discipline of suppressing the old man serves our neighbor by restraining our self-gratification. He writes,

---

28.   Lull, p. 610.

29.   See the first of Luther's *Ninety-Five Theses*: "The Christian life consists of daily, lifelong repentance."

"We must, however, realize that these works reduce the body to subjection and purify it of its evil lusts, and our whole purpose is to be directed only toward the driving out of lusts."[30] By lust, he does not mean what is often meant today, that is, libidinous preoccupation; he means any "selfist" preoccupation, regardless of what form it takes, whether virtuous or vicious. To subdue our residual self-preoccupation is to give free expression to another preoccupation; namely, the service of our neighbor; therefore, says Luther, the neighbor is the immediate beneficiary of our subduing the old man. Once again, Luther surprises us here, for we tend to think that we are the exclusive or at least the primary beneficiary of our pursuit of godliness—a mistake, obviously, that we must avoid lest self-preoccupation re-appear in the guise of the pursuit of sanctity.

SERVING THE NEIGHBOR

Having introduced this topic, in the rest of the tract Luther magnifies the significance of serving the neighbor as an expression of faith. When his opponents claimed that his elevation of faith underserved the neighbor, he replied that faith clings to the Christ who unfailingly directs us to serve the neighbor in love. The Christian "cannot ever in this life be idle and without works toward his neighbors."[31] Faith in Christ commits us to the service of our neighbor, simultaneously freeing us to carry out this service so that the neighbor is no longer the occasion of our veiled self-serving. True, we become righteous only through faith in Christ, not through serving our neighbor. Nevertheless, a Christian "should be guided in all his works by this thought and contemplate this one thing alone, that he may serve and benefit others in all that he does, considering nothing except the need and the advantage of his neighbor."[32] The faith that justifies releases us from

---

30. Lull, p. 611.
31. Ibid., p. 616.
32. Ibid., p. 617.

the self-gratification and self-lordship that are the essence of sin. Only in this way are we freed to consider the need and advantage of our neighbor.

What is our motivation in serving our neighbor? Luther writes:

> Behold, from faith thus flow forth love and joy in the Lord, and from love a joyful, willing, and free mind that serves one's neighbor willingly and takes no account of gratitude or ingratitude, of praise or blame, of gain or loss...He most freely and most willingly spends himself and all that he has.[33]

One of the acid tests of whether we are genuinely serving our neighbor is our response when we receive no gratitude. If we stop, then we never were serving our neighbor in the first place; we were serving ourselves under the pretense, however sincerely we believed it, of serving our neighbor. An apparent ministry to others has been ultimately a way of ministering to our own neediness.

This does not mean that we must wait until we are certain of the purity of our motives before beginning to serve. While the breaking of our bondage to self precedes our service in terms of logical priority, we will be paralyzed unless we begin by forgetting about ourselves and our spiritual status. Every time we look into ourselves, wondering whether our bondage to self is broken yet, we are strengthening that bondage through our preoccupation with ourselves. If, on the other hand, we get on with serving, not withholding ourselves when we receive no thanks, we will find our bondage to self broken in Christ. We can judge our motives without introspection by the evidence after the fact—by how we handle ingratitude and loss. We are sure to encounter both at some point, because the people we are serving are sinners like ourselves. But even if we can only ever approximate genuine service, that is better than nothing.

Luther hinted already at the beginning of the tract that the freedom of the Christian is freedom from self: "The Christian is perfectly free,

---

33.   Ibid., p. 619.

subject to none. The Christian is the servant of all, subject to all." We discussed this point also in the context of *Two Kinds of Righteousness*— the fact that we gain freedom from ourselves by living in another. To live in ourselves is always to magnify our spiritual bondage to ourselves and intensify our psychological anxiety. We are delivered from both by living in two others instead: in Christ by faith, and in the neighbor by love. And therein our proper righteousness overtakes us.

"WORD OF GOD" IN THE THOUGHT OF MARTIN LUTHER[34]

The Freedom of a Christian gives us an occasion to look more closely at a key concept in the theology of Martin Luther, namely, the Word of God. It is a topic that receives considerable attention in this tract. It has also been the subject of intense controversy in North American Christendom for the last several decades, with terms such as 'infallible' and 'inerrant' becoming shibboleths for some.[35]

The present-day controversy about the Word of God would have seemed strange to Luther, although not to the Lutheran scholastics who succeeded him. Luther's understanding of the expression 'Word of God' is subtle and nuanced. One way to represent it is by means of a triangle whose apex is Jesus Christ, God's living, concrete self-utterance and self-bestowal. Since that gift is normatively attested in Scripture, Scripture is one of the two lower corners; but that Scripture, the prophetic apostolic Word, is announced or proclaimed in the church, making proclamation the other corner of the triangle. Luther would say that any one of these three presupposes and implies the others. If we begin with Jesus Christ, we say that Jesus Christ is *the* Word of God incarnate, proclaimed in the ministry of the church, which proclama-

---

34.   In this section I am indebted to John S. Whale, *Christian Reunion: Historic Dimensions Reconsidered* (Grand Rapids: Eerdmans, 1971), pp. 35ff.

35.   Gabriel Fackre has distinguished nine different meanings of inerrancy. See *The Christian Story* (Grand Rapids: Eerdmans, 1996), chapters I and II. One wonders about the utility of such an ambiguous word.

tion always has Scripture as its measure and substance. Or we can start with Scripture: the content of Scripture is Jesus Christ, and Jesus Christ is known only through the proclamation of the church. Or we can start with proclamation: the substance of proclamation is Jesus Christ, and he (as opposed to a false Christ) is proclaimed only when our proclamation is formed and informed by Scripture.

This formulation can be found in Luther's own writings, and is also restated by Karl Barth in *Church Dogmatics*.[36] The main point, however, is that Jesus Christ is a person, while Scripture is a book. A person and a book are categorically different; they cannot both be Word of God in exactly the same sense. Scripture, moreover, is the writing of persons who are now dead, while proclamation is a pronouncement by a living one. In what sense are both the Word of God?

Luther maintains that the Word of God, in the first place, is to be understood as the essential content of the gospel. And the gospel, for Luther, is always the promise of God fulfilled in our midst in Jesus Christ: his five-word summary of the gospel is *Christus Gottesohn ist unser Heiland*, Christ the Son of God is our Savior.[37] Luther's use of the word "promise" always implies the fulfilment of the promise in Christ. For example, he says, "The promise is the content of the Lord's Supper," or "We cling to the promise in dark moments." That is his first meaning, then, of the Word of God: Jesus Christ, the living fulfilment of the promise, the essential content of the gospel.

The second meaning is the Word as medium or vehicle of revelation. Not only is the Word of God the content of the gospel, it is also the means of communicating it. The gospel benefits no one unless it is communicated. As Luther says, "The Word conveys, pours out, proffers and gives to me the forgiveness won on the cross." On the one hand,

---

36.   See Karl Barth, "The Word of God in Its Threefold Form," *Church Dogmatics*, Vol. I, par. 4.

37.   The same thought is captured by the well-known Greek acrostic from the early church, *Iesous Christos Theou Huios Soter*, whose initials form the word *ichthus*, meaning "fish."

then, the Word of God is itself the efficacy of the cross, Christ himself saving us; but that efficacy must be communicated to us, and the Word of God is the means of that communication. We must be careful, in this instance, to take the notion of 'communication' in its fullest sense: to communicate is not simply to relay information, but to impart a reality. Luther would say that apart from the Word of God as vehicle, meditating on Christ's death would be like thinking hard about a treasure chest filled with gold, buried safely but never brought to light and made over to us. It would be useless. The Word as vehicle brings to light the truth and the reality of Christ's work and makes it over to us.

The third form of the Word of God is that which makes the past and present contemporaneous. Here Luther has in mind the idiosyncratic Hebrew or Jewish understanding of remembering. Our Communion tables traditionally bear the inscription, "This do in remembrance of me," from 2 Corinthians 11:24. Remembrance, however, means more than just calling to mind Jesus' death two thousand years ago whenever we look at the elements. Similarly, when Paul exhorts us to "remember the poor" in Galatians, his meaning is not that we should think about them from time to time. In Hebrew, to remember something is to make an event or actuality operatively real in one's life. Jesus commands us to remember him—that is, we are to render him the operative reality of our life.

It is the Word of God, according to Luther, that enables us to do this by making past acts the operative reality of the present. The bread and wine, by the action of the Word of God, are not a souvenir or memory aid of something marooned in the past; they are the occasion of Christ's act two thousand years ago becoming the operative reality of our lives right now, so that the Christ who meets us Sunday by Sunday in the Lord's Supper is the same Christ who ate and drank with the disciples in the upper room. In other words, past and present have coalesced. The Word of God accomplishes this.

Fourth, the Word of God is that which can be received only in faith. In other words, everything spoken of in the promise is already possessed now by the believer. Sermon and sacrament bring us Christ not as they are performed, says Luther, but as they are trusted. It is as we trust the Word that the substance of the Word is made good to us. This is not to say that faith is something we generate and bring to the Word; it is rather the case that faith is quickened in our cold and stony hearts by the approach of the Word to us. However, we must still own that faith in a fully human act of affirmation.

Fifth, the Word is that which quickens a faith inherently personal and individual, yet also necessarily social. Luther liked to say that everyone must do his own believing, just as everyone must do his own dying: faith is inherently an individual act of the person. However, it invariably and necessarily has the profoundest social consequences. As Luther also liked to say, we are justified by faith alone, but faith never *is* alone; it is always accompanied by love. The Lord's Supper, wrote Luther in a 1526 sermon, makes fellow believers into a cake whose ingredients interpenetrate each other; we are inextricably joined together in Christ. In short, the faith fostered by the Word anticipates the Messianic banquet at which all are fulfilled individually and corporately, in fellowship with each other and with him who is Lord of all.

The Word is also that which witnesses to the absurdity of Christian truth. We see this most starkly in Luther's *theologia crucis,* the theology of the cross. From the world's perspective, the cross is the height of folly and absurdity. Jesus says, referring to his approaching death, "Now it is time for me to be glorified"; the glorification of Christ, in John's gospel, is in fact his crucifixion—not the sequel to his crucifixion (as if the Resurrection supplied a glory that the cross was unable to furnish). The world sees only shame at the cross, for ancient Rome crucified only the most contemptible types of criminal: rapists, military deserters, and insurrectionists. In reality, however, the cross is the occasion of a singular glory. While it is human degradation in the eyes of the world, from God's perspective it is our exaltation. The world understands it as utter weakness, but it is where God does his mightiest work, redeeming and reconciling the world; it is similarly where God reveals his heart most clearly as he recovers a rebellious creation for himself by means of the love that he is. This absurd truth is witnessed to by the Word of God; obviously this Word never dovetails with human categories but instead forges new ones in terms of which alone the Word can be understood.

Luther loved the paradoxes and seeming contradictions of the gospel: the last shall be first, those who lose their lives will keep them, whoever would be greatest must be the servant of all. He found that such paradoxes bring us the reality of our redemption and renewal in Christ; if we try to resolve them, we are left with no gospel at all. He coined the word *nihilitudo*, not found in Latin dictionaries, to express the ultimate nothingness of a rationalistically tidy, paradox-free gospel.

The seventh meaning of Word of God for Luther is Scripture. It is notable that he never wrote a treatise on the subject of Scripture. A warrior who wields a sword every day and triumphs with it in battle does not write a book about his sword, for its efficacy is evident from what he does with it. As Luther had recourse to Scripture over and over again and demonstrated its power, he expected people to get the point that it was the powerful and authoritative Word of God.[38] People come to recognize Scripture as Word of God as they are brought to faith in Jesus Christ through our faithful handling of it. It is the work of the church to use Scripture in such a way as to demonstrate the authority of Jesus Christ, and in so doing to persuade people also of the authority of the Scripture that attests him.

Luther said that the canon of Scripture is to be found within Scripture, but is not equated with Scripture. He was distinguishing the canonical collection from the canon itself—the former being the sixty-six books of the Bible, and the latter the pattern of the apostolic confession of Jesus Christ. The argument appears circular, since it is only through the canonical collection that we discover the pattern con-

---

38. Three hundred years later, Charles Spurgeon (1834-1892) compared Scripture to a tiger. To convince skeptics of the ferocity of a caged tiger, he said, the thing to do is not to write a book on the subject, but to let the tiger out of the cage. Not everyone will be convinced by a treatise on Scripture as the Word of God, but if we wield it authoritatively in the Spirit, no one can deny its power and reality.

stituting the canon. But as we become familiar with the canon in this way, it becomes, in turn, our measure of the collection. It was on this basis that Luther judged the epistle of James to be outside the canon: he believed that it failed to confess Jesus Christ in the way Matthew and John and the epistles to the Romans and Galatians did.

The later Lutheran scholastics compromised this distinction, tending instead to identify the canon with the canonical collection, the Bible. Moreover, they blurred the distinction between Word of God and Scripture. For them, the authority of Scripture derived from its having been verbally dictated: the Holy Spirit wrote the book, and therefore it is the authoritative revelation. For Luther, as we have seen, it was precisely the other way around: Scripture derives its authority from the authority of Christ to which it witnesses. It is revelatory in that it points normatively and uniquely to Jesus Christ, but it is Christ himself who is the revelation of God.

One final point is to be noted in Luther's understanding of Scripture. "Since the gospel is the sword of the Spirit," he writes, "We will not long preserve the gospel without the biblical languages. The languages are the sheath in which this sword of the Spirit is contained." If we are serious about Scripture as the sword of the Spirit, we must be serious about the scabbard or sheath in which it rests: Greek and Hebrew. It is not that Scripture is untranslatable, or that only the highly educated can apprehend the truth of God in it. But if we are serious students of Scripture, we ought to make use of all the normal tools accessible to us for understanding texts in general, not least the original languages in which they are written. Any soldier knows that if the scabbard is neglected, the sword is soon mislaid, even lost.

The contrast between Luther's understanding of the Word of God and that of the Lutheran orthodox scholastics who succeeded him is notable. For the latter, the Word of God is nothing more than the book. This is the mentality that gave rise to the evangelical Bible wars of the last forty years. Much anguish and accusation could have been spared the church if, instead of insisting on fine distinctions between infallibility and inerrancy, or between different kinds of inerrancy, we had held on to Luther's understanding. The authority of Scripture is a derivative of the authority of Jesus Christ, who is the authoritative Word of God. Scripture must be used to preach Christ, and in the encounter with Christ in Scripture, people will come to recognize the authority of Scripture derived from Scripture's Lord. We must let the Tiger out of the cage.

7

The Lord's Supper

Throughout his theological career, Luther found himself contending with two major disputants: Rome and the radicals. He articulated his struggle with Rome in 1520 in *The Babylonian Captivity of the Church* and his struggle with the radicals in 1526 in *The Sacrament of the Body and Blood of Christ—Against the Fanatics.*

In 1215, the Fourth Lateran Council had promulgated the doctrine of transubstantiation, articulating it in a way that presupposed an Aristotelian framework. The doctrine in brief was that when the elements are consecrated, the *substance* of bread is changed into the substance of Christ's body while the *accidents* remain. "Substance" and "accident" are foundational Aristotelian vocabulary: the accidents of a thing are that which can be noted through any of the five senses—shape, colour, texture, taste, and so on—while the substance is that which makes a thing what it is. Bread can be oval, rectangular, or circular; it can be brown, white, or black; it can taste like sourdough or cinnamon; it can be dense or light, coarse or smooth. In Aristotelian thought, all of these things are the bread's accidents, while its substance is that which makes it *bread.*

According to the doctrine of transubstantiation, bread on the Communion table (or, in Roman churches, on the altar) has the appearance of bread, and a chemical analysis would find it to be bread. But in terms of its true substance, it effectually becomes the body of Christ. In the same way, the wine continues to resemble wine (and would still intoxicate a person), but it effectually becomes the blood of Christ. This change of substance, moreover, is effectuated by a priest who has the capacity to do so in virtue of his ordination by the church of Rome—an institution defined by the hierarchy of priest, bishop, cardinal, pope. And finally, as put forward by the Roman church in Luther's day, transubstantiation presupposed the sacrifice of the Mass. It was understood to be an unbloody repetition of Christ's bloody sacrifice on Calvary.[1]

Luther objected to the Roman position on several fronts. He maintained that the notion of transubstantiation was yet another instance of Aristotelian obscurantism that be clouded, even denied, the directness and simplicity of Christ's "This [i.e., bread] is my body." It was enough for him that the real body of Christ is present in the Lord's Supper "by virtue of the words."[2] The apostles had not needed Aristotelian concepts in order to grasp the meaning of the Lord's Supper and profit from its force. Then why should anyone need such at any time, especially since "the church kept the true faith for more than twelve hundred years . . . until the pseudo philosophy of Aristotle began to make its inroads into the church"?[3] According to Luther transubstantiation "rests neither on the Scriptures nor on human reason."[4] He maintained that, apart from the impropriety of resorting to Aristotle, the church's reading of the philosopher was defective. Aristotle had maintained that "all of the categories of accidents are themselves a subject—although he grants

---

1.   Although the Roman Catholic Church today retains the vocabulary of sacrifice for the Mass, the understanding appears different. It would be that Christ keeps the promise he makes, that the significance and force of the death that was fully effectual on Calvary are appropriated every time someone receives Holy Communion.

2.   *The Bablyonian Captivity of the Church* in Lull, *Martin Luther's Basic Theological Writings* (Minneapolis: Fortress Press, 1989), p. 289.

3.   Lull, p. 287.

4.   Ibid.

that substance is the chief subject."[5] "This white" is a subject of which something else is predicated. Luther, perhaps waggishly, insists that if transubstantiation has to be invoked lest Christ's body be identified with the bread, then "transaccidentation" should be invoked lest Christ's body be identified with the accidents.[6] Admittedly, Luther never pretended to understand *how* the bread is the body of Christ; he remained content with the dominical assertion: "For my part, if I cannot fathom how the bread is the body of Christ, yet I will take my reason captive to the obedience of Christ, and clinging simply to his words, firmly believe not only that the body of Christ is in the bread, but that the bread is the body of Christ."[7] One of Luther's major objections to transubstantiation, it is evident by now, was the implication not that Christ is present but rather that bread is absent, since only "seeming" bread remained once its substance was altered.[8]

Along with other reformers, Luther insisted that there was one sole and sufficient sacrifice offered up for the sins of the world: Jesus Christ at Calvary. The significance and merits of that death are appropriated in the sacrament, but the sacrifice itself is not repeated; any talk of the Mass as sacrifice diminishes the significance and sufficiency of Christ's sacrifice on Calvary. Tersely Luther comments, "If it had been necessary to offer the mass as a sacrifice, then Christ's institution of it was not complete."[9] Any talk of the mass as "a good work or sacrifice"[10] (and for Luther to uphold one was to uphold the other) landed spiritually needy people in a meritocracy that offered no relief but only worsened their

---

5. Ibid., p.289.

6. Ibid.

7. Ibid. p. 290.

8. While subsequent to Luther his position has been described as "*con*substantiation" (Christ's body is received *with* the bread that remains bread in all respects), Luther himself never used the term and Lutherans have largely repudiated it. To deploy "consubstantiation" is to land oneself again in Aristotelianism, privileging philosophy over the pronouncement of Christ and faith in it.

9. Lull, p. 308.

10. Lull, p. 291.

predicament. Moreover, to speak of the mass or Lord's Supper as a good work was to deny that it is the "promise of Christ",[11] where "promise", for Luther, always means a declaration of forgiveness that is more than mere pronouncement but is rather a divine pardon determining the believer's existence now.[12] The promise does not merely announce forgiveness; the promise *bestows* it.[13]

The promise of God and the believer's faith are correlates. Only the promise (of forgiveness) quickens faith, and faith alone seizes the promise: "Without the promise there is nothing to be believed; while without faith the promise is useless, since it is established and fulfilled through faith."[14] According to Luther "God does not deal with, nor has he ever dealt with, man otherwise than through a word of promise . . . . We in turn cannot deal with God otherwise than through faith in the Word of promise."[15] Laconically Luther adds the reminder that no one would dare to be so foolish as to assert that "a ragged beggar does a good work when he comes to receive a gift from a rich man."[16]

The mass as good work, then, denied the reality of promissory gift, while the mass as sacrifice denied the sufficiency of Christ's finished work and thereby advanced what we can give instead of what we can only appropriate as the "last will and testament" of a benefactor who has sealed his munificence with his death.[17]

What is more, the effectiveness of the Lord's Supper cannot depend on ordination by the Roman hierarchy. All Christians are part of the priestly ministry vouchsafed to the church by Christ himself in his unique priesthood. Luther's insistence that the cup not be withheld

---

11.   Lull, p. 297.

12.   Like the Apostles' Creed, Luther used "forgiveness of sins" to stand for the gospel in its totality: "For what is the whole gospel but the forgiveness of sins?" (Lull, p. 312).

13.   Ibid., p. 299.

14.   Ibid., p. 298.

15.   Ibid.

16.   Ibid., p. 307.

17.   Ibid., p. 308.

from the laity (the withholding of the cup he regarded as the "first" of the three "Babylonian Captivities"[18]) presupposes his denial of sacerdotal privilege and power. In view of the non-distinction between clergy and laity before God, the laity should receive both elements of the Lord's Supper, just like the clergy.

As mentioned above, Luther objected to the power said to be vested in clergy to effect transubstantiation partly on the grounds that it ignored the priesthood of all believers. He also objected that this power seemed to subject Christ to human control: a priest consecrates the elements, and by that act bread and wine become Christ's body and blood. Christ thereafter resides in the elements as if he had been imported into them.

The Roman position, however, was more subtle than many Protestants seemed to understand. The Latin formula used by the Roman church to describe the effectiveness of the Eucharist is *ex opere operato*, "from the work performed." It means that the Eucharist operates simply by virtue of being performed, regardless of our faith. The church of Rome said that the sacrament was objectively operative: our faith does not bring Christ to the elements, for Christ is *in* the bread and wine by virtue of his promise. Unless we place an 'impediment' (i.e., a mortal sin) between ourselves and the elements, we cannot fail to receive Christ in them. This was Rome's way of recognizing that the elements are never empty, and that our faith is too weak and fitful to be a condition of the sacrament's effectiveness. Rome argued that if our appropriation of Christ hinges on the quality of our faith, and our faith is always weak (riddled as it is with unbelief), what can such faith appropriate except a weak and fitful "Christ"? Luther was aware of this consideration, and attempted to address the matter in his own way (as we shall see). Notwithstanding the issue here, Luther remained adamant: ordination does not confer the capacity to render Christ's presence effectual. Speaking of the celebration of the Lord's Supper he

---

18. Ibid., p. 283.

bluntly asserted, "As far as the blessing of the mass and sacrament is concerned we are all equals, whether we are priests or laymen."[19]

Given these objections to the Roman view of the Lord's Supper, what was Luther's own account of that rite? He believed that Christ is really, truly, present in the sacrament. The sacrament does not merely symbolize or represent Christ; it is the vehicle of his real presence. In the Marburg Colloquy of 1529, where he contended with Zwingli (whose position he never understood), Luther said, "Before I drink mere wine with the Swiss, I will drink blood with the Pope." In other words, even though he regarded transubstantiation as a defective understanding, he preferred it to an 'empty' Eucharist. While he opposed transubstantiation, Luther regarded it as "less grievous" than the "captivity" of withholding the cup from the laity,[20] and vastly less grievous than "by far the most wicked abuse of all", the mass as good work or sacrifice.[21]

Too few Protestants understand Luther's complaint regarding transubstantiation. He never objected to the effectual presence of Christ in the sacrament. (What Christian would?) He objected, rather, to the disappearance of the bread. Since the substance of bread had been transmuted, it was *bread*—not Christ—that was now absent. Absent the bread, the Eucharist lacked the creaturely material element essential to the definition of sacrament.

When Luther speaks of the real presence, he says that the sacrament gives us the same companionship with Jesus that his disciples and saints had. Just as Peter, James, and John met Jesus in the flesh in the days of his earthly ministry and were able to touch him, we have in the Eucharist a concrete, physical proximity to Jesus Christ that is no less intense and no less real. The saints in heaven have an equally intimate proximity to him now. The purpose of the Eucharist, said Luther, is to bring the communicant into contact with the glorified body of Christ, and Christ must be truly present in order for this to happen.

---

19. Ibid., p. 310.
20. Ibid., p. 284.
21. Ibid., p. 291.

Luther insisted that the sacrament benefited only those receiving it in faith; not that our faith adds Christ to the elements, but rather that Christ can be received savingly at the Eucharist only in faith because that is the only way Christ can be received savingly at *any* time, under *any* circumstance. At the same time, the real presence of Christ in the Eucharist meant that *everybody* receives him, with or without faith: "It all remains the same sacrament and testament, which works its own work in the believer but an 'alien work' in the unbeliever," the alien work being the recipient's condemnation.[22] The point that must be stressed here is that unbelief fails to apprehend the Christ who gives himself with the elements, rather than that unbelief fails to "posit" Christ in the elements.

The words, "This is my body, broken for you. Take and eat," and so on, are therefore not an incantation that transmutes substance, but the expression of a promise attached to the liturgical rite wherein Christ's availability is pledged unfailingly.

Luther wanted to have a defensible understanding of the Eucharist that genuinely involved the presence of Jesus Christ without transubstantiation. Transubstantiation presupposed the Roman Catholic hierarchy, an effectiveness independent of faith (*ex opere operato*), and a notion of the repetition of the sacrifice of Christ—all three of which Luther regarded as anathema. His understanding of the Lord's Supper, he believed, had preserved the truth and spared the church the loss of the gospel.

A COMPARISON WITH CALVIN

For Calvin, Luther's notion of Christ's body being consumed along with the bread was no improvement over transubstantiation. For one thing, to Calvin it suggested cannibalism.[23] Luther did in fact instruct

---

22.   Lull, *op. cit.,* p. 312.

23.   See Calvin, *Institutes,* 4.17.27-30 for his opposition to Luther's notion that Christ's body is mandicated and to Luther's notion that Christ's body is ubiquitous.

Melanchthon to write, in opposition to Zwingli and Calvin, that Christ's body is "partaken, eaten, and chewed with the teeth."[24] Luther did not want to suggest cannibalism, of course, and the *Formula of Concord*, written by his followers in 1580, called the idea of chewing Christ's body with the teeth a "malignant and blasphemous slander". Still, for Luther if the body of Christ is present together with the bread, then it is in the communicant's mouth and between her molars; to deny this was to have a Eucharist from which the real presence of Christ had evaporated.

Calvin disagreed. He objected that when the Lutherans talked about Communion, they sounded like butchers handling meat. He also took exception to Luther's idea that Christ is received by unbelievers to their condemnation. How is it possible to receive the Savior of the world to one's condemnation? How can it be detrimental for anyone to receive Jesus Christ? Calvin insisted that Christ is received by faith alone, and that therefore unbelievers do not receive him at all in the Eucharist. To the Lutherans and Romans, this immediately meant that there was such a thing as a Eucharist from which Christ was absent.

Calvin did not believe that Jesus Christ is "in" the elements in the Lutheran or Roman sense of spatial presence. He is not *in* the elements, but is received along *with* the elements by faith. According to Calvin, Jesus Christ is not ubiquitous but located in heaven, spatially remote from earth. It was the role of the Holy Spirit (the operation of the Holy Spirit is crucial everywhere in Calvin's theology) to bring us into contact with Christ in heaven, not by bringing him down but by taking us up. "By the strength or power of the Holy Spirit," said Calvin, "believers are drawn up to heaven where they receive Christ to their blessing."[25]

---

24. Quoted in A.M. Hunter, *The Teaching of Calvin* (London: James Clarke and Co.), p. 181.

25. Calvin, *Institutes*, 4.17.10. In the same passage Calvin states, "The Spirit truly unites things separated in space." Luther, unlike Calvin, rarely refers to the Holy Spirit in his discussion of the Lord's Supper.

Having been so drawn up, communicants receive Christ in the totality of his reality: body and blood. Believers receive him "spiritually," but this never means that they receive a disembodied spectre or an abstract influence. When Calvin says that Christ is received spiritually, he means that what is received—the totality of Jesus Christ in the reality of his body and blood—is received *in the power of the Spirit.*

Calvin's understanding of the Lord's Supper presupposes a different understanding of substance. Whereas Luther understood substance in terms of its extension in space, Calvin understood it in terms of power—that is, a substance is present wherever it is acting. Christ is not present in the elements per se but in the event of the Eucharist, for that is where he acts by the power of the Spirit.

When the Jesuit martyr Edmund Campion (1540-1581) was executed in England under Elizabeth I, he was ridiculed by his theological assailants for upholding transubstantiation. They maintained that since Christ is in heaven, he cannot be in the bread and wine; his body cannot be in both places at the same time. Campion replied, in effect, "Heaven is Christ's palace, and you have made it his prison."[26] Campion's point was irrefutable, for if Christ cannot be both in heaven and in the elements at the same time, how can he be in heaven and in our hearts at the same time?

There is a sense in which Christ's body, the body of that particular human being who is also God, is now absent from earth. In John 14 to 16, Jesus seems to be saying that he must go away in order for the Spirit to come—not that he will be here on earth in a different way, but that he will actually be gone, and the Spirit will take his place. In Matthew 28, however, he says, "I am with you always, even to the end of the age." Both can be true if there is a difference, biblically speaking, between "body" and "flesh"—flesh in the sense of hair, skin, fingernails, muscle, and so on. Christ's flesh is plainly not with us in that sense. But can

---

26.   Evelyn Waugh, *Edmund Campion: Jesuit and Martyr* (New York: Image, 1956), p. 166.

Jesus Christ, the Incarnate One, be present to us *at all* without being embodied? How can we have a discarnate Incarnate One? That Christ is seated at the right hand of the Father is not in doubt. But are there scriptural grounds for believing, not that his Spirit is here *in lieu* of him, but that he is present here himself in the power of the Spirit? In the Corinthian correspondence, the Spirit is not conceived of as the *alter ego* of a remote Jesus Christ. Jesus Christ himself is understood to be vividly present to the worship and particularly the Eucharistic celebration of the Corinthian people. The word "flesh" with reference to Jesus Christ has no meaning following his ascension, but in terms of that which sustains the personality of anything creaturely, Christ will never be without a human *body*. It is not Christ's flesh that is offered to us in the Lord's Supper, then, but his body, for we cannot receive Jesus Christ unembodied any more than we can receive one another unembodied.

The point, in any case, is that when Calvin speaks of Christ as spiritually present in the Eucharist, he does not mean that the Spirit of Christ is present while Christ himself is absent; rather, that in his totality—humanity and deity, body and blood—Jesus Christ is present *in the power of* the Spirit. The term for this doctrine is virtualism, ultimately from the Latin root *vires*, plural of *vis*, meaning strength or power. It should not be misunderstood as meaning that Christ is "virtually" present in the modern sense of "almost"; a Christ whom we almost have we do not have at all.

For Calvin as for Luther, the primary purpose of the Eucharist is to strengthen weak faith; it is to strengthen in Christ those who remain sinners in themselves. Its secondary purpose is as a public pledge of loyalty to our Lord. Notice that for both Luther and Calvin, the Lord's Supper is not a memorial in the sense of harking back to a past event in our imaginations. Unfortunately that is how we English speakers typically understand the word "remembrance" used in Luke 22 and 1 Corinthians 11—as the recollection, in our minds, of a concept representing an event marooned in the past. The Hebrew understanding of remembrance, however, is significantly different. To the Hebrew mind, remembering is an act that renders a past event the operative reality of one's present existence. When we so 'remember' Jesus Christ, particularly his atoning death on the cross, that past event and its efficacy become the operative reality of our life in the present. In this way our faith is strengthened. This does not mean that we fail to 'remember' in the sense of reflecting on the past event as a past event; if we failed to remember in this usual sense, we would also fail to remember in the Hebrew sense; the cross could not be rendered the operative reality of our lives in the present.

Despite the dour reputation that more effusive, charismatic Christians have assigned to Calvin and his followers, Calvin has rightly been called "the theologian of the Holy Spirit." The place of the Holy Spirit is critical in Calvin's theology, including his theology of the Eucharist. He understood Jesus Christ always to act in the power of that Spirit whom the Son bears and bestows. In the Eucharist, the Spirit is conjoined to the elements in the same way that he is conjoined to Scripture; that is, by means of the Word. Of itself, Scripture is spiritually inert and can give rise only to bare doctrinal orthodoxy, ideationally correct yet lifeless. When the Spirit is added to the Word, however, Jesus Christ presents himself to us *in living person* as Scripture is read; he seizes us by his grace, quickening in us the capacity and the desire to receive him in faith. A similar thing happens when the unity of Spirit-and-Word (Calvin insists they may be distinguished but never separated) acts in the Eucharist. Jesus Christ seizes us afresh in the Spirit's power and the Spirit commends the elements to us as the assuring sign of our inclusion in Christ.

Finally, for Calvin as for Luther it is the promise—the promise of mercy, of forgiveness, of Christ's presence—that renders the sacrament sacramental. The sign always points to the promise. The order of priority in bringing this about is always Scripture, sermon, sacrament: Scripture supplies the logic and the content of the sermon, while the sermon (rather than a prayer of consecration, according to Calvin) grounds the efficacy of the sacrament. Without Scripture and sermon (both vivified by the Spirit), 'sacrament', said the Reformers, is mere superstition.

A COMPARISON WITH ZWINGLI

Zwingli began his understanding of the Lord's Supper with *sacramentum*, the Latin word for the oath whereby a Roman soldier pledged his loyalty to his commanding officer. Zwingli puts first what Calvin puts second: the force of the Lord's Supper is first of all to declare to the world that we are servants and soldiers of Jesus Christ, and secondly to strengthen weak faith.

Contrary to what is still heard in churches and seminaries, however, Zwingli did not espouse bare memorialism. It has been said that for Calvin the elements exhibit a Savior who is present, while for Zwingli they recall one who is absent.[27] This does Zwingli a disservice. It is hard to imagine any Christian upholding the absence of Jesus Christ, and Zwingli certainly did not. Luther accused him of reducing the Lord's Supper to a mere badge of one's faith, but this is not true either. Zwingli did say that participation in the Lord's Supper is first of all a declaration of one's loyalty to Christ, but he never claimed that this exhausts the meaning of the rite.

Although he is the most literal of the Reformers in his reading of Scripture generally, Zwingli is the least literal when it comes to the Lord's Supper. He maintained that in the statement of Jesus, *hoc est meum corpus* (this is my body), the word *est* means not 'is', but 'signifies'. It has the same function as 'am' in "I am the door" (John 10:7, 9). There Jesus is telling us not that he is rectangular and made of wood, but that there is something about him that functions as a door. Namely, he is the one who admits us to life and blessing.

Zwingli also pointed out that Jews have an abhorrence of drinking blood. Whatever else was meant by the words, "This is my blood, shed for you; drink you all of it," Christ's pronouncement could not have meant that the apostles thought they were drinking blood. Jews under-

---

27.   T. M. Lindsay, *History of the Reformation* (Edinburgh: T&T Clark, 1907), Vol. 2, p.58.

stand themselves to be divinely forbidden to drink blood, and hence abhor any suggestion of doing so.

At the Marburg Colloquy, Luther picked up a piece of charcoal and wrote in frustration, *"est* means *est"*—*"is* means *is."* If the cup is not really Jesus' blood, he insisted, then Christ is not in the elements. He refused to shake Zwingli's hand, since for Luther the entire gospel was at stake. Luther, horrified, could see Zwingli only as touting Christ's absence. Zwingli, no less horrified, could see Luther only as endorsing cannibalism.

Nevertheless, Zwingli never departed from his conviction that believers do receive Christ in the Lord's Supper. They *receive* him, but they do not *eat* him. Think of Zacchaeus: Jesus goes home with Zacchaeus and the two of them eat and drink together. Jesus Christ is truly present at the meal in the totality of his reality, and at the end of it he says, "Today salvation has come to this house" (Luke 19:9 ESV). At that meal, Jesus is present in every sense of the word; he is not absent. Zacchaeus receives Christ into his heart, but he does not take him into his mouth. Nor does Jesus say, at the end of the meal, "Well, it was nice eating with you, Zacchaeus; goodbye for now." Instead he pronounces Zacchaeus *saved.* Zwingli never hesitated to say that Jesus Christ was received salvifically by Zacchaeus in this event. The Lord's Supper, said Zwingli, is a similar event inasmuch as it is the occasion, but not the cause, of receiving Christ salvifically.

Zwingli was as horrified as Luther at any notion of *ex opere operato* because of the suggestion that Jesus Christ can be controlled by priestly activity. Nevertheless, he said, Christ's true body is received by communicants. When the gospel is preached and the preacher urges the hearers to receive Christ, there is no doubt that Christ is present, available to be received at that moment in the totality of his reality through faith. For Zwingli Jesus Christ never inheres in the elements, whether naturally or "sacramentally"; rather, Christ is received *in conjunction with* the elements.[28] His point was that Jesus Christ is not remote from the elements even though they do not contain him. Jesus Christ is received *with* the elements insofar as the elements are part of the meal; the meal is the occasion of Christ's being received in faith, but Christ is not *in* what is eaten and drunk.

The Holy Spirit is crucial to this process because the Spirit alone quickens faith; Christ cannot be received apart from the Spirit. For Zwingli, as for Calvin, the Spirit and Christ can be distinguished but never separated, the Spirit always being the power in which Christ acts as well as the power, consequently, in which the believer acts in response.

Zwingli stands out among the Protestant Reformers in massively emphasizing the binding of believers *to one another* in the sacrament. He maintained that the Lord's Supper is a sacrament not only of our life in Christ, but also of our life in fellowship with believers; in binding us to Christ so as to strengthen our faith, it also binds us to fellow believers so as to strengthen our love. This communal dimension of the Lord's Supper is largely overlooked in the writings of the other magisterial Reformers. Admittedly, they all opposed private Communion. Believers are to be present as a congregation for the Lord's Supper and reaffirm their faith in Christ together. Nevertheless, for Reformers other than Zwingli, even though several hundred people may be present in the congregation, the Lord's Supper is largely an event between individuals and their Lord. Individuals commune simultaneously, but not corporately. Zwingli emphasized a dimension of the Lord's Supper that has virtually been lost in the midst of controversies concerning *how* Jesus Christ is present to the creaturely elements of bread and wine. Any contemporary exposition of the Lord's Supper will have to take note of and develop the crucial point that Zwingli alone magnified.

---

28. See J. Courvoisier, *Zwingli: A Reformed Theologian* (Richmond: John Knox Press, 1963), pp. 72-78.

THE ANABAPTISTS

It is more difficult to specify an Anabaptist theology of the Lord's Supper in light of the movement's diversity.

In general, however, the Anabaptists objected to the notion of "thing-holiness."[29] In Scripture, holiness is predicated of God (holiness being that which renders God *God*), and derivatively of God's people. Holiness, at least in the New Testament, is never predicated of inanimate objects. Christ's people are holy, but there is no such thing as holy bread or a holy cup or a holy table; nothing distinguishes the elements of the Lord's Supper ontologically from other objects, since holiness does not inhere in any object. The Anabaptists insisted that the magisterial Reformers were just as fixated on the holiness of objects as the church of Rome was. Whether this was a fair characterization is debatable. In their own defense the magisterial Reformers would have said that the Communion table and elements are to be treated with respect, even "set apart from common use" (in the words of many contemporary liturgies); yet it is doubtful that they attributed to objects the kind of holiness that characterizes God himself or the life of his people.

Of course, the Reformers were equally unfair in identifying the Anabaptists as bare memorialists. This misunderstanding might find a defense, however, in the Anabaptists' insistence that the Lord's Supper is not a "sacrament" but (only) an "ordinance," since Christ is not *in* the bread and wine. He is not in inert elements; he is in—that is, he dwells in the midst of—the congregation. The Anabaptists believed that "sacrament" necessarily entailed the manipulability of Christ's presence *just because* the risen Lord inheres in creaturely items (in this view), and the latter are always subject to human control. An "ordinance" on the other hand, is simply a congregational activity that God has commanded. The point at issue, then, is not metaphysical speculation or a manipulation amounting to idolatry, but rather *obedience*.

---

29. See W. Klassen, "The Nature of the Anabaptist Protest," *Mennonite Quarterly Review* (October 1971), pp. 291-311.

None of the foregoing, however, means that the divinely appointed congregational activity has only psychological significance, that it is empty. God has appointed the ordinance precisely as the context in which he is present to the *congregation* to strengthen it, and thereby to strengthen the faith and love of those who comprise it. It is the *fellowship* of the obedient believers, and not inert elements, that is the vehicle of Christ's continual self-bestowal. In other words, the real or true presence of Jesus Christ pertains not to lifeless things but to "living stones" whom Christ has gathered into his body and to whom he has pledged himself.

The Anabaptists also saw the Lord's Supper as the event by which believers were bonded to one another in community and pledged to give up their lives for one another as Christ gave up his for them. Every time they came to the Supper, they were offering themselves afresh for martyrdom on behalf of fellow believers. Here once again is the communal or corporate dimension of Communion that the magisterial Reformers, apart from Zwingli, largely overlooked; it was a crucial one for the Anabaptists in particular, in light of the slaughters visited upon them from all sides in the sixteenth century. For good reason, then, when they pondered the Eucharist (a term they never used, of course) they related it to their baptism—a threefold baptism in water, in the Spirit, and in blood. On every occasion of the Lord's Supper they recommitted themselves to each other as followers of Christ who had been rendered such by the Spirit, had confessed themselves such by water baptism, and now were willing to love each other to the death.

THE SACRAMENT OF THE BODY AND BLOOD OF CHRIST—AGAINST THE FANATICS

Having situated Luther's position on the Lord's Supper with reference to other positions taken up at the time, we can now look at it in more detail as set forth in his tract, *The Sacrament of the Body and Blood of Christ—Against the Fanatics*.

The first thing to notice here is the exquisite balance maintained by Luther between *fides quae* and *fides qua*. The former is the faith which is believed—the substance of the faith, the faith "once for all delivered to the saints." The latter is the faith *by which* we believe—the faith which we possess and exercise. "In this sacrament," he writes, "there are two things that should be known and proclaimed. First, what one should believe. . . . Second, the faith itself, or the use which one should properly make of that in which he believes."[30]

The balance between these two, between objective content on the one hand and subjective appropriation on the other, is lost over and over again in the history of the church. Karl Barth is a recent theologian who has, perhaps more than others, emphasized the objective content of belief; he did so by way of response to the liberal school arising from Friedrich Schleiermacher (1768-1834), which has typically emphasized human appropriation instead. A one-sided emphasis on what is to be believed leads to sterile objectivism and a philosophically-controlled scholasticism, while a one-sided emphasis on human appropriation gives rise to romantic subjectivism and liberalism.[31] Characteristically, the church is never exactly on the line between these imbalances but continually staggers back and forth across it.

Referring to those he calls "fanatics" because they promote what he considers to be a hollow sacrament, Luther writes:

> Now they have two points in particular which they bring up against us. First, they say it is not fitting that Christ's body and blood should be in the bread and wine. Second, it is not necessary. These are about the best foundations that they have to build on.[32]

---

30.   Lull, *op. cit.*, p. 314.

31.   According to Emil Brunner (1889-1966), The earlier Karl Barth rightly recognized the one-sided objectivism of Protestant scholasticism, but the later Barth appeared to reflect it. See Brunner, *Truth as Encounter*, (Philadelphia: Westminster Press, 1964).

32.   Lull, p. 317.

That last statement is sarcastic, of course; he means that an appeal to the fittingness or necessity of divine activity or appointment is inappropriate, and he is correct:

> To the first point I might say equally well that it is not reasonable
> that God should descend from heaven and enter into the womb
> ... And I might conclude from this that God did not become man,
> or that the crucified Christ was not God.[33]

Luther's point is that we do not begin our understanding of the Eucharist, or any other part of the gospel, from the standpoint of rational speculation—what we find fitting or necessary. Where revelation is concerned, we do not judge but submit. He returns to this on page after page of the tract. It is never our place to tell the Lord of the universe where he can and cannot be; we are not the measure of what is fitting or necessary or even possible. If God has deemed the sacrament necessary for our spiritual heath it can only be folly (not to say ingratitude or sin) to second-guess him.

We could argue that he is attacking the Anabaptists unjustly here, since they never claimed that the Lord's Supper itself was not necessary, only that the inherence of Christ's body in the elements is not necessary for the Lord's Supper to have its divinely intended effect. They insist that Christ's body is not in the elements, but it does not follow that the Eucharist is empty or hollow. The Anabaptists are simply denying that there is any such thing as holy bread or holy wine, because holiness does not reside in things. For Luther, however, the material presence of Christ in the elements is exactly what edifies us; that presence, effected by the Word, is definitive of the Lord's Supper, and therefore to question its necessity is to question the necessity of the Supper itself.

Even though the Anabaptists were not making rational speculation the norm of revelation, the general point about making ourselves the

---

33. Ibid.

judges of what is fitting or necessary stands. Luther sets forth the consequences of our doing so:

> Thus the devil blinds people, and the result is, first, that they are
> incapable of seeing any work of God in the right light, and second,
> that they also fail to regard the Word, and accordingly want to find
> out everything with their own minds.[34]

He says there are two consequences, but four can be found here.
First, we are blinded by Satan. Second, this prevents us from correctly
understanding *any* work of God: if we falsify his work in the Eucharist,
we are going to falsify it elsewhere. Third, we forfeit the Word. And
fourth, we speculate where we should welcome revealed truth. This
last point, about finding out everything with our own minds, is not an
expression of anti-intellectualism on Luther's part but a denunciation
of philosophical speculation. It should be taken in the same spirit as
his declaration that "faith seizes reason by the throat and strangles the
brute." According to the apostolic testimony, says Luther, Jesus Christ
is in the sacrament; we can only receive this and adore him and thank
him for it.

Having made an appeal to the objective reality—that which is to
be believed independently of our own evaluation of it—Luther next
refers to our subjective experience. Wanting to avoid any suggestion of
rationalist orthodoxy, he speaks of hearing the living voice of Christ in
doctrine and Scripture:

> If now you truly believe, so that your heart lays hold of the word
> and holds fast within it that voice, tell me, what have you in your
> heart? You must answer that you have the true Christ, not that he
> sits in there, as one sits on a chair, but as he is at the right hand of
> the Father. How that comes about you cannot know, but your heart

---

34.   Ibid, p. 323.

truly feels his presence, and through the experience of faith you
know for a certainty that he is there.[35]

Notice that Luther can never quite rid his thinking of the idea of spatial
location. We cannot say exactly how Christ can be present simultaneously at the right hand of the Father, present everywhere in the world,
and present in our own hearts, but we know he is. And if this is true, we
cannot then deny that he can be in the elements as well. It is as Edmund
Campion said: heaven is Christ's palace, not his prison.

The telling point, however, is not Luther's argument around spatial
determination, but his treatment of doctrine as the vehicle of our
heart's living apprehension of the person of Jesus Christ. There is a
personalism and warmth here that was seemingly lost by the Lutheran
scholasticism following the Wittenberger. Schleiermacher attempted
to re-emphasize it, but the warmth of the heart in Schleiermacher's
theology was not essentially related to Jesus Christ; it was insufficiently
differentiated from the subjectivism of philosophical idealism and the
non-specific divine presence of pan(en)theism. Luther, by contrast,
exquisitely maintains that balance between the objectivity of Jesus
Christ, who is not reducible to our faith, and our subjective appropriation of him in faith, which in turn is not reducible to doctrine. Notice
that although he refers to the experience—*necessary* experience—of
the believer here, he does not appeal to it as the ground of truth. The
ground of truth is always Jesus Christ himself, through the Word, in
the power of the Spirit.

In his epistles the Apostle Paul mentions his wonderfully vivid
experiences, but he never makes them the ground of his preaching.
He preaches nothing but Christ crucified. Apart from his personal
experience of Christ, however, he would have no reason to preach, he
would be unable to preach, and he would not be who he is. Luther is

---

35. See Lull, p. 319. Here Luther's insistence on the reality of the "voice" and
the necessity of hearing him whose voice it is, is one with with what we have noted
elsewhere concerning the cruciality of the "voice."

making the same point. What he does not seem to understand is that the Anabaptists are in complete agreement with the idea that Christ is really available to believers even while seated at the right hand of the Father. They merely object to the idea of his being *spatially located* in the sacrament.

Luther continues,

> No one can say otherwise, than that the power comes from the Word. As one cannot deny the fact that she [i.e., Mary] becomes pregnant through the Word, and no one knows how it comes about, so it is in the sacrament also. For as soon as Christ says: 'This is my body,' his body is present through the Word and the power of the Holy Spirit. If the Word is not there, it is mere bread; but as soon as the words are added they bring with them that of which they speak.[36]

Several things ought to be noted here. First, there is the conjunction of Word and Holy Spirit, a rare thing in Luther with reference to the sacrament. He routinely conjoins the Word and the Spirit in preaching; but, unlike Calvin, around the sacrament he usually says virtually nothing about the Spirit. Second, he is making a connection between *the Word* and *words*. The words to which he refers are the words of institution, taken from the upper room, but they are not an incantation. They are a declaration of *the Word*. And *the Word* at bottom is always the mercy of God: pardon, forgiveness.

Luther is presupposing a Hebrew understanding of *dabar*, the Hebrew word for "word," meaning both "word" and "event." Whenever God speaks, in the Hebrew Bible, something happens; his Word never returns to him void (Isaiah 55:11) as an empty echo "returns." Instead he speaks, and the world comes into being; he speaks, and Jesus is raised from the dead. Luther would say that the Word, added to the elements, makes the sacrament an *event*—the event of the believer's being seized afresh at the hands of Jesus Christ.

---

36.   Ibid, p. 320.

A little further on, Luther refers to Paul's statement in Ephesians 4:10, that Christ "fills all things," to support his notion that Christ is 'located' everywhere in space. Christ fills all things, but he wills to be found where the Word is conjoined to the elements—that is, in the sacrament that he has ordained. "Although he is present in all creatures, and I might find him in stone, in fire, in water, or even in a rope, for he certainly is there, yet he does not wish that I seek him there apart from the Word."[37] We are to seek him, as ordained, in the bread and wine which are attended by the Word.

Not that this is the *only* place where Christ can be found; but every time we go to the Lord's Supper, or to Scripture, we can be sure of meeting him there. No Christian would deny this in the case of Scripture, and Luther is saying that Christ is present in the Lord's Supper in the same way and for the same reason. He would say this of preaching, too—always keeping in mind the order of priority: Scripture, sermon, sacrament. It is by conjunction with the Word that each of these is the occasion of Christ's self-giving.

Moreover, it should not surprise us that Christ can be present in the bread, "for that he enters the heart through faith is a much greater miracle than that he is present in the bread."[38] Why? Because the human heart is much more resistant to the Word. Bread, being inanimate, cannot resist the Word's approach, but the human heart is so petrified and recalcitrant that it takes a much greater miracle for the Word to penetrate the human heart than for Christ to be found with bread and wine. In other words, any time a human being comes to faith in Jesus Christ a miracle has occurred no less than the resurrection of Lazarus from the dead, no less than the grand miracle of *creatio ex nihilo*. In fact, every time a human being comes to faith, resurrection and *creatio ex nihilo* have happened anew.

More than once Luther repeats the reason for his contention. He wants to be able to say that we can be sure of finding Christ in the

---

37.   Ibid, p. 321.
38.   Ibid, p. 322.

Eucharist. He does not deny the possibility of finding Christ anywhere else in the universe, but the sacrament strengthens our faith because in it we encounter him for sure. If the encounter *depends* on our faith, how can it strengthen our faith?

Recall that the Roman church used the same argument to defend *ex opere operato*. Objecting to the Reformers' insistence that Christ is received in the sacrament *if* it is received in faith, they countered, Whose faith? How strong a faith? Do we only receive as much of Christ in the Eucharist as the quality of our faith will permit? If the weakest faith still receives all of Christ in the Eucharist, then plainly we are receiving vastly more than the quality of our faith will permit.

We must understand from all of this that there is a reality here so profound and glorious that we cannot articulate it exhaustively. Yet we must try to articulate it adequately, for otherwise we gain no understanding of it at all; lacking understanding (however partial and provisional), we cannot communicate it to anyone else. Still, however adequate our articulation, ultimately the final category is not explication but witness. We say, "Go to the Lord's Supper and find out for yourself." The same is true of preaching: we preach as intelligibly and as cogently as we can, but in the final analysis it is not our careful explication that is the substance of Jesus Christ. We must say, "Look to the Lord commended by the sermon, and see for yourself."

Addressing the matter of how the Lord's Supper should be conducted, Luther writes:

> Therefore one should shout it out publicly and hold such public commemoration, that even those who do not yet know of it will attend. That they hold such commemoration privately is worthless. It should take place publicly before the congregation, and there should be preaching at the mass at all times.[39]

Two things are to be noted here. One is the insistence, once again, on preaching. This is common to all the Reformers for whom the irrevers-

---

39. Ibid, p. 327.

ible order is—once again—Scripture, sermon, sacrament; there *must* be Scripture and sermon at every enactment of the sacraments. Second, note the rejection of private masses. Only the rich have the privilege of a private mass, since they alone can pay for it, and this "privilege" is already a denial of the unity of the Body of Christ. Even if there were no cost, however, the very fact of restricting a mass to a private group—for any reason—is also a denial of the commonality of the Lord's Supper.

Luther takes this point further, in the passage quoted above, by widening the Lord's Supper to include those who are not yet believers. Referring to 1 Corinthians 11:26, he says, of Paul:

> He uses the word 'proclaim,' in order to show that it is not to be done privately, only among Christians who know of it beforehand and who stand in need, not of proclamation, but only of admonition.

Unlike Wesley who states unambiguously that the Lord's Supper is not only a confirming sacrament but also a converting one (i.e., someone may be brought to faith through participation in the Eucharist),[40] Luther is content to *allude* to the Lord's Supper as a converting sacrament as well as a confirming one. In *The Babylonian Captivity of the Church* he had said not only that faith is increased in the sacrament but also that it is "kindled" as well.[41] He implies as much here. The promise in the sacrament is not to be announced only to Christians, but to those who have not yet been seized by the gospel. Not everyone in the church community is a believer, and even believers remain afflicted with sin. Therefore we need both admonition and proclamation.[42]

---

40. See Wesley's Journal entry for June 27 and 28, 1740 in W. R. Ward and R.P. Heizenrater, eds. *The Works of John Wesley*, Vol. 19, (Nashville: Abingdon, 1990), p. 158.

41. Lull, p. 306.

42. Proclamation is what we would call today *kerygma*, as opposed to *didache*. *Didache* is the edification of believers. *Kerygma* is the declaration of the gospel to unbelievers. While some New Testament scholarship has attempted to drive a wedge between the two, a closer reading of Scripture suggests that both were found together in apostolic preaching.

The gospel proclaimed in the Lord's Supper is forgiveness of sins. "Now we surely know," writes Luther, "what forgiveness of sins means. When he [that is, God] forgives, he forgives everything completely and leaves nothing unforgiven. When I am free of sin, I am also free of death, devil, and hell; I am a son of God, a lord of heaven and earth."[43]

As was noted above, the forgiveness of sins is comprehensive. We have narrowed it today to mean pardon only, great and wonderful as that is. For Luther, however, the expression 'forgiveness of sins' comprehends the totality of the Christian life; it entails the full freedom and servant lordship that characterize our discipleship as discussed in *The Freedom of a Christian*. The whole of our Christian life is enriched and enhanced and deepened by our participation in the Lord's Supper, whose substance is the forgiveness of sins.[44]

For this reason, moreover, we should not let feelings of unworthiness keep us from the Lord's Supper. Luther writes:

> The papists have taught: 'Beware, do not go thither unless you are pure and have no evil conscience,' so that Christ may be certain to have a pure abode. They have so stupefied and frightened the poor souls by this that they have fled from the sacrament and yet have had to receive it under constraint—with such trembling that they would as gladly have entered a fiery furnace.[45]

He was targeting the Roman church, but even in Protestant communities there are many Christians who feel that their faith is not strong enough, their life not good enough, or their conscience not clear enough to admit them to the Lord's Table. Luther has already said that the sacrament is given to strengthen and comfort us; if we are weak, or in need of forgiveness, we ought not to deprive ourselves precisely of the

---

43. Lull, p. 328.
44. As noted above, the Apostles' Creed assumes a similar understanding of "forgiveness of sins." Some, not realizing this, have called the creed deficient because they believe it makes no mention of the Christian life.
45. Lull, p. 330.

grace we sorely need. After all, if we were worthy, the sacrament would be superfluous. Besides, it is our Lord's invitation that is at issue, not our worthiness. To imagine that we are the judge of our own spiritual condition is a form of spiritual pride masquerading as humility; the real issue facing us is the invitation and the command of Christ, and whether we are going to respond to it—*obedience.*

Of course, if we have venom in our heart, or a deliberate spirit of anti-gospel contempt, it must be dealt with before we come to the Lord's Supper. The passage in 1 Corinthians 11:29 speaks against coming to the Lord's Table without discerning "the body." The body referred to there is the congregation as the body of Christ: we ought not to come while disdaining the congregation or any member of it. Therefore, if we have animosity or resentment in our heart, we ought to deal with this first. If we simply have a troubled conscience, however, Luther wants to assure us that we are welcome and should not be afraid.

LUTHER ON CONFESSION

In the same tract Luther addresses the question of confession, because he believes that the same theological arguments apply to confession no less than to the Eucharist. If we can accept the reality of Christ in the one, we can accept it in the other, and if we balk at the reality of Christ in the one, we will balk at it in the other. He speaks of three kinds of confession.[46]

First of all, we are to confess our sinnership before God. Although we have the Holy Spirit, we are still sinners "because of the flesh,"[47] in the Pauline sense of 'flesh'; that is, the old human nature. We are under two determinations. The determination of Adam or the "old creature" is inferior to that of Christ in us (or else we would not be Christian), but

---

46. Bonhoeffer's *Life Together* contains an updated statement of Luther's understanding of confession.

47. Lull, p. 334.

it is nonetheless operative. Therefore the Christian still sins, and still needs to confess to God.

The second kind of confession is confession to one's neighbor. No one knows shame as profoundly as Christians who are aware of their sinnership. But because we know our shame so profoundly, we have the freedom to confess it, both to God and to other believers: "A godless person will not humiliate himself so deeply as to shame himself. He does not see that to humble himself would be a great honor to him before God and before devout people."[48] Confessing sin to another human being whom we trust keeps us from perpetuating an illusion about ourselves. It also fosters accountability; we are motivated to resist temptation in future, because we do not want to experience the shame of having to confess the same sin again and so appear to have been insincere.

We ought not to be preoccupied with making a full inventory of all of our sins, however. For one thing, it is not possible to do so. Luther writes:

> Where Christians were few in number, each individual said the confession separately to the other. From this they reached a point where they tried to classify and enumerate sins. It would be better if they remained unenumerated, for you will never reckon up how much you have left undone of that which you ought to have done.[49]

The root problem is our systemic sinnership, not the particular sins we commit. If we attempted to enumerate all the ways in which we have fallen short, there would be no end to the endeavor—and no helpful outcome either. At the same time, when we confess to a brother or sister, we do more than acknowledge our sinnership in general; we must also confess concrete, particular sins. Everyone is cursed with systemic sinnership, but only *I* have done what I have done. If we are serious about confessing our sin, then, we will name the specific sin

---

48. Ibid., p. 337.
49. Ibid., p. 337.

that shames us. Otherwise we have not really made confession to fellow-believer *or* God.

With reference to this second kind of confession, confession to one's neighbor, Luther says something crucial at the outset:

> I am under obligation to everyone; in return everyone owes consola-
> tion and assistance to me when I am in need and require help. We
> are not zealous enough, however, in seeking out the people who
> need us and offering them our service. It seems too much for us.[50]

In other words, one aspect of confessing my sin to my neighbor, whom I have violated, is seeking out that neighbor in order to help him. It is a seamless robe: I confess my sin to the neighbor whom I have violated, but I also offer myself as helper to the same neighbor without her having to undergo the humiliation of seeking help from the one who has abused her. Indeed, unless I offer help to the offended neighbor, I am only pretending to confess the sin with which I wounded her.

The third type of confession is private confession with the pronouncement of absolution. Where Rome insists on confession to a priest as a condition of forgiveness, Luther says that the only condition is a believing appropriation of the gospel. We can receive absolution at the hands of any fellow-believer. "[T]he absolution, in which your neighbor absolves you in God's stead, is just as if God himself were speaking, and that should indeed be comforting to us,"[51] writes Luther. The words 'as if' here do not have the force of 'not really'. When my neighbor pronounces me forgiven in Christ's name, it is the *same* as Christ forgiving me. This truth is entailed in Luther's understanding of the priesthood of the believer. Christ acts in the absolution offered in his name by my neighbor, just as he acts in human preaching vivified by the Holy Spirit.

It is for this reason that Luther includes a discussion of confession and absolution in his tract on the Lord's Supper; Christ acts in the

---

50.   Ibid., p. 335.
51.   Ibid., p. 338.

penitential act as surely as he does in the Eucharist. Those who find one empty will dismiss the other, while those who are strengthened and renewed by their encounter with Christ in the one will seek the same benefit in the other. Luther's challenge to the church is unmistakable: is our theology rich enough to support a genuine absolution at the hands of Jesus Christ, pronounced through a fellow-creature? If so, Luther would say, then we will not cavil before the gift of Jesus Christ in the bread and wine of the Eucharist.

8

Law and Gospel

I f asked to identify the heart of Luther's theology, most people would
say, "justification by faith." Luther, however, disagrees. According to
him, an understanding of Scripture, and hence virtually the whole of
theology, depends on a true understanding of Law and Gospel. This is
the elemental distinction in Scripture, and anyone who can articulate
that is a theologian. Failure to make the proper distinction between
Law and Gospel was for Luther the arch error in theology, even though
he recognized this failure to be the normal state of affairs.

Before we continue, an explanation is in order for the spelling of
Law and *the law* in this chapter. For purposes of this discussion, *Law*
is used for Luther's concept of whatever makes us aware of our sinnership—anything that accuses and terrifies the conscience, whether we
find it in Moses or in Christ. It includes, but is not identical with, *the
law*, that is, the Torah, or any specific commands or commandments
of God. In fact, according to Luther we cannot even equate Law with
the Bible's deployment of the imperative mood. For example, the first
three petitions in the Lord's Prayer are not imperatives, but every time
we pray, "May your name be hallowed," we are tacitly confessing that it

ought to be hallowed as we have not yet hallowed it, and in that instant we stand convicted of sin. In this way even petitions may function as Law.

Similarly, every time Christ is held up as an example (which he certainly is, even though he is more than that), Law is operative in that Christ's example highlights our deficiency. Or consider the words of Jesus in Matthew 11:28: "Come unto me, all who labor and are weary and heavy laden, and I will give you rest." It sounds like the most winsome invitation in the world, pure Gospel. However, if Christ says, "Come unto me," then insofar as we do not come or have not yet come, his words are Law, and convict us of our sinnership.[1]

In a parallel way, we will use *Gospel* for Luther's concept of whatever assures us of God's unfailing redemptive love for us, no matter where we find this in Scripture, and *the gospel* for the story of how our salvation is accomplished by God becoming human in Christ, living, dying, and rising for us.

LAW AND GOSPEL CONTRASTED

Luther says that humankind has known God's law ever since Creation, because the law of God is written on the human heart. He is referring here to Romans 1 and 2, and specifically Romans 2:14: "For when Gentiles, who do not have the law, by nature do what the law requires, they are a law to themselves, even though they do not have the law" (ESV).[2] The law written on the human heart therefore predates Moses' Decalogue, but the content of both, and the ethical admonitions of the gospel, are the same. In the written gospel we are told to love our neighbor as ourselves and to treat our neighbor as we would wish to be treated, for this is the law and

---

1.   Rarely mentioned, of course, is the grammatical form of "Come unto me." It is an imperative. The invitation is in fact a command, and there is nothing optional about it.

2.   Many New Testament scholars regard Rom. 2:14 as referring to Gentile Christians. See, e.g., C. E. Cranfield, *Romans: A Shorter Commentary* (Grand Rapids: Eerdmans, 1985).

the prophets.[3] Even though that injunction is found in the written gospel, it is an instance of Law, Luther would say, and is identical with the law written on the human heart.

At the very least, then, for Luther, the law written on the heart renders every human being without excuse. No one can ever claim to be guilt-free before God and in no need of the gospel. At the same time, says Luther, the Fall has largely deafened us to the claim of the law written on our heart; hence Moses restates it for us, summarizing natural law in a much better way than any philosopher has done. The content of the law remains the eternal will of God; it states that we should let God be God and not usurp what he claims for himself. And in allowing God to be God, says Luther, we will find God to be gracious.

It can be seen already—even though Luther will say that Law and Gospel are distinct and ought never to be confused—that at some level he sees the law as an anticipation of the gospel: the law commands us to let God be God, and therein to find God gracious. It is in this sense that Luther says the law is good (Romans 7:12), for it shows us what we were before the Fall, and what we will be when we are glorified. As we proceed in our discussion we will see more of this delicate balance between the contrast and the unity of Law and Gospel.

Luther then goes on to develop two uses of the law. The first use is to restrain public evil and promote public order, and the second use is to move us to repentance.[4] In this second role, the law does not assist

---

3.   Matthew 19:19b, 22:39b; Matthew 7:12.

4.   Although he never explicitly used the expression "the third use", he did maintain that believers, upon coming to repentance in faith, need the law for guidance once they are in Christ. Disagreeing with some of the radicals who said that the Christian has been delivered from the law in all respects, Luther says that the Christian is delivered from the law as a principle of justification—for which the law was never intended in any case, Calvin and others will point out—but is not freed from the law with respect to obedience. In the *Formula of Concord* in 1577, years after Luther's death, explicit reference is made to a third "normative" use of the law to guide the life of believers. This was the influence of Melanchthon. It is interesting to note, incidentally, that in the Calvinist tradition the first two uses of the law are inverted.

us to become righteous, but instead exposes our unrighteousness by showing us God's requirement for a pure heart. In fact, in doing so, the law *intensifies* our unrighteousness. As we know from reading Romans, the law provokes the very thing it forbids. Luther is thinking here mainly of the second table of the Decalogue; as our violation of it increases and we become increasingly aware that we cannot fulfill it, we come to resent the Lawgiver himself, and so violate the first table of the Decalogue. We come to hate God, and resenting and hating God, we come to despair of his mercy and despair of ourselves. We now wish that God did not exist. In other words, says Luther, what lurks in the human heart is deicide, and this is what Paul means when he says that sin becomes sinful beyond measure through the law.[5]

This process becomes operative only as the Holy Spirit vivifies the law; it is not enough for us merely to hear it with our ears. And the despair just described is where the process would end up if it were not for the gospel. Only the gospel spares us the despair aroused by the law. According to Luther, the law on its own works "demonic terrors of conscience," but together with the gospel it works "evangelical terrors of conscience". Demonic terrors of conscience leave us hopeless; evangelical terrors of conscience are hopeful, because our smitten conscience is what orients us towards the gospel. To say the same thing another way: apart from the gospel, the law simply beats us up; *with* the gospel, it disciplines us as a schoolmaster and points us to Christ.

Repentance, says Luther, occurs as both the law and the gospel are efficacious. The law gives rise to pain in us, while the gospel gives rise to comfort and joy. Both are needed. It is only as we become aware of the

---

5. Luther is providing a psychological analysis of humankind under the law, whereas Paul's is strictly theological and describes our objective predicament before God independent of our feelings about it. Plainly, from a psychological perspective we are better off not knowing the law of God, but spiritually, of course—given that our predicament is objective—we are always better off knowing the law because our conviction at its hands is exactly what orients us, ultimately, towards the gospel.

work of the law within us causing us pain that we move on to the gospel and find comfort and joy there.

CONSCIENCE AND LAW

In the unfolding discussion of Law and Gospel, it is important to understand the distinction between natural or divine law on the one hand and the dictates of conscience on the other. What role does conscience play in the salvific process of conviction and repentance outlined above? How does conscience interact with the Word of God as Law and Gospel?

While children are often told that the voice of conscience is the voice of God, Luther goes so far as to say, on occasion, that it is the voice of the devil. Every human being, he says, possesses a conscience in the same way that every human being possesses two arms and two legs; it is simply part of our creatureliness. And this means that, like every other aspect of our creatureliness, the conscience is essentially good, but fallen. A fallen conscience is *not* an immediate awareness of God, nor does it have any ability to discern truth and falsehood. It simply alerts us to the contradiction between what we uphold and what we perform. What we uphold might be entirely false; our fallen conscience cannot tell us this.

As we saw at the beginning of this chapter, Luther says that natural law, which embodies God's will, is common to all people. However, this law is obscured both by Satan and by false teaching, with the result that our conscience reacts to what is not sin and fails to react to what is sin. Moreover, regardless of how much the conscience is stung, it continues to sense evil as a moral deficit to be countered by moral achievement. In this respect, says Luther, conscience always takes us farther away from the gospel; when it alerts us to the gap between confession and performance, it only prods us to try harder. Besides, our conscience accuses us on the basis of our works, but it also *excuses* us on the basis of our works. Hence it always moves us into self-produced righteousness, which is sheer contradiction of the righteousness of God. Our conscience operates in a non-gospel orbit.

Conscience portrays God characteristically as judge. God *is* judge, but he is characteristically Father. Conscience leaves us thinking that God is not Father at all but only the judge, someone hostile to us whom we must placate and satisfy. In this way, says Luther, conscience fosters idolatry: it mischaracterizes God by assuming that those who do good works have a gracious God while those who sin have an angry God, and it prescribes to us a false way of worshipping him.

Our fallen, corrupt conscience can only persist in such error, as it has no awareness of our systemic sinnership and estrangement from God. It can only respond to what we do or fail to do; it is unable to recognize the human predicament that gives rise to wrongdoing. And despite its constant attempt to acquit itself before God, conscience can never entirely eradicate the sense of sin or give us assurance concerning our standing with God. It can never pronounce, with certainty, that we are saved.

How do we react in the wake of this persistent condemnation or uncertainty? Luther describes three reactions:

(a)   indifference, leading to antinomianism: my conscience pricks me, but it pricks me regardless of what I try to do, so why bother? Who cares?

(b)   presumption: if my conscience faults me for wrongdoing, I will betake myself to rightdoing, and will incur God's favor.

(c)   despair: I will flee God.

What humankind needs, he says, is thoroughgoing condemnation, but at the hands of the law rather than at the hands of conscience. Condemnation at the hands of the law moves us towards pardon because it anticipates the gospel, while condemnation at the hands of conscience simply depresses us and precipitates despair.[6]

---

6.   For a sensitive discussion of this point see Randall Zachman, *The Assurance of Faith* (Minneapolis: Fortress Press, 1993).

The attempt by the conscience to know God is contradicted by God's self-revelation. We cannot know God through conscience, and will never know the acquittal of God through the acquittal of our conscience. According to the Word of God, says Luther, it is upon those who are condemned in their conscience that God pronounces his acquittal. Therefore, the law must never be preached so as to acquit or silence the conscience. Conscience cannot bring us to God, but it can alert us to the gap in our lives—whereupon God's law, if proclaimed, informs us that this gap is the result of sin, and leads us to the gospel. That is the proper use of the law in the life of the unbeliever. Conscience sees condemnation as the purpose of the law, whereas in reality the purpose of the law is to bring us to Christ.

In short, conscience never discloses sin; it only discloses moral failure, and moral failure as such never orients us to the gospel but only leaves us trying harder morally, in our orientation away from the gospel. The law must be added to conscience in such a way that the stricken conscience is seen to be stricken over violation of the law of God. Once sin has been revealed by the law, conscience confirms it. Under the impact of the law of God, then, the testimony of the law and the testimony of conscience coincide, and in this moment we correctly know our predicament before God. In other words, if conscience is to function in the economy of salvation it must be informed by the Word of God.

For this reason—and here Luther is adamant—revelation of the law, which discloses sin, must always precede revelation of God's mercy. We must acknowledge our sin before we can hear the gospel in our hearts. Insofar as this suggests a dualism of Law and Gospel, making them mutually exclusive, there appears to be a problem: how can revelation of the law lead the conscience to the gospel? How can the law lead the conscience to seek something beyond the law? How can the law, when it is the only word of salvation of which the conscience is aware, inform the conscience that it is not the "word" of salvation? Furthermore, is it really in the face of God's wrath that we acknowledge our sin, or in the face of God's mercy? These questions can be obviated only by an understanding that Law and Gospel are ultimately one Word of God, uttered simultaneously. This point will be developed more fully in the next section.

THE UNITY AND SIMULTANEITY OF LAW AND GOSPEL

At the end of the first section, we noted that Law and Gospel had two opposite functions or effects, both essential to bring us to salvation. However, we also saw hints that Law anticipates Gospel—that the law has a gospel-like function. Now we are going to see that the converse is true as well: the gospel has a lawlike function. We have described the gospel as the story of Christ, the Incarnate One who fulfills God's promise in our midst, accomplishing our salvation. But since nothing exposes our sinner-ship like the goodness of Christ, nothing is as piercingly Law as the gospel. This may sound strange, given Luther's insistence that the two are never to be confused; but if it is an inconsistency in his theology, it is a glorious one. While he contrasts Law and Gospel, he makes clear that they are both Word of God, and therefore cannot ultimately be antithetical.[7]

Moreover, we are left with the questions raised at the end of the previous section. If Law and Gospel are antithetical, how could there be any movement from one to the other? As we will see even more clearly when we discuss conscience at greater length, unless the law somehow anticipates the gospel, conviction under the law only drives us further from the gospel; it simply worsens us inwardly until finally we despair of ourselves spiritually and psychologically. Law and Gospel have opposite functions—the one terrifies and condemns, while the other comforts and pardons—yet they are not absolutely antithetical.

Indeed, in Luther's understanding, if conviction of sin arises at the hands of the law, confession and repentance arise only in the light of the

---

7.   Karl Barth greatly magnified this point in the twentieth century, declaring that the gospel is the content of the law, and the law is the form of the gospel. See his *Church Dogmatics*, Vol. II, part 2, sections 36-39. Calvin also underlines this point, repeating again and again that the gospel is the substance of the law; if not, we have a two-headed deity.

gospel. The revelation of the gospel is always necessary to penitence; therefore the priority of Law to Gospel, as discussed above, is always balanced by their simultaneity. Law is prior to Gospel in the salvific process as it unfolds in an individual, but theologically the two are simultaneous, since both are Word of God. Sometimes Luther even describes the gospel as revealing both the condemnation of sin and our redemption from it, and to the extent that it reveals the former, it is functioning as law.[8]

There is another way in which the gospel exercises a lawlike function, and this is in the life of the believer. It has to do with the relationship between promise and command, two manifestations of the Word of God in Luther's theology that parallel Gospel and Law. A command is a specific direction stipulated by the law, and is always the voice of the living God directing us to concrete obedience in the moment. Believers can obey the command of God, says Luther, because God visits them with both grace and gift—grace being the forgiveness of sins, and the gift being the Holy Spirit who heals the sinful heart and strengthens the will.[9] Grace is our being in Christ, and allows us to find God merciful; gift is Christ's being in us, and allows us to find God holy. Having heard

---

8.   This lawlike function of the gospel was made more explicit by other theologians, most notably Calvin and Barth. There is an important theological reason for the tension in Luther between the contrast of Law and Gospel, on the one hand, and their simultaneity and overlap on the other. He says that simply to hear the law of God with our ears will never convict us of our sinnership; we must hear it suffused with the Holy Spirit, as only the Spirit can give us awareness of spiritual conviction. A problem lurks here, for if a hard and fast line is drawn between Law and Gospel, or between Law and Christ, then there is a work of the Holy Spirit with respect to Law which is not a work of Christ. Luther says that the law, promulgated and suffused with the Spirit, convicts us of sin, but the gospel promulgated and suffused with the Spirit brings us to Christ and to salvation. Romans 8:9-11 says in three different ways that the Spirit is the Spirit of Christ, and that Christ is the bearer and bestower of that Spirit. Can there be, then, a work of the Spirit concerning the law which *is not* a work of Christ? If there can, we end up with the Spirit divorced from Christ, a major theological problem. Luther recognizes this problem and is trying to avoid it.

9.   See Zachman, *Assurance of Faith,* p. 69-70.

the law of God, having been convicted of our sinnership, and having been moved thereby to embrace the gospel, we become new creatures in Christ, whereupon we hear with specifically Christian hearing the command of God appointing us to a specific obedience.

Luther points out that God never gives a promise without also giving a command.[10] All the promises of God are covered commands, in that every promise contains a responsibility as well as a benefit. The fact that we are the beneficiaries of God's mercy means that we are also commanded to praise God for it and to extend the same mercy to our neighbor. In this respect, then, Gospel is Law at the same time.

The gospel gives us freedom from the law, but without emptying the law of its content or its claim on us. It frees us from the law in three different ways.[11] First, we are freed from the law's condemnation and therefore from pursuing self-justification in order to assuage our consciences. Second, we are freed from the law's coercion, for the Christ who claims our obedience does so graciously, without twisting our arm or threatening us, so that we delight in the law. Third, the gospel frees us from legalistic subservience to human laws and traditions (what were called, in Luther's era, *adiaphora* or non-essentials). We may observe or ignore these freely, making use of whatever facilitates our praise of God, so long as love of our neighbor is not violated. Luther was strong on this point, believing that anything not forbidden by Scripture was permitted, including many of the devotional aids used by the Roman church. Scripture forbids worship of images or saints, for instance, but it does not forbid the presence of a statue in a church. It does not forbid making the sign of the cross. Since Scripture makes no pronouncement on these things, the gospel that frees us from the law frees us also from human 'laws' about matters such as these, laid down by tradition.

Elsewhere Luther speaks of the law being both "suspended" and "preserved" in the gospel. The law is suspended in the gospel because we

---

10. The Puritans emphasized the converse: that God never gives a command without at least implicitly giving us the promise of his grace and gift.

11. Zachman, *Assurance of Faith*, p. 71-74.

have moved from condemnation to pardon, but it is preserved in the gospel because we still need its guidance and direction in our life in Christ. As believers, we are freed from the power of the law to accuse and condemn, but its content continues to express God's will for our discipleship. The difference is that our obedience is now Christ's Torah-keeping within us, so that instead of hating the law as the convicted unbeliever does, we now rejoice in the law and find it precious and good.[12] But precious and good, it must be recalled, are characteristics Luther normally predicates of the gospel. Thinkers who followed him, such as Melanchthon, Calvin, the Puritans, Barth, and others, will pick up this theme: if the law is precious and good, then the law must, in some sense or in some form, be the gospel.

We must always be careful of making Law larger than Gospel, because to do so is to offer no hope to anyone. Once again, that is why Luther seems to move back and forth between primacy and simultaneity. If Law and Gospel are announced simultaneously, Law will never eclipse Gospel so as to leave needy people in a worse condition than ever.

LUTHER'S *PREFACE TO THE OLD TESTAMENT*

Luther develops the above-mentioned themes in his tract *Preface to the Old Testament*, written in 1523 and revised in 1545. The first thing to notice is that Luther finds both Law and Gospel in the Old Testament just as in the New, and considers them to be of one substance. He writes, "Similarly in the Old Testament too there are, beside the laws, certain promises and words of grace, by which the holy fathers and prophets under the law were kept, like us, in the faith of

---

12. Notice that this moves into a "third use" of the law: to order the believer's new life in Christ. For Calvin, this is the principal use of the law, in the sense that it is the law's ultimate goal; it is only on the way to this ultimate goal that the law convicts us of sinnership. Again, Melanchthon was the first Reformer to speak formally of the "third" use of the law, a use that is anticipated but not rendered explicit in Luther's work.

Christ."[13] In other words, we find Gospel and grace under the economy of Torah, Torah being that which kept Israel in the faith of Christ. This is another way of saying that Gospel "is the substance of" Law, although Luther did not express himself in precisely these words.

In the same tract he states, "Genesis, therefore, is made up almost entirely of illustrations of faith and unbelief, and of the fruits that faith and unbelief bear. It is an exceedingly evangelical book." Genesis is "an exceedingly evangelical book" because it speaks of faith. The only person in whom anyone can have faith is Jesus Christ; therefore, says Luther, the book of Genesis is full of discussion of faith in Jesus Christ. In fact, Luther sees faith in Christ as the substance of book after book in the Older Testament.[14] Again a little further on he writes:

> Thus Moses, as a perfect lawgiver, fulfilled all the duties of his office.
> He not only gave the Law, but was there when men were to fulfill it.
> When things went wrong, he explained the Law and re-established
> it. Yet this explanation in the fifth book really contains nothing else
> than faith toward God and love toward one's neighbor.[15]

If the book of Deuteronomy "contains nothing else than faith toward God and love toward one's neighbor," then the book of Deuteronomy contains the gospel.

Having established that the gospel can be found in the Old Testament, Luther directs his attention to the law and its specific function. He writes:

---

13.   Lull, *Martin Luther's Basic Theological Writings* (Minneapolis: Fortress Press, 1989), p. 120.

14.   At one point Luther seems to contradict this, writing, "[J]ust as the chief teaching of the New Testament is really the proclamation of grace and peace through the forgiveness of sins in Christ, so the chief teaching of the Old Testament is really the teaching of laws, the showing up of sin, and the demanding of good." He corrects this later on the same page.

15.   Lull, p. 121.

[W]here there is no Law of God, there all human reason is so blind that it cannot recognize sin. For human reason does not know that unbelief and despair of God is sin. Indeed it knows nothing about man's duty to believe and trust in God.[16]

Luther makes two important points here. First, he says that apart from the law of God we never recognize sin. Reason can recognize immorality, socially destructive behavior, or activity that is personally ruinous, but it can never recognize sin, and never understands that morality and immorality are equally sin. In particular, reason does not know that hatred of enemies is sin. Fallen humankind naturally regards hatred of one's enemies as proper and right, whereas Jesus insists that we are never closer to God than we are to our worst enemy. In short, only the law of God as the Word of God discloses sin to be sin; there is no natural knowledge of sin.

Second, he points out that the essence of sin is unbelief. In the church we tend to regard pride as the arch-sin, thanks to the influence of Augustine. For the synagogue, however, the arch-sin is unbelief and despair—particularly despair of God, which underlies any despair of oneself. Reflecting Israel's conviction here (we must always remember how much "at home" he was in the Old Testament), Luther speaks of unbelief not as it pertains to the religious furniture of one's mind but rather as the "set" of one's heart. Unbelief is not a matter of cerebral error; it is rather the refusal to trust the promises of God.

Luther goes on to describe the human condition with respect to the law:

Every law of God is good and right . . . . Accordingly, whoever does not keep this good law—or keeps it unwillingly—cannot be righteous or good in his heart. But human nature cannot keep it otherwise than unwillingly.[17]

---

16.   Ibid., p. 125.
17.   Ibid., p. 127.

Human nature resents the claim of God, because we all want to be our own lord, and as Calvin was later to say repeatedly in his commentaries, where the law of God is not kept willingly, gladly, and cheerfully, it is not kept at all. It is only once we are brought to acknowledge the Lordship of Jesus Christ that we can obey the law of God willingly, continues Luther: "For through Christ sin is forgiven, God is reconciled, and man's heart has begun to feel kindly toward the law." Unbelievers resent the law when they first hear of it, but when they are brought to Christ, they at least *begin* to feel kindly toward the law as their affections are transformed.

This brings us to the sweetness of the law as described in Psalms 19 and 119, a sweetness in which believers characteristically "delight" (Psalm 1). In the psalmist's view, outside the sphere of God's law there is only self-contradiction, agony, anguish, and death, but within the sphere of God's command, there is freedom. It is hard for Christians to understand this, because we have heard from infancy the note in Galatians and Romans that the law is a curse. The law is a curse when it is abstracted from the gospel and misunderstood in terms of its proper end, that is, when perverted into a vehicle of our self-justification; it does nothing more, then, than arouse the conscience. Paul describes it as an intolerable burden. But Luther, reading Paul more accurately than most, is never confused by the apostle's description of a perversion of the law as if it were the law.

Law is never spoken by God apart from Gospel or as contradiction of Gospel; it is given to be the vehicle of our glad honoring of God, an expression of the life he has given us and the presence of Christ in us. In other words, it is given as Gospel, and we pervert it by our tendency to use it for self-justification. When the law is misappropriated as the vehicle of our ascent to God, it becomes an insuperable mountain on whose slope we die of exposure before we have made any progress. The psalmist, however, who is not thinking of the law as the vehicle of his justification but as God's self-bestowal, says that it is sweeter than honey, a delight that profoundly satisfies without satiating.

This brings us back to the integrity of the Word of God with respect to Law and Gospel. However much we may contrast the two with respect to how they function, we cannot divorce them with respect to their substance, or else we would have two Words of God. As Calvin came to say later—and Luther would agree—the person of God is present in all the acts of God; that is, the Word of God is not simply something God says, it is God himself speaking.[18] Therefore, since there is only one God, there can only be one Word of God. There must be, then, a relationship of Law to Gospel besides antithesis; there must be an inherent unity.

A wonderfully subtle dialectic characterizes Luther's discussion of Law and Gospel. We need to hear the law of God in order to be awakened to our sinnership, but can only bear to do so while hearing the gospel of God that we are secure in Christ. Similarly, once we are on the road of discipleship we need to hear the law of God again to direct us on that road, but not without also hearing the gospel of God that our performance—the obedience we have resolved and declared through our faith in Christ—is not the condition of our continued acceptance. Luther whipsaws us back and forth between Law and Gospel throughout the Christian life. In truth, the dialectic between Law and Gospel is, finally, two aspects of the one gospel, or else we have a two-faced God.

That God has two faces is the position of those who dismiss the Older Testament or pit it against the New, confining Law to the former and Gospel to the latter. Marcion (c.85-144) made this error; he dismissed the Old Testament, thinking it spoke of a different God from the New. Luther is always at pains to make the point that it is Israel's God who has come to humankind in Jesus of Nazareth. Law and Gospel are found in equal measure, in equal proportion, in both Old and New Testaments.

Let us return for a moment to the Decalogue. In both Exodus and Deuteronomy, the first commandment includes the preface, "You were slaves in Egypt and I saved you with my outstretched arm ..." "I brought you out of the house of bondage". It is obvious from this why Luther

---

18. For example: ". . . the highest proof of Scripture derives in general from the fact that God *in person* speaks in it" (Calvin, *Institutes,* 1.7.4, emphasis added).

hears the first commandment as Gospel, and why the psalmist delights in the law of God: it is in the law that the pardoning, delivering, vindicating God gives himself to his people and pledges himself to them forever. The law is therefore a gift first of all, and only on that basis a claim. It cannot be fulfilled by works, as Luther points out,[19] even though it enjoins obedience. It can be fulfilled only in faith, trusting the One who both gave the law and fulfilled it himself as the Incarnate One by rendering it the human obedience it demands. By faith, then, believers cling to that Incarnate Son with whom they are now identified as Torah-keeping sons and daughters of God. It is in this sense that Luther never relents in his insistence that the law of God can be fulfilled only through faith.

Admittedly, the law can be perverted—as can the gospel—so deep-rooted is our addiction to self-justification. The gospel is pure gift; yet so many people in church life, as Luther knew and as any pastor or counselor will testify, hear the gospel with their ears and turn it into the occasion of attempting to justify themselves before God by self-promotion, substituting moral achievement for the self-abandonment that is faith. That self-abandonment is the meaning of Luther's oft-repeated "first commandment righteousness." As fallen beings bent on self-justification we characteristically turn the purest announcement of the purest life-bringing gift of God into its death-dealing antithesis.

A BRIEF INSTRUCTION ON WHAT TO LOOK FOR AND EXPECT IN THE GOSPELS

Most of this chapter has been spent examining the distinction between Law and Gospel in the context of their ultimate unity. In his *Brief Instruction On What to Look for and Expect in the Gospels*, Luther examines the distinctions among the various accounts of the gospel in the context of their ultimate unity. As an astute reader of Scripture he knew that there is finally only one gospel, but there are angles of vision on that one gospel provided by the testimony of many different apostles. In other

---

19.   Lull, p. 129.

words, Luther ultimately upholds a unity of the New Testament while admitting differing emphases, just as he upheld the ultimate unity of the Word of God while distinguishing Law and Gospel.

The notion of the theological unity of the New Testament has attracted relentless criticism in the last several decades, but it is essential concerning the gospel. We cannot deny that Matthew, Mark, and Luke have recognizably different emphases, but if there is no common witness on the part of the apostles, we must ask ourselves whether there is such a thing as "the gospel" at all.

All of the New Testament gospel writers agree that Jesus is Lord, Messiah of Israel, Son of God, Savior. For Matthew, however, Jesus is also the new Moses; to be sure, he is greater than Moses, but he is not less. Matthew divides his written gospel into five "books" or sections, plainly drawing a parallel with the five books of Torah, and seeing the gospel as the Torah renewed and fulfilled rather than opposed to it. For Mark, Jesus is Victor: wherever Jesus comes upon sin, sickness, sorrow, suffering, demonic activity, and death, he conquers them. In Luke's gospel, Jesus is the helper especially of all who are voiceless, defence-less, abandoned, lost, and forlorn. He comes to the assistance of the poor and marginalized, the outcast, Gentiles, women, and—be it noted in this age—the not-yet-born.

Those are different angles of vision on Jesus Christ which give rise to peculiarities in each written gospel. Luther remained convinced, however, that beneath all this lies the gospel which presupposes the apostles' unitary confession of Jesus. He writes, "One should thus realize that there is only one gospel, but that it is described by many apostles...The gospel is a story about Christ, God's and David's Son, who died and was raised and is established as Lord."[20] The phrase "God's and David's Son" is particularly important. Luther recognizes Jesus Christ as God Incarnate—God's Son—but also, and necessarily, as the fulfillment of Israel. Luther grasped the inconsistency in pretend-

---

20.   Lull, pp. 104-105.

ing to uphold the Incarnation while setting aside Israel; he knew that whenever this omission occurs, the Incarnation becomes the divine legitimation of a humanistic agenda. Erasmus, for example, preferred to speak of *philosophia Christi*, the philosophy of Christ, but appeared never to grasp the jarring *novum* that Luther knew the gospel to be as something that can never be humanly anticipated. (As Luther liked to remind Erasmus' fellow travelers, What philosopher ever speculated that the world's cure is accomplished in the manger of the Incarnate One and the cross of the crucified God?) Not surprisingly, Erasmus was also one of the worst anti-Semites in Europe. To neglect the Older Testament, seeing Jesus as God's Son but not David's son, can only spell the disappearance of the gospel.

This is no surprise in view of what has already been said about the unity of the Older and New Testaments, both of which are replete with Law and Gospel. Luther continues:

> Yes, even the teaching of the prophets, in those places where they
> speak of Christ, is nothing but the true, pure, and proper gospel,
> just as if Luke or Matthew had described it. For the prophets
> have proclaimed the gospel and spoken of Christ, as St. Paul here
> [Romans 1:2] reports and as everyone indeed knows.

Reading Romans more closely than most, Luther gives full weight to Paul's declaration that the law and the prophets (that is, the Old Testament in its entirety) attest the gospel.[21] The law and the prophets can bear witness to the gospel only if the gospel is the substance of both—that is, if Gospel is the content of Law, and here Luther harbours no doubt; he maintains that the teaching of the prophets is nothing but the "true, pure, and proper gospel." He finds purest Gospel as well as Law in the Old Testament, just as he finds Law as well as Gospel in the New Testament. He confirms this about the New Testament, saying of the evangelists:

---

21.   Romans 3:21.

They want themselves to be our guides, to direct us to the writings
of the prophets and of Moses in the Old Testament so that we might
there read and see for ourselves how Christ is wrapped in swaddling
cloths and laid in the manger, that is, how he is comprehended in
the writings of the prophets.[22]

The law and the prophets are the swaddling cloths—the diapers—in
which we find Christ in the manger; Christ is comprehended in the
writings of the prophets. Crucial here is the truth that the prophets
do not merely *point to* Christ—every Christian will acknowledge this
much—but *comprehend* Christ. In other words, Christ is the substance
of Old Testament prophetic teaching, and the evangelists recognize
this by in turn incorporating the Old Testament in their account of the
gospel. Ever perceptive, Luther is aware of the church's tragic neglect of
the Old Testament and the consequences of this negligence:

> But what a fine lot of tender and pious children we are! In order
> that we might not have to study in the Scriptures and learn Christ
> there, we simply regard the entire Old Testament as of no account,
> as done for and no longer valid. Yet it alone bears the name of Holy
> Scripture. And the gospel should really not be something written,
> but a spoken word which brought forth the Scriptures, as Christ
> and the apostles have done. This is why Christ himself did not write
> anything but only spoke.[23]

As Luther correctly points out, Scripture in the apostolic church
consisted of the writings of the Older Testament from Genesis to
Malachi. He urges us to regard the gospel as the spoken word which
brought forth these Scriptures. In other words, the gospel is the living
self-utterance of Jesus Christ, simultaneously self-interpreted and self-
communicated, which brought forth the Old Testament Scriptures in
the first place. Clearly then, the gospel cannot be at odds with the Old
Testament.

---

22.   Lull, *op. cit.,*p. 109.
23.   Ibid., p. 110.

Luther also makes an interesting distinction here between the written text and the spoken word which is its source. We assume today that anyone who has something to say is going to write a book. Christ did not. If he had, we would venerate the writing and ignore Christ himself; the book would take the place of a personal engagement with the living Christ and so become the antithesis of faith. Scripture is the only book which is essential to our engagement with Christ, but reading Scripture is not the same as engaging Christ; the book is not a substitute for a personal engagement with the living Savior.

For Luther, then, Holy Scripture means principally the Old Testament, and Gospel ought not to be understood as something that supersedes this, but rather as its content. Nor should Gospel be understood chiefly as something written, but as the self-utterance of the living Lord Jesus Christ which brought forth Scripture. If these two points are understood, Christ will always be found in the Old Testament. Moreover, we will never confuse testimony to Christ (prophetic, apostolic witness) with the living person himself, whom faith alone encounters, engages, and comes to know incontrovertibly.

9

Marks of the Church

LUTHER'S UNDERSTANDING OF THE CHURCH1

I believe in one holy, catholic church, the communion of saints, asserts the Apostles' Creed. With reference to that ringing affirmation Luther writes, "Here the creed clearly indicates what the church is, namely, a communion of saints, that is, a crowd or assembly of people who are Christians and holy, which is called a Christian holy assembly, or church."[2]

"Yet this word *church,*" he goes on to say, "is not German and does not convey the sense or meaning that should be taken from this article." Luther struggled over the best word to use for the holy assembly. He particularly disliked the word *Kirche,* the standard German word for "church," because for him it principally evoked the institution. A definition of the church in terms of institution violates biblical ecclesiology in any case, but because of its exclusive application to Rome at the

---

1.   Paul Althaus, *The Theology of Martin Luther* (Philadelphia: Fortress Press, 1963) has been helpful with respect to this chapter.

2.   Lull, *Martin Luther's Basic Theological Writings* (Minneapolis: Fortress Press, 1989). p. 540.

time, the word *Kirche* also suggested a hierarchical constitution of the church. Other words available to Luther in his writing on ecclesiology included *Hauffe*[3] (group or crowd), *Gemeinde* (community), *Sammlung* (gathering), and *Versammlung* (assembly); there were also the Latin *congregatio* and the Greek *ekklesia*. Luther moves ultimately in the direction of the church as community, regularly speaking of *Gemeinschaft*, or participation, and contrasting this with the Roman understanding in which the hierarchy of priest, bishop, and pope is what defines and constitutes the church.

There are three levels at which this Christian community is formed. In the first place, we put ourselves and our goods, time, and talents at the disposal of others in the local Christian fellowship. Second is the level at which doctrine is forged and apprehended, for without doctrine there can be no church. At this level, too, we console others and intercede for them. But it is at the third level, he says, that the Christian community exacts the greatest cost from us, for there we share the weakness and sin of our fellow Christians.

To share the sin of fellow Christians is to share their disgrace. Recall Luther's teaching that, as Christians, we do not live in ourselves; we live in Christ by faith and in the neighbor by love. As we saw in an earlier chapter, living in our neighbor involves sharing his need—not all that costly for us; sharing his suffering—a little more costly; and sharing his disgrace—costliest of all. This element of disgrace is something the church can never escape. Not only does it suffer public disgrace in the form of outright scandal from time to time; there is also the disgrace of the church's overall obedience, forever falling lamentably short of its profession of Christ. Christian community means that everybody in the congregation—pastor and people alike—owns that disgrace.

It is relatively easy to put ourselves and our goods, time, and talents at the disposal of the congregation, and relatively easy, at least for cerebral types, to forge and apprehend doctrine. It is even relatively

---

3.　Spelled *Haufe* in modern German.

easy to console those who are suffering and intercede for them. But to share the weakness and sin of fellow Christians, as the Crucified has shared ours, exacts the greater and *characteristic* price. Only at this level, says Luther, is Christian love worthy of the name. He cites the example of Christ in Philippians 2, "who, though he was in the form of God, did not count equality with God a thing to be grasped, but made himself nothing, taking the form of a servant, being born in the likeness of men" (ESV). In a similar way, Luther adds (quoting Paul), "We who are strong have an obligation to bear with the failings of the weak, and not to please ourselves" (Romans 15:1, ESV). He refers also to the example of Jesus washing the disciples' feet, and finishes with the parable of the Pharisee and the publican from Luke 18.

In that parable, the Pharisee feeds on his brother's sin. There is often a pharisaical element in church life which perversely rejoices in the failure of some other woebegone Christian and uses that to feel superior; such an attitude, however, destroys community. We are all sinners carried along in the fellowship of the congregation, and the real test of Christian love is our willing identification, in imitation of Christ, with one another's shame and disgrace. Where would any of us be if Jesus Christ had refused to identify with our disgrace—and refused to continue living with it even now?

This, then, is how Luther understands that community which is the church, and it reflects his characteristic realism. Lest it be thought, however, that Luther fostered an indulgent attitude towards sin, notice what he says about the holiness of the church:

> Now there are many peoples in the world; the Christians, however, are a people with a special call, and are therefore called not just *ecclesia*, 'church,' or 'people,' but *sancta catholica Christiana*, that is, 'a Christian holy people' who believe in Christ. That is why they are called a Christian people and have the Holy Spirit, who sanctifies them daily, not only through the forgiveness of sin acquired for them by Christ (as the Antinomians foolishly believe), but also

through the abolition, the purging, and the mortification of sins, on the basis of which they are called a holy people.[4]

It has been suggested that it was only with the appearance of Dietrich Bonhoeffer's *The Cost of Discipleship* that holiness received its proper emphasis among Lutherans. But Luther, we should note, was already saying explicitly that Christ's people do not merely claim forgiveness for sin; they repudiate it "through the abolition, the purging, and the mortification of sins." If we are to know and enjoy forgiveness, in other words, we must repudiate sin as quickly as we discern it in our own hearts; otherwise we are on the road to Antinomianism, the lawlessness which Luther abhorred.[5]

Further on in the same tract, Luther writes,

> This is still bearable; but they are the holy Christian people of a specific time, in this case, the beginning. *Ecclesia*, however, should mean the holy Christian people, not only of the days of the apostles, who are long since dead, but to the end of the world, so that there is always a holy Christian people on earth, in whom Christ lives, works, and rules, *per redemptionem*, 'through grace and the remission of sin,' and the Holy Spirit, *per vivificationem et sanctificationem*, 'through daily purging of sin and renewal of life,' so that we do not remain in sin but are enabled and obliged to lead a new life, abounding in all kinds of good works, as the Ten Commandments or the two tables of Moses' Law command, and not in old, evil works. That is St. Paul's teaching.[6]

This is as close to a definition of the church as Luther comes. The first point he makes is that the church is a people *on earth*; it is the earthly, historical manifestation of Christ's body. Luther will not permit an understanding of the church that flies off into mystical,

---

4.   Lull, p. 540.

5.   Similarly Calvin, while maintaining that it is by forgiveness and not by perfection that we are retained in the church, insisted that although justification and sanctification can be distinguished they can never be separated.

6.   Lull, p. 541.

inner spiritualism devoid of earthly rootedness. It is a people *on earth* through whom Christ lives, works, and rules.

In the second place, he says, this living, working, and ruling of Christ takes place through grace and the remission of sin. That is, grace and the remission of sin comprehend the totality of the Christian life. When the Apostles' Creed affirms, "I believe in the forgiveness of sins," it is speaking of the Christian life *in its entirety*.

His third point is the necessity of the Holy Spirit for vivification and sanctification. We have come to see over and over again how rich the whole category of Christian experience is in Luther; the association of Christian experience with the Holy Spirit may not always be explicit in his writing, but is always implicit despite the tendency of later Lutherans to diminish the Spirit's importance in proportion to their approach to rationalism.

Fourth, the church is to be noted as the appearance of the new life on earth: a people on earth whose deeds attest their renewal at God's hands. Faith is invisible, and in that sense the church is invisible; the sociologist can never measure faith, and therefore can never establish by that criterion the identity or boundaries of the church. The confession and works of faith, however, are undeniably visible, and render the church a public event.

In this regard, Luther and the other Reformers all stress the importance of *public* confession of faith.[7] In Romans 10:9, Paul writes, "If you confess with your mouth that Jesus is Lord and believe in your heart that God raised him from the dead, you will be saved" (ESV). In other words, wherever there is faith, there is concomitant public confession; there is no such thing as a secret or anonymous disciple.[8] This scriptural insistence was particularly significant in the sixteenth century, when the costliest price tag was attached to public confession

---

7.   In the spirit of the Reformers see Karl Barth, *Church Dogmatics,* Vol. III.

8.   See Calvin, *Excuse aux Nicodemites.* The English translation by Seth Skolnisky is found in *Come Out from Among Them* (Dallas: Protestant Heritage Press, 2001.

of evangelical faith. Faith itself is invisible—God alone searches the human heart and knows who are his—but the profession of faith, which is essential to faith, is as visible as a "city set on a hill."

To return to Luther's point about the Holy Spirit and the church: he writes,

> For Christian holiness, or the holiness common to Christendom, is found where the Holy Spirit gives people faith in Christ and thus sanctifies them (Acts 15); that is, he renews heart, soul, body, work, and conduct, inscribing the commandments of God not on tables of stone, but in hearts of flesh (2 Corinthians 3).[9]

One reason for this emphasis on the Spirit's sanctifying work in the lives of believers is that Luther, aware that his understanding of justification by grace through faith continues to attract the charge of lawlessness, is always anxious to repel that charge by distancing himself from the Antinomians. About the latter he writes:

> For they, having rejected and being unable to understand the Ten Commandments, preach much about the grace of Christ, yet they strengthen and comfort only those who remain in their sins, telling them not to fear and be terrified by sins, since they are all removed by Christ. They see, and yet they let the people go on in their public sins, without any renewal or reformation of their lives.[10]

The Antinomians, Luther insists, are wrong: we cannot glory in the forgiveness of sins unless we are horrified by our residual sin. Paradoxically, our sin has indeed been removed by Christ, yet the sin that has been so removed ought to continue to horrify us. In fact, this Reformer who is always aware of the deleterious consequences of poor theology puts indifference to the need for godly integrity in the same category as explicit heresy:

---

9. Lull, p. 542.
10. Ibid., p. 544.

Therefore it is certain that they neither have nor understand Christ or the Holy Spirit, and their talk is nothing but froth on the tongue, and they are as already said, true Nestoriuses and Eutycheses, who confess or teach Christ in the premise, in the substance, and yet deny him in the conclusion or *idiomata;* that is, they teach Christ and yet destroy him through their teaching.[11]

Unholiness of life among Christians, he says, is as heretical and Christ-denying as the work of Nestorius or Eutyches.[12] The importance of right theology is often highlighted by Luther as the corrective to deficiencies in the church; here, however, he warns that unholiness among Christ's people is worse than poor theology. People can embrace incorrect theology and yet apprehend Christ, but people who show a cavalier indifference to sin "neither have nor understand Christ."

We have noted, above, Luther's point about the visibility of the deeds and confession of believers. Holiness cannot be reduced to inner mysticism; rather it is necessarily outward and embodied.[13] This outwardness, however, is not that of physical objects and rituals, for it is also true that holiness cannot be institutionalized or reified. It is not a quality attached to things. Luther writes sarcastically of the kind of holiness favored by the pope: "He has to have one that is much holier, namely that found in the prescription of chasubles, tonsures, cowls, garb, food, festivals, days, monkery, nunning, masses, saint-worship, and countless other items of an external, bodily, transitory nature."[14]

---

11. Ibid., p. 544.

12. Nestorius (d. 451) taught a dualistic view of Christ's person, in which his deity and humanity are joined together like two blocks of wood which meet only at the edge. Eutyches (c. 375-454), in opposing Nestorius, advanced the opposite heresy that Christ's deity and humanity are combined in one, single nature.

13. Cf., John Wesley's characteristic "holiness of heart and life." Holiness of heart (so-called) without holiness of life, said Wesley, is but romantic self-indulgence. Holiness of life (so-called) not rooted in holiness of heart is but one more attempt at moralistic self-salvation and religious superiority.

14. Lull, p. 544. It is important to understand that Luther never objected to the papacy in principle. He objected only to its occupants' failure to function as the chief

Far from minimizing sacramental life, Luther judges that the papacy, misreading Scripture and thereby advocating a mechanistic view of holiness, is shortcutting true holiness and so has gone as far astray as the Antinomians.

We would be naïve if we attached this error to any particular denomination or generation. In every place and age there is a tendency among Christians to treat holiness mechanistically by attaching it to a given activity, religious exercise, object, role, or church structure. According to Luther, this is a form of cheap grace that shortcuts true Christian holiness.[15]

THE SEVEN MARKS OF THE CHURCH

The Word

"First," declares Luther, "the holy Christian people are recognized by their possession of the holy word of God. To be sure, not all have it in equal measure, as St. Paul says. Some possess the word in its complete purity, others do not."[16]

The first mark of the church is the Word of God: the Word as the living self-utterance of Jesus Christ, never known apart from Scripture, yet not reducible to Scripture. If the Word were identifiable with

---

pastor, the gospel-informed shepherd of Christ's people. See Scott Hendrix, *Luther and the Papacy* (Philadelphia: Fortress Press, 1981), *passim*.

15.   With regard to holiness, the gap between John Wesley and Luther is much narrower than many people, including Wesley himself, have imagined. Wesley always taught that there was no salvation without holiness, often citing Hebrews 12:14 which refers to "the holiness without which no one will see the Lord" (ESV). But it is clear from Luther's writing that he too believed holiness was essential to the Christian life. The so-called pietistic emphasis on holiness in Bonhoeffer's *The Cost of Discipleship* is a direct reflection of this motif in Luther.

16.   Lull, p. 545. The Pauline text alluded to is 2 Corinthians 3:12-14. Note that in German, all nouns are capitalized; *das Wort* has been translated here by *the word*, but on the basis of what Luther says about this word we are justified in understanding it as *the Word*.

Scripture, it would not make sense to say that some people possess it in its complete purity while others do not, for there are no degrees of possessing Scripture. People and congregations are, however, more or less fogged by accretions other than that Word which is the living self-utterance of Jesus Christ. Nevertheless, even where there are many such accretions, the Word still shines through, sufficient to save, and this presence of the Word is the first mark of the church.

One could say that it is not only the first and chief mark but also the comprehensive and determinative mark of the church; this Word, the living Word, gathers up every other word and every other mark of the church. The Word is the ground of all the other marks. For example, while Luther maintains that an ordained ministry is essential to the body of Christ, he does not consider it as having the same weight as the Word, because the Word is what generates, forms, and informs the ordained ministry. In the same way, crossbearing, another of Luther's marks of the church, is dependent on the Word, since it is not simply suffering but specifically that suffering which is visited upon us on account of our possession of the Word—or better, the Word's possession of us.

The Word of God, then, is the determinative mark of the church, and everything else flows from it. Luther calls it "the principal item, and the holiest of holy possessions, by reason of which the Christian people are called holy; for God's Word is holy and sanctifies everything it touches; it is indeed the very holiness of God."[17] The Word of God is the holiness of God because it is God—not Scripture, but God himself in his self-revelation. The whole life and nature of the church is in the Word of God in that the Word repeatedly creates and constantly sustains the church; the church lives only as the Word "administers" the crucified One.[18] In other words, the church is the ever-renewed miracle of the power of the Word, as the Word brings it to life and shapes the life it brings.

---

17.   Ibid., p. 546.

18.   John S. Whale, *Christian Reunion: Historic Divisions Reconsidered* (Grand Rapids: Eerdmans, 1973), p. 36.

If the Word is not Scripture, it is also not preaching, though clearly all three are related. On the relation of the Word to preaching, Luther says, "But we are speaking of the external word, preached orally by men like you and me, for this is what Christ left behind as an external sign."[19] The Word of God must be embodied in the external sign of preaching: it must be spoken and heard. It is embodied not only as it is declared, but as it is received and becomes embedded in a community. It is not enough for individuals to read Scripture on their own, or for the congregation simply to convene, read the Bible together, and then return home. Much as he believed in the perspicuity of Scripture, Luther knew that the Bible is a difficult and perplexing book for untrained people. He believed it to be transparent enough that a serious, sincere reader can be illumined by the Spirit in such a way as to come to saving faith, but he never settled for such a minimalist approach. Scripture is not transparent in *all* respects, and must be expounded, articulated, and illustrated by people called to and equipped for that particular ministry.

Another reason for the necessity of preaching is the effect of what we see in the world and in our own lives. What we see contradicts the truth to which faith clings; namely, that God loves us even more than he loves himself (having given up his Son for us). Marriages fail, children die, people suffer cruel reversals or are devastated by disease. What can be apprehended naturalistically appears to contradict the bedrock apostolic affirmation, "God is love" (1 John 4:8). In the midst of this, the Word must be spoken, heard, and embedded in our hearts through the activity of the Holy Spirit, because only in that way will what is *heard* overturn or refute the conclusion drawn from what is *seen*. Every day, what we see supports unbelief; what we *hear* is the Spirit-quickened Word.

The Word is also intimately related to confession—not confession of sin, but confession of faith. Luther writes, "We also speak of this external word as it is sincerely believed and openly professed before

---

19.   Lull, *op. cit.,* p. 546

the world; as Christ says, 'Everyone who acknowledges me before men, I will also acknowledge before my Father and his angels' [Matthew 10:32]. There are many who know it in their hearts, but will not profess it openly."[20] At the time of the Reformation the "Nicodemites" were those who knew the Word in their hearts (having come to admit the truth of the Reformers' understanding of the gospel) but would not profess it openly for fear of persecution. Luther maintained that the Word had to be acknowledged openly; we must both believe the Word in our hearts and confess it in public with our lips.[21]

All this is to underscore Luther's insistence that the Word is determinative as nothing else is. "Now, wherever you hear or see this word preached, believed, professed, and lived," he says, "do not doubt that the true *ecclesia sancta catholica*, 'a Christian holy people' must be there, even though their number is very small."[22] Notice the four participial adjectives: the Word must be "preached, believed, professed, and lived" in the church because it is by that Word that the church is constituted. All other human institutions aspire to meet genuine human needs and for this reason are self-invented. The church, on the other hand, does not constitute itself out of recognized human need. The church is constituted by Another, by the Word, and this Word must be preached, believed, professed, and lived. Where the Word meets with that fourfold human response (whose order cannot be reversed), there you have the church.

"God's word cannot be without God's people, and conversely, God's people cannot be without God's word," the Reformer continues. That is to say, God's Word invariably fosters a people, and this people could not endure as God's people for a minute without God's Word. As God declares through the prophet Isaiah, "For as the rain and the snow come down from heaven and do not return there but water the

---

20.   Ibid., p. 546.
21.   See Romans 10:8, 9.
22.   Lull, p. 547.

earth, making it bring forth and sprout, giving seed to the sower and bread to the eater, so shall my word be that goes out from my mouth; it shall not return to me empty, but it shall accomplish that which I purpose, and shall succeed in the thing for which I sent it" (Isaiah 55:10-11, ESV). God's Word will never finally be fruitless; it will always constitute, claim, and commission a people, and that people will be made, directed, and known by that Word alone. In this connection it should be noted that while Luther never minimizes the significance of theology or doctrine, he never equates theology or doctrine with the Word. The Word always transcends, is lord of, Scripture, doctrine, and theology. It is not merely a verbal pronouncement *describing* the victory of Christ, but is itself *charged* with that victory. Always aware of Pauline pithiness, Luther recognizes the gospel to be the *power* of God unto salvation (Romans 1:16), not primarily a statement concerning such power. "Word of God" gathers up the power of Christ, his victory, and his atoning efficacy, with the result that when the Word is declared, the living Christ invariably acts. The gospel is *operative* good news, an announcement effecting what it announces. Simply put, the Word is Jesus Christ himself acting upon us and within us.

Baptism

The second mark of the church, in Luther's list, is baptism. He writes:

> Second, God's people or the Christian holy people are recognized by the holy sacrament of baptism, wherever it is taught, believed, and administered correctly according to Christ's ordinance. That too is a public sign and a precious, holy possession by which God's people are sanctified. It is the holy bath of regeneration through the Holy Spirit, in which we bathe and with which we are washed of sin and death by the Holy Spirit.[23]

---

23.   Lull, p. 548. Note the allusion to Titus 3:5, "He saved us, not because of works done by us in righteousness, but according to his own mercy, by the washing of regeneration and renewal of the Holy Spirit" (ESV). One could question whether this verse necessarily points to baptism. Paul describes regeneration in terms of the

Notice the *realist* understanding of baptism here, that is, the understanding that baptism is efficacious. Baptism, viewed sacramentally, is more than confession; it is not primarily the expression of our response to Christ (important as that is), but the sacrament of what Christ has done for us preveniently to anticipate and facilitate our response.

In some Christian circles the question is raised whether baptism is essential to salvation, by which people mean to determine whether it is permissible to forgo that step. Luther would see this as an altogether inappropriate question. He believes that Christ has appointed and ordained baptism, and has pledged himself unfailingly to us in this act. It remains normative for the church. To step around it, therefore, is an act of willful disobedience. Prayer is also not explicitly identified in Scripture as "essential to salvation", but Luther would find puzzling (if not ludicrous) any Christian who argued that for this reason it was acceptable to forgo prayer.

Communion[24]

The third mark of the church is Holy Communion: "God's people, or Christian holy people, are recognized by the holy sacrament of the altar, wherever it is rightly administered, believed, and received, according to Christ's institution."[25] Once again, because Holy Communion has been

---

metaphor of washing, but there is no reason to assume that every use of this metaphor is to be interpreted as baptism any more than the evangelist's comment on the interstitial fluid ('water') that flowed out of Jesus' side together with the blood.

24. For an amplification of the relation of Word to Eucharist see the chapter on Luther's understanding of Holy Communion.

25. Ibid., p. 549. It is interesting that Luther refers to the holy sacrament of the *altar*. The altar is the venue of Old Testament sacrifice, which Jesus Christ has rendered obsolete by offering himself once for all and living to make intercession for us in heaven as our high priest. On the one hand, as we saw when we studied his view of the Eucharist, Luther distances himself wholly from the Roman Catholic notion of the sacrifice of the Mass. He regards it as a blasphemy because it encroaches upon and in fact denies the sufficiency of Christ's one sacrifice. His use of the word *altar* here is therefore inconsistent.

instituted by Christ, we are not at liberty to absent ourselves from it. The Word is the substance of both baptism and the Lord's Supper, and the Word of God consecrates the people in their priestly ministry. Luther writes:

> Moreover, you need not ask whether you have a tonsure or are anointed. In addition, the question of whether you are male or female, young or old, need not be argued—just as little as it matters in baptism and the preached word. It is enough that you are consecrated and anointed with the sublime and holy chrism of God, with the word of God, with baptism, and also this sacrament; then you are anointed highly and gloriously enough and sufficiently vested with priestly garments.[26]

Since the Word-empowered sacrament qualifies the people of God for their priestly ministry, Luther indicates at this point what would constitute disqualification. Reflecting a long tradition in the church, he discusses Holy Communion in terms of discipline. While he describes discipline as essential to church life, he does not consider it a mark of the church (that is, part of the definition of the church), but rather as an aspect of the correct administration of Holy Communion.[27] "[T]he church, or God's people, does not tolerate known sinners in its midst," he avers, "but reproves them and also makes them holy."[28] Of course, all of us are known in the church, and all of us are sinners; obviously, if "sinners" are expelled categorically, no one will be left. By "known sinners", Luther means the obdurately impenitent, the proudly flagrant. His insistence that the church not tolerate impenitence is in full accord with his declaration that the Word must be *lived* as well as preached, believed, and professed in order to be embodied in the church community.

---

26.   Ibid., p. 549

27.   In fact, the only Protestant Reformer to call discipline a mark of the church was Martin Bucer.

28.   Lull, p. 549.

One might well ask what the difference is between something that is *essential* to the church and something that is a *mark* of the church. After all, once we have recognized the Word as the ground and source of all the other marks, without which they would not be marks of the church at all, we have put the Word in a distinct category. All the other marks are only implicates of the Word, and the same could be argued of discipline. In this respect it is like any other mark of the church. Why, then, does Luther not designate it as such?

One reason that the magisterial Reformers shied away from naming discipline a mark of the church is that they were aware that a church could have discipline while lacking the Word—in which case discipline could never be a mark of the (Word-engendered) church. Another reason is that they wanted—here as elsewhere—to distinguish themselves from the Anabaptists. For the Anabaptists, discipline was a mark of the church, and in the view of the magisterial Reformers they administered it in a way that appeared both punitive (as discipline in connection with sin inherently is) and counterproductive. Miscreants could not only be denied access to worship, but could even be placed under an all-encompassing ban prohibiting members of the religious community from doing any business at all with them. Clearly, anyone subjected to such strictures would be driven to the margins of life.

The magisterial Reformers perceived a one-sidedness in the Anabaptist approach to discipline that undervalued the aspect of restoration. The Anabaptists would say that it *was* restorative, that the hardship of the ban was exactly what would drive people to repent, forsake their sin, and recommit themselves. In all of this, of course, there must be kept in mind what the Anabaptist communities understood and intended, and what appeared to occur among their people—just as there must also be kept in mind what the magisterial Reformers perceived as outsiders and what they would never be able to understand, let alone observe as spiritually helpful, just because they remained outsiders.

It has been traditional to discuss discipline in the context of the Lord's Supper. Even today, many churches use admission or non-admission to Holy Communion as a vehicle of discipline.[29] Those under discipline may be welcome at worship but are asked to refrain from taking the elements. The passage about eating and drinking judgment upon oneself (1 Corinthians 11:29) is customarily recalled to the congregation on such occasions.[30] One wonders, however, whether the measure of non-admission to Communion is taken primarily to protect people from spiritual danger, or to expose them to public recognition and humiliation. The pain of humiliation, rather than the withdrawal of the blessing of Communion, then becomes the vehicle of discipline.

In any era discipline is a difficult area of church life; it requires Solomonic wisdom. On the one hand, moralistic faultfinding is out of place; on the other, notorious sin cannot be winked at. Luther was aware that it is difficult to know how to proceed so as to recognize the assault of scandal upon the church's Lord (not to mention the spiritual threat to others) while aiming compassionately at the restoration of the person under discipline. The risk of seeming to promote one's own moral superiority is always present. Moreover, Luther knew how the church tends to focus arbitrarily on certain categories of sin—especially the sexual—while ignoring others. The Wittenberger, reading Galatians 5:19-24 with practiced eye, knew that strife, jealousy, and dissension are no less ungodly than fornication. Luther knew that covetousness is mentioned in the same verse as fornication in both Ephesians and Colossians, and is explicitly underlined as "idolatry." He recognized that covetousness destroys the community of God's people as little else does, and for this reason he grasped the Old Testament's prohibition against the plundering of defeated enemies, and under-

---

29. E.g., the Brethren assemblies.

30. The judgment to which Paul refers surely has to do not with "unworthy" participation on the part of those who are insufficiently informed as to what the Lord's Supper means or those who lack the requisite sanctity. The church situation in Corinth supports the interpretation, rather, that those who do not "discern the body" are those whose proclivity to bickering, quarrelling, and general contentiousness has advertised them as having failed to recognize the congregation as the body of Christ.

stood why the plundering and hoarding that Achan and his family tried to hide had to issue in their execution.

The Office of the Keys

This fourth mark of the church is crucially important in terms of Reformation history, and, for that matter, in terms of the church's understanding of its life and witness today.

Our Lord says to the disciples after the resurrection, "If you forgive the sins of anyone, they are forgiven; if you withhold forgiveness from anyone, it is withheld" (John 20:23, ESV). This power to forgive and withhold forgiveness has been called the office of the keys, after a similar passage in Matthew in which Jesus refers to the "keys of the kingdom."[31]

There has been much controversy as to the meaning of these words. At the time of the Reformation, Luther and others of like conviction denied that the *institution* of the church possessed the power of the keys through priestly mediation; they denied the prevailing belief that if a priest pronounced absolution in response to confession, the penitent was forgiven, and if the priest did not pronounce absolution, the penitent was not forgiven.[32] The power of the keys did not inhere in the institution, Luther insisted, nor was it vested specifically in the clergy.

Calvin was soon to echo this conviction: the power of the keys is not in the institution, but in the gospel, in the Word. Moreover, for Calvin the Word was a congregational event. The Word forms and enlivens the congregation, and is therefore always found with the congregation. He nevertheless minimized the congregational dimension of the power

---

31.　"I will give you the keys of the kingdom of heaven, and whatever you bind on earth shall be bound in heaven, and whatever you loose on earth shall be loosed in heaven" (Matthew 16:19, ESV).

32.　Given this belief, there were few graver threats in the Reformation era than that of placing a town or city under "interdict." Interdiction meant that all sacramental ministries were withdrawn: no one could be married, baptized, absolved, or given the last rites.

of the keys. The power of the keys is the Word of the gospel, according to Calvin—but then he insists that it is only the ordained ministry that proclaims the gospel. Hence, in his understanding, the power of the keys still ends up effectively vested in the ordained ministry.

Luther, in what might be considered a sounder approach, also relates the keys to the Word, but more particularly to the congregation as Christ's people who are the vehicle of the gospel heard and believed. He writes:

> Fourth, God's people or holy Christians are recognized by the office
> of the keys *exercised publicly* [emphasis added]. That is, as Christ
> decrees in Matthew 18[:15-20], if a Christian sins, he should be
> reproved; and if he does not mend his ways, he should be bound
> in his sin and cast out. If he does mend his ways, he should be
> absolved. That is the office of the keys . . . If God's people are not
> there, the keys are not there either; and if the keys are not present
> for Christ, God's people are not present. Christ bequeathed them
> as a public sign and a holy possession, whereby the Holy Spirit
> again sanctifies the fallen sinners redeemed by Christ's death, and
> whereby the Christians confess that they are a holy people in this
> world under Christ.[33]

In other words, just as Word and people imply and presuppose each other, people and keys imply and presuppose each other: where Christ's people are, the keys are. Where the keys are not, the people are not. Notice the high calling and efficacy of the people of God: they are not merely a ragtag collection, or a group of people with a religious yen. They are not even a community formed around a common interest, however noble. Christ's people are that community whose ministry is to attest Christ's ministry and therein be rendered a vehicle of it.

On the one hand, Christ alone forgives; on the other hand, the church possesses the power of the keys, whereby Christ alone forgives. In other words, the church "unlocks the door" to remission of sin. This

---

33.   Lull, p. 550.

does not mean, however, that the church can manipulate Christ, or that it can decide either to turn the key in the lock or not. The church does not possess the gospel; the gospel possesses the church. The church does not possess Jesus Christ, but forever remains his possession. Still, as a matter of fact, Jesus Christ is known and believed upon for forgiveness of sins only where the church exercises a ministry faithful to him. Apart from that ministry, Christ cannot be heard, known, called upon, and enjoyed. This is a momentous and sobering understanding of the church's vocation. The whole question of the keys—"Whoever's sins you remit are remitted; whoever's sins you retain are retained"—which loomed large at the Reformation and was surrounded with immense controversy, is rarely discussed in church life today, yet it continues to be crucial.

Luther's point is seen also in the commissioning of the Seventy, or the Seventy-two, in Luke 10. "Whoever hears you, hears me," says Jesus in Luke 10:16. That is not to say that the disciples *are* Jesus, that he has collapsed himself into his missioners, for Christ collapses himself into nobody and nothing. Nevertheless he makes his people the vehicle of that ministry by which he is known. The office of the keys, therefore, is the exercise of the church's ministry in the name and spirit of Christ himself. The words of Christ's witnesses are not synonymous with Christ's word, and yet when the former are heard, the latter is heard; specifically, when they are heard he acts—and is received. Luther's understanding of the "keys" is intimately related to his theology of witness, including preaching.

It would appear, then, that according to Luther, Rome institutionalizes the keys and Calvin professionalizes them. Luther said that the power of the keys is the power of the gospel. And the gospel, without being the possession of the church, is nonetheless the truth and reality of the church—and not of the clergy only, but of the whole congregation. The whole congregation articulates and embodies and attests the gospel so that it unlocks the heart of the unconverted. The whole congregation, therefore, and not just the ordained minister, is vested as successor to the apostle in holding the office of the keys.

The Ordained Ministry

When it comes to this fifth mark of the church, there are two lines of argument in Luther. On the one hand, Luther says, "The church is recognized externally by the fact that it consecrates or calls ministers, or has offices that it is to administer."[34] On the other hand, Luther's understanding of the priesthood of the believer, and of the whole congregation holding the power of the keys, seems to cut against the idea of the ordained ministry as a mark of the church. If the whole congregation exercises a priestly ministry and the power of the keys, then perhaps the only function served specifically by the ordained ministry is the preservation of order. Certainly there is a place for ordained ministry as a way of preserving order in church life, lest four hundred people all be clamouring to bear witness aloud on Sunday. But that is different from saying that ordained ministry is essential to the church.

In addition to this administrative function, a number of other functions are often assigned to the minister in Protestant churches: many lay people today see the minister as the *representative* or *spokesperson* of the congregation, or the *rallying point* of the congregation. None of these roles, however, implies that the ordained ministry is essential to the being of the church. To say that the ordained minister maintains order, or acts as the spokesperson or rallying point, renders the ordained ministry purely functional rather than definitive: it serves the well-being of the church, but does not help to define the church. Luther appears to support both sides of this question, but ultimately comes down on the side of ordained ministry as a mark of the church. Once again, he is reacting to the radical Reformers, whose ecclesiology tended not to include the office of pastor and the rite of ordination.

In the quotation at the beginning of this section, Luther uses the term *office*. He also refers to *gift* in this discussion. Speaking of the gifts that God's people have, he says, "The people as a whole cannot do these things, but must entrust or have them entrusted to one person."

---

34.   Ibid., p. 551.

In other words, gifts are given to the church in the form of specially endowed individuals who exercise the gift on behalf of the church as a whole. But what is the relationship of office to gift?

It is debatable whether office, as understood historically, is a concept found in the New Testament at all. The historical understanding of office has been that certain powers pertain to an office, and are conveyed to an individual by virtue of installation in that office. Some scholars would argue, however, that this notion does not occur in the New Testament. It is not the case that someone is brought in and invested with a pre-existing office of apostle, for example, and suddenly has the powers of an apostle. Rather, it is the apostle's vocation in Christ that lends him the power. According to this view, the office does not generate the gift; the church does not start with offices and fill them with people who are then endowed, by virtue of that installation, with the necessary gift. Luther, however, seems in some places to suggest that this is what happens. In others, he emphasizes the gifts of the Spirit that forge the "office", with the congregation in turn recognizing and endorsing the ministry of those upon whom the Spirit has acted.

It is also significant that, despite what he says in the context of baptism about males and females being equally consecrated and anointed to a priestly function, Luther restricts the office of the ordained ministry to males. He writes, "It is, however, true that the Holy Spirit has excepted women, children, and incompetent people from this function, but chooses (except in emergencies) only competent males to fill this office, as one reads here and there in the Pauline epistles that a bishop must be pious, able to teach, and the husband of one wife."[35] That women spoke at worship in Corinth, and that they were leaders in the house churches as mentioned at the end of the book of Romans, is unquestionable. Yet four-fifths of Christendom still does not ordain women: none of the Eastern Orthodox churches ordains women, the Roman Catholic church does not, and large parts of the Protestant church do not. It

---

35. Ibid., p. 551.

has been assumed, on the basis of what are arguably slender exegetical foundations, that women are not to be ordained, and Luther did not question that assumption.

In addition, he makes a rather surprising comment about apostles, evangelists, and prophets: "Now, if the apostles, evangelists, and prophets are no longer living, others must have replaced them, and will replace them until the end of the world."[36] His point here seems to be that the ordained minister replaces all of these essential offices. His remark is odd, however, for whereas evangelists and prophets *must* be replaced in every era, the apostles are by definition unique and irreplaceable; they are normative. When the apostles were alive, it was their living witness that was normative for the church; the apostles having died, we retain their written testimony in the form of Scripture. Their ministry remains normative for the ministry of all others in the church, and in our era this is an enscripturated normativity. This is why the apostles are always mentioned first whenever the New Testament lists the gifts of ministry.[37] We will revisit the relationship between the apostleship and ordained ministry below.

Luther also emphasizes the servanthood of the ordained minister, and does so by contrasting it in his characteristically graphic way with the perceived conduct of the Roman Catholic clergy. "Popes and bishops, indeed, are fine fellows to be bridegrooms of the church—yes, if she were a brothel-keeper or the devil's daughter in hell," he writes. "True bishops are servants of this bride, and she is a lady and mistress

---

36. Ibid., p. 552.

37. Nevertheless, it is notable that Luther includes evangelism among the ministries of the ordained. The evangelist is specified in the New Testament lists of gifts, because all other gifts presuppose the ministry of the evangelist. Without evangelism, there will be no people brought to Christ, hence no one to teach or be taught, no one to exercise the gift of healing, and no one to prophesy. Yet we tend to undervalue this ministry today or confine it to mass evangelism by famous people. Evangelism must take place continuously even inside the church, because not all in the congregation are believers.

over them."[38] With this strong language he intends to convey that the clergy are not the church's masters but its servants. At the same time, when the church is called their "lady and mistress," this does not mean that the ordained minister takes orders from the congregation, but rather that he is to act for the good of the church as a whole and not for his own interest. While the minister is the congregation's servant, the congregation is never the minister's master; Jesus Christ ever remains that, incontrovertibly, since he alone is Lord.

In non-congregationalist denominations today, structures are in place to make clear that the congregation is not the minister's master. For example, in some denominations the minister can be called by the congregation but can be inducted only by the presbytery. Even then, it is only at a still higher level of church government that the minister is ordained, and at an even higher level that he is defrocked if necessary. All this is a way of saying that the minister is not the employee of the congregation and is not at the mercy of the congregation's wishes. At the same time, Luther reminds us, the ordained minister is not lord or boss of the congregation, either; his ministry is that of a servant. He is a shepherd, and while a shepherd has authority over the sheep, the mark of a *good* shepherd is that he gives his life for them. This distinction between authority and authoritarianism is crucial. The Lord and Shepherd of all, of course, is Jesus Christ. Ultimately the ordained minister, pastor of the congregation, has his authority and commission from the hand of the Crucified himself, and exercises his authority in accordance with the example of his Lord.

The metaphor of sheep and shepherd introduces another point about the function of the ordained ministry. Sheep tend to wander and need to be continually kept by the shepherd from going astray. In the same way, a congregation left to itself will invariably drift from the pattern of the apostolic confession by small but cumulative degrees. The apostles, as noted above, are unique and normative, and the ordained minister

---

38.   Ibid., p. 556.

cannot replace them; however, he exercises an apostle-like function by ensuring that the congregation adheres to the pattern of their confession. He is the witness to the apostolic witness, in other words, and in that limited sense carries on the apostolic ministry.[39]

Public Worship

"The holy Christian people are externally recognized by prayer, public praise, and thanksgiving to God," continues Luther. "Where you see and hear the Lord's Prayer prayed and taught; or psalms or other spiritual songs sung, in accordance with the word of God and the true faith; also the creed, the Ten Commandments, and the catechism used in public, you may rest assured that a holy Christian people of God are present."[40]

The sixth mark of the church is *public* prayer, praise, and thanksgiving, and Luther speaks of this in terms of the Lord's Prayer, psalms, hymns, the Apostles' Creed, the Ten Commandments, and the catechism. Plainly, there is a correlation of this notion with that of public confession of Jesus Christ as per Romans 10:9. However, there is more here than confession of faith; this public witness is multidimensional and also includes petition, praise, and instruction in the faith. These four things must all be present, and they must be done *in public*. Christ was not crucified in a corner. His crucifixion was a public event, the church is a public event, and these are its features.

---

39. Nevertheless, given that some theologically sound denominations deny the need for an ordained ministry, one might ask whether it can be considered a mark of the church. It is rather telling that in such denominations, there is still recognized formal spiritual leadership of the congregation. There are elders whose mandate it is to exercise servant authority. They not only keep order; they also minister to the spiritual needs of the congregation and, through their preaching, they evangelize and keep the congregation faithful to the apostolic witness. Even without the formal office or the ceremony of ordination, the gifts associated with it are recognized and exercised precisely because this is essential to the life of the church.

40. Lull, p. 561.

Notice the substance of this public witness. Luther does not say that *any* public display is a mark of the church, but only that public event whose content is the truth of God. Luther knew only too well that much occurs in church life that has little if anything to do with the gospel. The sixth mark of the church, then, is that public dimension of church life which attests the truth and the reality of God.

Crossbearing

Finally, says Luther, the church is marked by crossbearing:

> The holy Christian people are externally recognized by the holy possession of the sacred cross. They must endure every misfortune and persecution, all kinds of trials and evil from the devil, the world, and the flesh (as the Lord's Prayer indicates) by inward sadness, timidity, fear, outward poverty, contempt, illness, and weakness, in order to become like their head, Christ. And the only reason they must suffer is that they steadfastly adhere to Christ and God's word, enduring this for the sake of Christ, Matthew 5[:11], 'Blessed are you when men persecute you on my account.'[41]

Luther has picked up something here which the Protestant churches have largely neglected. We do not expect a mark of the church to be something so physical and gritty, but Luther insists that suffering is one of these marks—not just any suffering, but suffering visited upon Christ's people because of their loyalty to him. By calling it a mark of the church, he is saying that such suffering is part of the church's definition, and that the church does not exist without it.

There is suffering which is simply part of the human condition, such as disease. There is other suffering, however, which is visited upon Christ's people because of their faithfulness to him in conformity to his crossbearing. "No people on earth have to endure such bitter hate," writes Luther, "And all of this is done not because they are adulterers, murderers, thieves, or rogues, but because they want to have none but

---

41. Ibid., p. 561.

Christ, and no other God."[42] This is a suffering that does not loom very large in most congregations, at least in the western world, but it is huge in the New Testament; in fact, Jesus says that there is no discipleship without crossbearing. In Mark 8:34, he calls the crowd and disciples to himself and says, "If anyone would come after me, let him deny himself and take up his cross and follow me" (ESV).

Today, in common discourse, we do not distinguish between suffering and affliction. Where suffering is mentioned in the New Testament, the church's mandated response is to relieve it. In the case of affliction, however, the response for which we pray is *hupomine*, steadfastness. Affliction (the New Testament reserves the word *thlipsis* for "affliction" but not for "suffering") is pain visited upon us because of our loyalty to Jesus Christ; for this reason the only way to relieve it would be to commit apostasy.[43]

Needless to say Luther would disown the chorus sung in churches today wherein worshippers repeat the erroneous proposition, "He bears my guilt, my shame, my cross." It is erroneous because although Christ bears our guilt and our shame, he does not bear our cross. He bore his own, and because he did so, he appoints us to bear ours. We cannot bear his; he will not bear ours. He will help us in the cruciform service to which he has appointed us, and the Holy Spirit will minister to us as Christ was ministered to by the angel in Gethsemane. Still, just as his crossbearing was essential to his vocation as Savior, ours is similarly essential to our vocation as disciples. To the mother of James and John, wanting positions of honor for her two sons, Jesus said, "Can they be baptized with the baptism wherewith I am baptized? Can they drink the cup that I drink?"[44] Claiming a position of honor has nothing to do with discipleship; crossbearing has everything to do with it.[45]

---

42. Ibid., p. 562.

43. One of the finest expositions of this distinction is by Karl Barth, *Church Dogmatics*, Vol. IV, Part 3, "The Christian in Affliction".

44. See Matthew 20:20-28 and Mark 10:35-45.

45. Although crossbearing was a mark of the church for Luther and also for the Anabaptists, it was not explicitly stated to be such by Calvin. Yet Calvin suffered

This is hard for us to hear. We would much rather have the Lord's Supper as a mark of the church than bear a cross. Whereas Luther lived in a truth culture whose two questions were "What *is*?" (that is, what is the nature of ultimate reality?) and "What is *right*?" (that is, what ought we to do in light of what is?), we live in a therapy culture, whose only question is "How does it feel?" When the purpose of life is merely to feel better, crossbearing of any kind is dismissed since it invariably entails feeling worse. Luther, oceans deeper than contemporaneity, maintains that crossbearing always conduces to our sanctification. "[W]hen you are condemned, cursed, reviled, slandered, and plagued because of Christ, you are sanctified," he writes. "It mortifies the old Adam and teaches him patience, humility, gentleness, praise and thanks, and good cheer in suffering ... [I]n that way we learn to believe in God, to trust him, to love him, and to place our hope in him."[46]

These words are paradoxical; we would think that crossbearing bends us away from faith, because we can always relieve ourselves of our suffering by ceasing to believe. Profoundly Luther contradicts us: crossbearing intensifies our faith, because it is only as we are afflicted that we learn to trust God. It is easy to say that we trust him if our lives are pain-free; we do not really know whether we trust God, however, until we are put to the test. It is when our supposed trust in God brings on the world's assault that we learn real trust.

We must remember, too, that it is not only the world that is hostile to the gospel. To the extent that the world, or the spirit of the world, has invaded the church, there is a cross to be borne even within the church. Suffering inflicted by those who are or profess to be our brothers and sisters in Christ is always more painful because of the disappointment and betrayal that accompany it. Luther, we should note, came to face

---

as much as anybody, and an acknowledgment of suffering as a mark of the church is implicit in his writings. His correspondence with the widows of martyred pastors, or with men who suffered extraordinarily, is moving in its tenderness.

46. Ibid., p. 562.

as much opposition from within the Reformation as he had to endure from without it.

In light of his career-long anguish, Luther remained aware that the necessity of crossbearing is not a lesson learned once but instead something that Christians must ever learn anew. One of the most haunting New Testament verses is Hebrews 5:8: "Son of God though he was, he had to learn obedience through suffering." Jesus had to *learn* obedience, and could learn it only through suffering. Luther knew that if this was true of the incarnate Son of God, there is surely no other way for God's people to learn obedience.

10

Church and State

L uther's reputation is undeservedly bad when it comes to the matter of the proper relationship between Christians and the state, mostly because of two misconceptions which are not in fact borne out either by his writing on the topic or by his personal conduct. This chapter aims at providing a more balanced view of his position.

One of the two misconceptions—that Luther believed the authority of the state should never be resisted no matter how unjust—is based on his support of the princes in the peasant uprising of 1524–1525, already alluded to in this book. The uprising was one of several similar insurrections during the Middle Ages and issued directly from the grievous oppression of the peasants. Luther railed repeatedly against the conscienceless, exploitative, and cruel conduct of the princes; he warned them of the inevitable consequences, and when the trouble broke out he supported the peasants in their grievances. However, once the revolt threatened territories with murderous lawlessness, he approved its suppression.

Luther never spoke in a mealy-mouthed way. His edicts about "stabbing the murderous raving hordes of the peasants" must not be read as *carte blanche* for cruelty by the authorities. Luther recognized the wickedness of class exploitation, but he also recognized that today's victim is tomorrow's victimizer. As events in many Latin American and African countries have shown, simply exchanging one oppressor for another does not bring shalom to a society, because the human heart is equally dark in the case of victim and perpetrator. Only the Kingdom of God provides genuine newness. Meanwhile, social order of some kind is necessary for living, and needed no less for the church as it attempts to spread the gospel.

The other popular misconception is that Luther's theology laid the groundwork for the rise of the Nazi regime. According to William Shirer (1904-1993) in his famous book *The Rise and Fall of the Third Reich*,[1] Luther encouraged political quietism. Lutheran Christianity is so occupied with evangelizing and discipling souls, says Shirer, that it completely neglects the political order, leaving a vacuum that can be filled by anything and anyone. Then when the vacuum is filled by someone as wicked as Hitler, it is not the church's business. But this is a wholly inaccurate understanding of Luther, whose idea of the two kingdoms— as we shall see—intends the opposite of political quietism. Church and state are distinct but nevertheless always related, and Christians are never absolved of political or social responsibility. On the contrary, we are freed by the gospel for critical, redemptive service to the state as a vehicle of neighbor-love.

TWO KINGDOMS, TWO KINDS OF GOVERNMENT

The first point to be made is that Luther's teaching on the relationship of church and state is rooted not in philosophy but in Scripture.[2] Traditionally it is philosophers who write ethics, and the ordering of public

---

1. William L. Shirer, *The Rise and Fall of the Third Reich* (Greenwich: Fawcett Publications, 1960).

2. For a concise overview of Luther's teaching on church and state I am indebted to P. Althaus, *The Ethics of Martin Luther* (Philadelphia: Fortress Press, 1972), chapters 4 and 8.

life is a branch of ethics. Luther, however, says that his understanding of the state comes not from Aristotle or Plato or any other philosopher, but from the Word of God.

According to Luther, Scripture contains two kinds of assertions governing life in community. The first is exemplified by the Sermon on the Mount, and pertains to how the disciples of Jesus govern themselves. They do not resort to force, they do not avenge themselves, and they serve one another in love. This is not a way of ordering society; it is a way of ordering life in the Kingdom.

Then there are passages such as Romans 13 and 1 Peter 2, which pertain to secular government—how it has been instituted by God, and for what purpose. Luther would also include here the teaching of the Old Testament that evildoers are to be punished, and the New Testament attitude towards armed combat. He notes that John the Baptist, for example, in his conversation with the soldiers, recognizes their occupation as a legitimate undertaking; he enjoins them not to be cruel or exploitative, but he never says that soldiering is wrong in principle. Even our Lord himself, living in a land occupied by Roman soldiers, does not speak ill of them in principle; as a matter of fact, there is much about soldiering that he finds commendable and co-opts illustratively to describe life in the Kingdom. In the same way, Peter recognizes in Cornelius a God-fearing man brought by grace into the Kingdom, at no point finding this man's vocation as a soldier to be in conflict with his becoming a member of the church.

The point there, of course, is that Luther wants to distinguish himself from the Anabaptists. They saw passages like the Sermon on the Mount as a blueprint for the ordering of all public life, and considered the state and the army, as sword-bearing institutions, to be inherently in conflict with God's Kingdom. Not so, says Luther. Secular government is one of two distinct but related governments, each ordained by God for its own purpose. The other is spiritual government.

THE FUNCTIONS OF SECULAR AND SPIRITUAL GOVERNMENT

Secular government, according to Luther, serves the preservation of the world by protecting physical life and social order. This is the purpose for which God ordained it. The Bible does not teach a body-soul dualism according to which the body is inferior and therefore what happens to it does not really matter.[3] Bodily life is a God-ordained good and is essential to our existence; to be human is to be embodied. The body is the vehicle of the Incarnation, and as such has been dignified and even glorified by that event, since Christ was resurrected and ascended bodily.

To assault my body, therefore, is to assault me, and has far-reaching consequences. The worst feature of such an assault is not that my nose is broken or my eye blackened, but that I am psychologically terrorized and come to fear physical assault, as do those who witness the event or hear about it. Bodily security is always at risk in society and must be preserved by the state in order for life in society to be possible.

But the state is not simply the invention of humankind, the way a society orders itself to preserve itself. Secular government is given by God for the good of everyone, says Luther, to order life in society—if not according to the second table of the Decalogue, then according to the natural law which he believes anticipates it. The state restrains evil negatively, mitigating the outward effects of the Fall, but also exercises positively what Luther calls a parentlike, nurturing office so as to enhance the public good. It nurtures people in those goods which pre-existed the Fall and which remain in spite of it, such as marriage.[4]

---

3. The Lutheran theologian Dietrich Bonhoeffer offers a nuanced discussion of the significance of the preservation of bodily life. See *Ethics* (New York: MacMillan, 1975), chapter IV.

4. Notice that the state considers the preservation of marriage part of its mandate in recognition of the fact that this institution is essential to the well-being, even the preservation, of society. In fact, in the Puritan era in New England, it was not clergy but magistrates who presided at weddings. The point was to ensure that the

The secular government does not announce the gospel, says Luther, but it does express the goodness of God in that social order is a God-ordained good; in upholding a God-ordained good, secular government points to the gospel without actually articulating the gospel. Moreover, insofar as the state maintains social order, it also makes possible the spread of the gospel by the church—even if it perversely opposes that activity.

If secular government serves the preservation of the world, spiritual government serves the redemption of the world by making us truly righteous, and is given by God only to the church. In the Kingdom of God, Christ is King and Lord, and Christ exercises his Lordship by saving those in bondage to sin and death, freeing them from all the demonic powers and the powers of this world. In other words, to be saved by Jesus Christ means that the world no longer has the oppressive thrall over one that it once had. The world can no longer dazzle, capture, or enslave. And it is by means of Word, sacrament, and brotherly consolation, says Luther, that this Lordship of Christ becomes effective in believers.[5]

It is not the case, however, that secular government rules unbelievers exclusively, while believers are ruled by Christ and therefore require only spiritual government. The earlier Luther tended towards this position, but the mature Luther recognized that even the Christian, with his heart renewed at Christ's hand, lives under both governments.

---

whole community—the society, the state—recognized in a publicly-owned ceremony that these two people were married.

5.　　See Althaus, *The Ethics of Martin Luther*, p. 46. No one is surprised to hear Luther mention Word and sacrament, but "brotherly consolation" has an unexpectedly Anabaptist ring. Though he disagreed with the Anabaptists so vehemently on so much, here he agrees with them. In the Puritan era, one hundred years after Luther, we find the Puritans saying that Christian conversation, or brotherly consolation, is a means of grace, and this is echoed one hundred years later still by John Wesley in the eighteenth century. When Paul urges us in Ephesians 4:29b to engage in edifying conversation "that it may impart grace to those who hear," this is what he means. If our speech actually imparts grace to those who hear, then our speech has sacramental force.

We continue to be dogged by the "old" man, and remain part of the earthly society whose order is secured by secular government. Therefore Christians live under both spiritual and secular governments. In other words, God's blessing is twofold.

Similarities Between the Two Governments

With respect to similarities between the two governments, it is important first of all to begin with the fact, already noted, that one and the same God has established both governments. Sin is not the source of secular government. Nor is secular government a function of the state to order itself because it sees, in its great wisdom, that there is a need for some capacity to coerce. Rather, it is God who ordains it for this reason and who is its source. This means, in turn, that rebellion against the state is ultimately rebellion against God. We can see how this statement on its own might be taken as an encouragement of political quietism, but Luther has more to say.

Just as physicians and lawyers assist us where we could only perish by ourselves, says Luther, so do political authorities, and for this reason he refers to them as "saviors." In so doing he is not encroaching on the sole saviorship of Jesus Christ; he is only imitating Joshua, who called the judges of Israel "deliverers" or "saviors."[6] Political authorities are "saviors" in the sense that they preserve the social good and keep society from succumbing to lethal evil.

In fact, secular government is to be a symbol of salvation and the Kingdom of Heaven—not the Kingdom of heaven itself, but a symbol or hint of it. Since Luther understands by the word 'lord' a helping power that we may trust for our earthly good, both Jesus Christ and secular government are lords, even if the latter exercises this office most imperfectly. Now, if we live in a political environment in which the state cannot be trusted at all for our earthly good, we have a different problem on our hands, and this is something we will address later.

---

6.   E.g., Judges 2:16-18.

With respect to evildoers, Luther says, the secular government exercises wrath, force, and punishment, but always in the service of mercy. Criminality must be restrained, and such restraint presupposes the use of force. The ultimate purpose of the restraint of evildoers, however, is their restoration to society; eventually, the person will be released back into the community and we will have to live with him or her. Clearly, then, attention should be given to the manner in which force is used to restrain such persons, lest they be affected in such a way as to make a return to society virtually impossible. Whatever force the state exercises, then, must serve mercy, and this "bottom line" of mercy is something both governments have in common.

After all, Luther says, even under the spiritual government, a preacher must do something besides offer comfort and encouragement. The preacher must exercise a ministry of severity with the congregation, but always guided by the ministry of mercy. Note that severity is not to be understood as lovelessness. The severe word spoken by a pastor might be the most loving thing a parishioner has heard in a long time, if ultimately it serves restoration. In the same way, Luther mantains, the severity and wrath of the secular government may seem unmerciful, yet they are not the least of God's mercies.

It may appear that Luther overemphasizes the legitimacy of political authority and coercion. It is always important to remember that in the sixteenth century people lived constantly on the edge of social chaos, and they knew how terrible such chaos was. Today, for the most part, we do not. Life under a tyrannical government may be exceedingly unpleasant, but at least life is possible. Life in the midst of anarchy soon ceases to be "life." Nevertheless, Luther stops short of promulgating the divine right of kings or upholding political absolutism.

Differences Between the Two Governments

The two governments have their similarities, but also their differences. First, they differ in rank. Spiritual government plainly has the higher rank, because the righteousness it inculcates is the ultimate righteousness, that "alien" righteousness of Jesus Christ by which sinners are set right with God. The righteousness inculcated by the state, on the other hand, is simply right behavior, and not reconstitution of the heart.

The two governments also differ in their *modus operandi*. Spiritual government levels all distinctions: in Christ we are one and we are equal. We often say in the church that the ground at the foot of the cross is level, meaning that I as clergyman have the same standing in Christ as the newest Christian convert. We are alike sinners saved by grace.

Secular government, on the other hand, maintains a hierarchical distinction. The Prime Minister is the Prime Minister, and no one else is; the professor and the parent exercise an authority that the student and the child lack; a physician may write a prescription, whereas others may not. Luther insists that the form of government maintained by the state, unlike that of the church, is necessarily hierarchical—that is, this hierarchy is necessary for social order. Secular government recognizes that not everybody is equally intelligent or talented or qualified; it recognizes a natural inequality which is not thereby unjust. In the spiritual kingdom, however, there are no such distinctions.[7]

A third difference between the two kingdoms lies in the expression of their rulership. In spiritual government, rule is exercised through love, while in secular government it is exercised through justice. That justice must always be modified by equity, says Luther, lest it turn out to be unjust. That is, a principle applied with absolute consistency to all persons regardless of mitigating circumstances, and without accounting for need, ability, motive, and so on, ends up being unjust. Consider a theft committed by a woman whose husband has left her with four young children, who has just been discharged from the psychiatric hospital and has no money to feed her family; we recognize that this situation should be dealt with differently from theft by someone unencumbered by these

---

7.   It is important in this discussion not to confuse spiritual government with the institutional government of the organized church. Clearly, differences in gifts, experience, and so on are relevant for the latter, which is actually a form of secular government.

pressures. Nevertheless, it is the concern for justice that accommodates, and even mandates, all such considerations.

The kind of response elicited by each government is also different. Under spiritual government, the authority attempts to elicit free, glad, voluntary obedience, whereas under secular government, obedience is enforced by the power of coercion. It is interesting to note that in our democratic society we are sometimes surprised and even outraged when the government exercises its powers of coercion—for example, to end a strike that is damaging to the social order. We forget that a monopoly on power is part of the very nature of secular government. In our democratic system we can vote a government out if we do not approve of it, but all we are doing in that case is changing the platform; we are not altering the principle that government monopolizes power. Some readers of Luther bristle when they find him saying that the state has authority to coerce. The fact is, however, that every state has such authority to coerce, or it is not a state.

The two governments differ, fifthly, in their relation to sin. In the spiritual government, forgiveness is exercised by the Word, while under secular government, retribution and punishment are wrought by the sword. Note that Luther uses the word 'sin' in both cases. Today we would use the word 'crime' for that wrongdoing to which the secular government responds with the sword. We would say that sin is to be forgiven by the Word, but crime is to be punished and restrained by the sword, sin being a violation of God and crime a violation of the state, by definition. Luther recognizes this distinction between sin and crime but, living as he did in Christendom, he gathers both up under the heading of sin.[8]

---

8. Although the distinction between sin and crime is defensible, obviously there are actions which belong to both categories. The line between them is drawn differently, of course, in different jurisdictions; but in general, as the society is secularized the line between sin and crime becomes wider and wider. In most jurisdictions it is not a crime to seduce someone's spouse, but it is a crime to steal someone's car. Yet which causes a greater or more harmful loss? Against what sort of harm should

Finally, spiritual and secular governments differ with respect to the role of reason. Under spiritual government, reason always subserves revelation, and it should be clear from all we have said so far about fallen humanity why this must be the case. Under secular government, which is not a vehicle for the reconstitution of humanity, reason rules. Luther says that positive law—the the law enacted by the state—is grounded in natural law, to which we have access by reason. It is to be tested by reason. We do not test the gospel by reason, because the gospel corrects our reason (vitiated by the Fall with respect to the truth of the gospel) and brings us that reality to which reason itself has no access. Christians, in other words, honor God by remaining rational without becoming rationalists.

Mutual Dependence of the Two Governments

As we have seen, the two governments are distinct, each having its own jurisdiction. However, they are related to each other and belong to each other, according to Luther.[9] In his tract *Temporal Authority* (1523), he writes:

> [One] must carefully distinguish between these two governments. Both must be permitted to remain; the one to produce righteousness, the other to bring about external peace and prevent evil deeds . . . . Where temporal government or law alone prevails, there sheer hypocrisy is inevitable, even though the commandments be God's very own. For without the Holy Spirit in the heart no one becomes truly righteous, no matter how fine the works he does. On the other hand, where the spiritual government alone prevails over land and people, there wickedness is given free rein and the door is open for all

---

we be able to invoke the protection of the state? Such questions bear on the issue of the Christian's penetration of society in general, but also the Christian's role with respect to informing the state and holding political office. It is a much subtler and more nuanced issue than we often think.

9.   He is not unique in this view, as Calvin says the same in his *Institutes*, Book IV.

manner of rascality, for the world as a whole cannot receive or comprehend it.[10]

Only the spiritual government facilitates true righteousness—that of Christ—and it does so only in believers through justification and sanctification. Secular government can only attempt to restrain evil deeds, and can do nothing about evil inclinations or aspirations. At the same time, secular government is necessary, not only because there are unbelievers who behave without consideration for the Law of God, but also because of the residual sin that haunts believers; it would be naïve to suppose that all Christians can be trusted to do what is right just because they are Christians.[11] To be sure, "...Christ did not wield the sword," Luther continues, "or give it a place in his kingdom. For he is a king over Christians and rules by his Holy Spirit alone." At the same time, Luther is aware that the "old" man or woman continues to dog Christians. For this reason even the godliest require the state. Luther would acknowledge, with Calvin, that Christ is indeed king over the whole cosmos; yet his rule is effective or operative in the hearts of Christians and is exercised by the Holy Spirit. The Holy Spirit is not the power of Christ's rule in the state, on the other hand.

Moreover, while the spiritual government alone pertains to the eternal, the secular government serves it indirectly by maintaining the temporal earthly order without which the gospel cannot be preached. Had it not been for the *pax Romana*, for instance, the Christian faith would never have spread beyond Palestine. Admittedly, Peter and Paul

---

10.　Lull, *Martin Luther's Basic Theological Writings* (Minneapolis: Fortress Press, 1989), p. 677.

11.　A page later in the same tract, Luther describes the rule of the state as "not essential" to the Christian. Although the tract is not one of the earliest of Luther's writings, statements such as this one are more in keeping with the earlier than the later Luther. In later life, Luther would insist on the reality of residual sin in the life of the believer. But even where he describes the state as inessential to the Christian, he writes that the Christian submits willingly to its authority so that it will continue to function for the good of all.

perished in the reign of Nero (37-68), and the state has harassed Christians at different times. But as a matter of fact, apart from the Roman road system and Roman order and security, the first Christian missionaries could not have survived to bring the gospel to hearers, nor would the latter have been able to listen and respond.

This mutual dependence of spiritual and secular government involves a fine balance in the exercise of temporal authority, concerning which Luther writes:

> We must now learn how far its arm extends and how widely its hand stretches, lest it extend too far and encroach upon God's kingdom and government. It is essential for us to know this, for where it is given too wide a scope, intolerable and terrible injury follows; on the other hand, injury is also inevitable where it is restricted too narrowly.[12]

Temporal authority cannot extend limitlessly, or the state will control the church, as happened in Nazi Germany. On the other hand, if temporal authority does not extend far enough, society will break down, and with it the conditions essential to the church's mission. No little wisdom is required by the public administrator in order to maintain this balance; Luther describes the responsibility as a heavy burden that incurs for its bearer "much envy and sorrow."[13] At the same time, he is quick to recognize that very few officeholders have the requisite character: "You must know that since the beginning of the world a wise prince is a mighty rare bird, and an upright prince even rarer. They are generally the biggest fools or the worst scoundrels on earth."[14] Secular government is therefore usually badly executed, but remains God-ordained and is manifestly better than the alternative.

There is all the more reason then for Christians, who are under spiritual government, to contribute by acting as leaven as well as by holding office. Spiritual government ought always to inform secular

---

12. Lull., p. 678.
13. Ibid., p. 700.
14. Ibid., p. 687.

government, for a society properly maintains law and order only as it knows God and his truth. Only the proclamation of the Word, says Luther, enables us to see that secular government is of God, but is not itself divine; that its authority is legitimate, yet is not the ultimate authority. Without the gospel, without an awareness of accountability to God, secular government will invariably move in the direction of tyranny and self-idolization; it will always absolutize itself. Such self-idolization Luther never supports.

THE SERMON ON THE MOUNT

The Roman church said that the Sermon on the Mount was a counsel of perfection for people who enter a religious order, but was not applicable to Christians in the secular world.[15] Christians in a convent or monastery were deemed spiritually superior to lay Christians living in the world, who could not be expected to follow the letter of Christ's teachings in, for instance, the Sermon on the Mount. Luther disagreed. First of all, he declared that lay people are not spiritually inferior. Second, the Sermon on the Mount is the word and gift and command of God for all Christians.

The radical Reformers, far as they were from the Church of Rome, maintained that in order to obey Christ, all Christians must extricate themselves from the world and turn their back on the state. Christians must have nothing to do with private property, the courts or penal system, the swearing of oaths, the holding of government office, law enforcement, or war. In fact, in their withdrawal from the world and its corrupt systems they have no accountability to the state at all. They may occupy the same territory as others, but they are not citizens of it inasmuch as they are citizens of another kingdom and live under a different Lord. The Sermon on the Mount and similar passages supersede state law.

---

15.   See Lull, p. 656f. and Althaus, pp. 62-66.

Luther opposed the view of the radical Reformers as well. As far as private property is concerned, Luther never supported rampant acquisitive capitalism, but he did support the right to private ownership, and believed that the government was mandated to preserve this right. At the same time he maintained that the gospel gives us freedom from this world's goods; our possessions are not to possess us. Whether we own much or little, we must view our possessions with detachment, "having nothing, yet possessing everything" (2 Corinthians 6:10). Moreover, our goods ought to be used in the service of the community. Luther's word here is as startling as it is unwelcome today: "Anything left over that is not used to help our neighbor is possessed unjustly, it is stolen in God's sight, for in God's sight we ought to give and lend and let things be taken from us."[16]

In fact, we must be willing to surrender everything, if necessary, for obedience to the first commandment, our confession of faith, and our discipleship. Luther points out that Jesus Christ—who himself wore a robe so fine that the soldiers gambled for it—did not require all disciples to abandon all possessions, but he did require them to be prepared to do so if God so called them. Different levels of material renunciation are required of different Christians, just as celibacy may be required of certain believers and not others: Paul says that the other apostles have the comfort of a wife, whereas he does not. For the sake of our discipleship the Lord may require the renunciation of something that is good in itself but that now impedes our obedience.

With respect to our relation to the state, Luther disagreed with the Anabaptist claim that we do not live under its authority, but he did speak of an emergency situation in an extraordinary hour that might call for unusual action from believers. Although these situations cannot call into question the principle that governs the ordinary situation—namely, submission to secular authorities—they do arise. Dietrich Bonhoeffer, a thoroughgoing Lutheran, would have had in his bloodstream all of

---

16. See Althaus, op. cit., p. 65.

Luther's thought on this topic, including his recognition that most princes are "fools or scoundrels." It is not to the perfect secular government that the Christian owes obedience, said Luther, for that can never be found. Rather, we owe obedience to the secular government that exists by God's mandate.

On balance, secular government is stupid and mean, but the alternative, again, is anarchy. At what point, then, does it become so stupid and mean that it can legitimately be resisted by force of arms? What constitutes the emergency that calls for unusual action? Bonhoeffer, having agonized over this question, became involved in a plot to assassinate Hitler. He felt that he was living in an "extraordinary hour" of the kind Luther mentioned, that the state had so violated its God-ordained mandate that submission to it was no longer required—or even permitted. Bonhoeffer could have survived if he had remained silent and taken no action, but he was acquainted with Luther's writing concerning civil disobedience and agreed that *in extremis,* the Christian can kill legitimately. The agony of the heart is in determining when this point is reached.

What of the Christian's participation in government? Luther points out that we are related directly to others as Christian persons, and indirectly to others through social structures. Both kinds of relationship are ministry, and both entail a readiness to serve the neighbor in love. I am related directly to my immediate Christian brother and sister in congregation and life, but I am also indirectly related to the woman on welfare in a distant city through the social structures of the state. Both my direct and my indirect relationships ought to be a ministry of love.

One of the ways we can fulfill the ministry of love in our indirect relationships is through active participation in government. In other words, secular government can be a vehicle of neighbor-love. Luther believed that holding political office was a divine calling and that Christians should offer themselves for such service in order to minimize the likelihood of abuse of power. In our day there is enormous cynicism around politicians; we look upon them as treacherous, and some may be. But unless someone in our society is willing to shoulder the burden of political office, what is the alternative? The office is necessary for the public good, and as such it ought to be occupied by the best people possible. In contradiction of the Anabaptists, therefore, Luther said that Christians ought to be willing to hold political office.

At the same time, Christians in political office exercise a secular mandate. They do not use their secular office as a means of privileging themselves, the church, or Christian causes. Neither do they let their reactions as Christians—for example, to heinous crime—control their work in secular office. Regardless of how they feel about victim or perpetrator, Christians in secular office are pledged to uphold the criminal justice system of the state, without which there remains only a form of 'justice' that is no more than lawless vigilantism.

In other words, says Luther, the severity of secular government as exercised by the Christian in office is not the Christian's personal severity, but the necessary severity of the state. By the same token, a Christian civilian, while pledged to the forgiveness of offenses, may nonetheless invoke the retribution of the secular courts in order to uphold public order, and these two positions are entirely compatible. If our car is stolen, we are called to forgive the offender his offense against us, but the theft is not an offense against the individual only. It is an offense against society, and therefore requires a societal response. The individual Christian's renunciation of revenge and offer of forgiveness to the offender attest a gospel spirit, but they do not undercut society's response to criminality.

In *Temporal Authority*, the tract already referred to, Luther writes, "Although you do not need to have your enemy punished, your afflicted neighbor does."[17] As a Christian I may, and should, forgive the offender from my heart. However, I must ensure that he is also punished, lest I fail my neighbor in love by neglecting to safeguard her from further offence. If someone is assaulted, everyone is at risk of being similarly assaulted unless the situation is dealt with. In the absence of retribution by the

17.   Lull, p. 669.

state, not only will the offender likely re-offend, but others will follow his example so that my neighbor is increasingly violated as offences multiply. There are, of course, those victims of offense for whom the punishment of the offender is a vehicle of personal vengeance; they relish the offender's suffering. That does not mean, however, that the action the state takes in punishing criminality is inherently vengeful. It is serving the neighbor in love by maintaining safety and peace.

Luther's point in all this is that we need the response of the Christian in both roles. We need the response of Christians to their neighbors in direct personal relationship and in indirect relationship as agents of the secular government. "Therefore," he writes in *Temporal Authority*, "if you see that there is a lack of hangmen, constables, judges, lords, or princes, and you find that you are qualified, you should offer your services and seek the position, that the essential governmental authority should not be despised and become enfeebled or perish. The world cannot and dare not dispense with it."[18] We may be a little uncomfortable with this exhortation to take on the office of the most heavy-handed in a society—the executioners as opposed to the social workers—but this is simply Luther's realism. Having made clear that punishment by the state is necessary, he is saying that unless office in the secular government is filled, particularly by the right people, the whole society is at risk.

We may not want the job of prison guard. As a matter of fact, however, someone in the society must do this job. Law enforcement is one of the hardest jobs in society. On the one hand, if the police operate always according to the letter of the law, the public will quickly become enraged at them. On the other hand, if they wink at violation of the law, they will be accused of failing the public. It is extremely difficult to know how rigorously to apply the law. The same is true for judges, who must decide when true equity requires that they make an exception; after all, as noted above, perfectly consistent justice is inevitably unjust

18. Ibid., p. 669.

and oppressive. In view of this delicacy, Luther would ask, whom do we want exercising the job of constable, hangman, and judge on behalf of society?

In defending the right of the state to wield the sword, Luther does not lose sight of the fact that secular government is ordained by God, and as such is not a parallel authority to God's but rather an authority under God and answerable to God. The Sermon on the Mount does not represent an inherent conflict with secular government, but such conflict may arise. We must disobey secular government if it asks of us anything that contradicts God. Clearly, as in the case of Bonhoeffer, this requires discernment, but we must not decline exercising such discernment for fear of being wrong.[19]

COMMON CRITICISMS ADDRESSED

There are two main criticisms of Luther's doctrine on church and state. One is that it limits the claim of Jesus Christ to be Lord of all areas of life and of the world, confining his lordship to the church and issuing in a compartmentalization that fails to acknowledge the Christian's task as an agent of transformation in the world.

The second criticism is that Luther fails to take account of Revelation 13, in which the state is revealed to be the monster, that beast from the abyss who devours the saints of God. According to this view, the two kingdoms do not serve each other at all but are antithetical.

In response to the first criticism, Luther would reply that Christ is acknowledged as Lord by the Christians who serve in the secular orders, whereas the orders themselves acknowledge no such lord. However, the fact that the orders do not acknowledge Christ as Lord never means that they are lords unto themselves. When Jesus is challenged about paying taxes in Matthew 22 and asks whose image is on the coin, the implication is that by God's appointment Caesar has a legitimate claim in Caesar's

---

19.   In a subsequent section of this chapter, the question of legitimate resistance to temporal government will be addressed at greater length.

sphere. Luther would say that Jesus Christ is ultimately Lord of the state because he is Lord of the entire cosmos; however, he rules the church and the Christian by the gospel and the Holy Spirit; that is, in a way that he does not rule in the state. His lordship of the church is owned and confessed, while his lordship elsewhere is hidden and even disputed. The resurrection has established Jesus Christ as Lord of the cosmos, but the *parousia* (literally, 'presence') will render this lordship incontestable. Until then, Christ's sovereignty is disputed.

In any case, we cannot expect the state to be the church, according to Luther; it has a different function. Recall that the state is not mandated to obey the gospel; it is mandated, rather, to promote social order so that the church may obey the gospel.

Concerning the second objection, that according to Revelation 13 the state and church are not servants of each other but seem to be entirely at cross-purposes, Luther would say that the real conflict is not between the Kingdom of God and secular government but between the Kingdom of God and the kingdom of Satan. The "kingdoms of this world" by definition oppose God and are hence identical with the kingdom of Satan; they are not the state, because the state does not oppose God by definition, although it may come to do so in practice. It is God who institutes both spiritual and secular government for our good, and Satan who attempts to undo both. In other words, what is antithetical is the work of Satan on the one hand and divinely mandated government, whether secular or spiritual, on the other.

Luther would also say, however, that secular government is far less at risk through Satan's molestation than spiritual government; Satan can do far more damage in the church than in the state, and therefore church office is a greater spiritual risk than office in the state. To see his point one need only think of the damage done, for example, when a church officeholder betrays the gospel.

Luther's teaching here on the work of Satan vis-à-vis the two kingdoms is important for us today. The political right today tends to see the state and the church as hand in glove, while the political left sees the state and the church as wholly antithetical. Both positions are wrong, according to the Wittenberger. While God mandates different functions for church and state, one is not in principle the contradiction of the other. Rather, Satan is the contradiction of both.

Luther was able to proceed on the assumption of Christendom— not that everyone in Christendom was a *bona fide* believer, but at least everyone, including those in political office, admitted that the gospel was the "indirect lighting" of the society. (Those who were not even apparently Christian—Jewish and Islamic people, for example—would not have been allowed to hold office in Luther's era.) Given today's pluralism it is considerably more challenging for a Christian to hold political office and maintain a Christian witness. The much-touted separation of church and state, which really means that the state is not allowed to encroach upon the faith that the church upholds, has come to mean that people of faith must not permit that faith to influence how they think about politics. Any officeholder perceived to be doing so is faulted and risks being ousted in the next election.

In such a society it might seem that the radical Reformers were right: it is impossible to hold political office and maintain a Christian witness. Christians who are descendants of the magisterial Reformers, however, will not give up the struggle so readily, knowing that their abandonment of public life can only leave society in worse condition.

The demands of the state or of political office may at times conflict with what God requires of us, though we know that believers will never reach agreement on where to draw the line. An Anabaptist would deny the state the right, in principle, to conscript Christians for military service, because the Christian by definition cannot bear arms. Luther would say that the state does have the right to conscript, for otherwise it cannot wage a war to resist aggression—this being the only kind of permissible war in his view. However, even if we grant that the state does have the right, in principle, to conscript, that does not mean that it has the right to conscript for any and every military objective. Should a Christian ever resist the draft, or even work against the military objectives of the state? The same questions apply to other acts of civil disobedience. That is why Bonhoeffer and others like him—such as Martin Niemöller (1892-1984),

Franz Hildebrandt (1909-1985), and other members and martyrs of the Confessing Church in Germany—suffered such anguish. There is no denying the torment in the Christian mind and heart concerning such matters.

Similarly, we might as Christians be committed to public education yet be unable to defend a particular practice or notion embraced by the public school system. At what point do our legitimate concerns render us unable to support public education? The answer will vary from one believer to another. The bottom line, for Luther, is that although the state may come to oppose the Kingdom of God, it does not do so by definition. It is mandated by God and remains answerable to God, even while its function differs from that of the church.

WHETHER AUTHORITY MAY BE RESISTED

The tract *Temporal Authority* has been cited several times above. Notably, it was subtitled *To What Extent It Should be Obeyed,* making clear that, at least at that point in his life, Luther was prepared to discuss limits to the authority of the state.

Luther tended towards the view that any resistance people offer the state is to be passive, because mob rule—social chaos—is worse than political tyranny. He did not support the destruction of social order in the name of resisting a tyrant. He even said that when tyranny becomes unbearable, God himself will depose the tyrant—a view that seems naïve.

However, Luther also declared it permissible to remove a ruler by force if he or she is insane. The question, of course, is how such insanity is to be recognized. We can recognize the worst derangements of the psychotic, but where is the boundary between behavior that is extremely ill-advised and destructive and behavior that is clinically pathological?

There were other situations which, according to Luther, justified taking up arms against a tyrant, one being the threatened re-imposition of Roman Catholicism: in this case, said the older Luther, the people had a right to mount armed opposition. His point was not that force was legitimate only when it was a question of establishing Lutheranism, advancing his own theological interests, or spreading the gospel; he knew the gospel could not be spread by force. His point, in view of the real possibility of the Holy Roman Emperor wanting to re-impose Catholicism by force of arms, was that such an action would be a violation of the people by the state. Any attempt to impose a religion by force may appear to be a religious cause, but in fact the resort to armed invasion makes it a political one. (The question can always be raised about the re-imposition of Roman Catholicism by non-foreign authorities. Before we dismiss Luther as an anti-Catholic bigot, we should ask ourselves how Christians would respond, or should respond, if a duly sanctioned government outlawed Christian faith.)

Luther, Jonas (1493-1555), Bucer (1491-1591), and Melanchthon (1497-1560) agreed that armed resistance is permissible if a ruler perpetrates injustice, since natural law teaches that official violence dissolves all obligations between subjects and rulers. The appeal to natural law is something we have come across before in Luther's understanding of the state, and it is problematic. Today there is little recognition of natural law; and among those who uphold it, little agreement as to its content. In any case, Luther said at the outset that his teaching on church-state relations was to be grounded not in philosophy but in Scripture, and while one might recognize natural law as an occasional motif in Scripture (e.g., Romans 1 and Acts 17), it is adduced only to expose the sinner's lack of excuse; it is not advanced as the foundation of the state.

The Magdeburg Confession, a Lutheran ecclesiastical document written in 1550, stated that no obedience is owed a ruler who endeavors to lead people "away from the true fear of God and honorable living," for then the ordinance of God has become an ordinance of the devil and is to be resisted "with good conscience." In other words, if the state, not content with preserving order and exercising its proper parental function, inculcates immorality or unbelief or engages in idolatrous self-aggrandizement, it forfeits its claim to the citizen's obedience.

There is a fine line, however, between what the state mandates and what it permits, and what it permits today it often encourages or even requires tomorrow. For example, a state may lay a charge of infanticide against someone who stabs a child just as it emerges from the mother's body, but permit partial birth abortion, or even recommend abortion as population control. At what point is the state deemed to be leading people away from the fear of God and honorable living, and therefore to have forfeited its claim on the citizen's obedience? Would forfeiture of its claim in one instance (or in several) nullify the legitimacy of that state as a whole? If so, who or what would maintain public order instead?

Whether or not we agree with Luther on the applicability of his criteria for resisting state authority, the point to be taken is this: while it is not easy to disentangle our obligation to the state from the requirements of God, we must endeavor to do so. We must resist the tendency, as well, to sacralize a particular political position. Neither the political left as such nor the political right is closer to the Kingdom; all political parties and perspectives are equidistant from it. The church of Jesus Christ, which is necessary to attest the Kingdom of God, is yet not synonymous with it; how much less synonymous are the Kingdom of God and any political party.

WAS LUTHER A WARMONGER?

A previous section raised the question of the Christian's attitude to war, and identified Luther as supporting wars of defense only. He has, however, come under attack from some quarters as a warmonger. This may seem an odd accusation in view of the charge of political quietism also leveled at him, but in fact he has been criticized from both sides. Both charges are hard to justify.

Luther tirelessly insisted that people must protest and resist governmental evil, and considered that the pulpit ought to exemplify public rebuke of the state's malfeasance. He maintained that cowardly preachers who would not speak up were "unfaithful pigs." This is scarcely an exhortation to quiescence or quietism.

Luther also opposed all wars of aggression, declaring that the state has a right to defend itself against invasion but not to wage war for territorial acquisition. It is hard to imagine how this understanding of the state could underlie German expansionism, particularly in World War II.

Finally, Luther insisted that soldiers should disobey any order that clearly contradicts God's commands. Soldiers too ought to obey God rather than human authorities, in light of the apostolic precedent of Acts 4. Even in the context of a legitimate war, therefore, he was unwilling to give the state *carte blanche*.

Even Luther's response to the peasant revolt argues against his theology providing justification for German aggression, if only because it indicates his refusal to sacralize any political cause. As noted earlier, Luther first faulted the princes for oppressing the people and sympathized with the peasants' grievances, but later opposed the peasants' bloody anarchy and their attempt to baptize their grievances as holy war. Then, after the princes had put down the revolt with his support, Luther rebuked them for their excesses, denouncing them as "furious, raving, senseless tyrants who, after the battle, still don't have their fill of blood."[20] "I have feared both," he wrote. "Had the peasants become lords, the devil would have become an abbot, but if tyrants become lords, the devil's mother becomes an abbess . . . Hellfire, trembling, and clattering teeth will be their eternal reward if they do not repent."[21]

There is one holy cause, said Luther, and that is the gospel: gospel, church, and Kingdom. Far from undergirding the idolization of the state in the Nazi era, Luther's doctrine of the two kingdoms actually de-idolizes the state and all political causes, and recognizes the supreme authority of God over both kingdoms.

---

20. Uwe Siemon-Netto, *The Fabricated Luther: The Rise and Fall of the Shirer Myth* (St. Louis: Concordia Publishing House, 1995), p. 77.

21. Ibid., p. 78.

It should be clear by now that Luther was neither a political quietist who created a vacuum to be conveniently filled by Hitler, nor a warmonger who is prepared to co-opt the power of the state to advance his theological interests and put down people he finds objectionable. Luther is far more subtle and nuanced. He is also realistic, because he knows how treacherous the human heart is. This reality underlies the very necessity of the state as well as its vulnerability to abuse and its fundamental inability to produce genuine righteousness. Meanwhile, the spiritual government is able, insofar as Christ is its operative Lord and insofar as social order is maintained by the due exercise of temporal authority, to be a leavening and transforming force; it is also the source of enlightenment as to the true nature and mandate of secular government. Christians have a responsibility to serve their neighbors, both directly as private individuals and indirectly as participants in social systems. They must forgo vengeance and the pursuit of selfish gain, and if qualified—only if qualified, for the demands are as great as the inherent spiritual risk—should be willing to assume the high calling of public office. Since all government is, in principle, ordained by God, submission to it is proper; for the same reason, however, it must be resisted if it contradicts, in practice, the commands of God—a situation easy to declare but often extraordinarily difficult to discern.

11

Luther on Marriage

Three things typified the spread of the Reformation in German-speaking lands. The first and most notorious, of course, was the teaching of justification by faith, a doctrinal issue that stood at the center of the Reformation: God justifies the ungodly through the merits of Jesus Christ his Son. The second, less well known, was the practice of allowing the laity to receive Holy Communion in both kinds, a change whose significance we have already discussed. The third, related to the other two, was marriage among the clergy.

THE PREVAILING MEDIEVAL VIEW OF MARRIAGE[1]

The Reformers' estimation of marriage differed from the view, both written and unwritten, that prevailed during the late medieval era.

---

1. For a more detailed discussion of this topic see Steven Ozment, *Protestants: The Birth of a Revolution* (New York: Doubleday, 1993), chapter 7 and *The Reformation in the Cities* (New Haven: Yale University Press, 1975), chapter 3; and Paul Althaus, *The Ethics of Martin Luther* (Philadelphia: Fortress Press, 1972), chapter 5.

Generally speaking, in the church of that era, marriage was deemed to be an unhappy estate, frequently problematic. For one thing, it was considered inferior to a life of celibacy, for reasons we will examine. In addition, marriage was seen to be vitiated by the depravity of women. Women were thought to pose an extraordinary threat to the faith and the integrity of males. They had, after all, been the downfall of Adam, Samson, David, and Solomon. There was even, in the Aristotelian school of thought, the idea that women were botched males; Aristotle had said that if copulation and conception were error-free, a male would result every time.

Luther became the primary critic of this Aristotelian view of women. He also faulted the church fathers—Jerome, Cyprian, Augustine, and Gregory in particular—for not having written positively about marriage. Augustine, for instance, had said that the pleasure inherent in sexual intercourse betokened the problem of original sin passed on in conception. He had maintained that if sexual intercourse could occur without any hint of pleasure on the part of either participant, the child so conceived would be born without taint of original sin.[2] All such notions Luther opposed in such pithy pronouncements as, "Whoever is ashamed of marriage is also ashamed of being and being called human...."[3]

A vernacular catechism that made its way around Germany in 1444 exemplifies the sort of teaching the Reformers had to contend with. It expatiated on the various ways in which lay people commit the third deadly sin—that is, the sin of lust—in what it called the "marital duties"; the latter posed a danger only to the laity, of course, since the

---

2.   Concerning human genitalia, Augustine wrote, *"Ecce unde.* That's the place! That's the place from which the first sin is passed on." In the same vein Augustine assumed, and appealed to, his congregation's sense of shame at nocturnal emissions. (*Sermon,* 151, 8. Quoted in P. Brown, *Augustine of Hippo* [Berkeley: University of California Press, 1967], p. 388).

3.   *Weimar Ausgabe,* 18.277; quoted in Heiko A. Oberman, *Luther: Man Between God and the Devil* (New Haven: Yale University Press, 1982), p. 272.

clergy were not married. "Unnatural" acts and positions in intercourse were one way of committing the third deadly sin, an unnatural act or position being one that maximized pleasure while minimizing the likelihood of conception; masturbation, that is, stimulation of one's spouse to orgasm without actual penetration, was an unnatural act, as was any form of contraception or birth control. A second way of sinning in the marital duties was to fantasize about sex with a non-spouse while having intercourse with one's spouse. Another way was to withhold sex for no good reason, thereby precipitating one's spouse into adultery. Having intercourse at forbidden times—for example, during periods of penance and Lent, during the woman's menstrual period, during the final weeks of pregnancy, or while the woman was lactating—constituted another sin, as did continuing to have relations with one's spouse when he or she was known to be adulterous. Finally, it was a sin to engage in sexual intercourse for the sheer pleasure of it; that is, without intention to conceive.[4]

In light of the above, marriage had come to be viewed as "second-best" compared to the purity of celibacy. It was less than unambiguous blessing—and this despite the inclusion of marriage among the seven sacraments.

Luther and his followers inverted the late medieval understanding by transfering the praise of monastic life to marriage. They wholly revalued the institution of marriage by allowing clergy to marry and commending marriage to the laity, but it must be asked whether, in so doing, they made a misstep in the other direction. In light of Luther's insistence that matrimony befits everyone, did they fail to understand that marriage might not be for everyone?[5] The Reformers tended to assume that, since marriage was good in light of the doctrine of creation, it was normative for everyone. In the wake of the Fall, however, it is evident that there are some people who ought never to marry, since

---

4. See Ozment, *Protestants*, pp. 152-153.

5. *Weimar Ausgabe*, 12.94; quoted in Oberman, *Luther: Man Between God and the Devil*, p. 272.

they are constitutionally incapable of sustaining a marriage. There are also people who are called to the discipline of celibacy, and there are others who simply never have the opportunity to marry, whether they want to or not.[6]

Jesus said, in Matthew 19, that there are some men who are born eunuchs; that is, they are born genitally unequipped for marriage. There are some who become eunuchs for the Kingdom of God, and there are some who become eunuchs thanks to the violence of other men. These categories might be said to correspond roughly to those who, for many different reasons, are incapable of sustaining a lifelong union with one other person; those who forgo marriage because of a vocation to celibacy; and those who, through war or other misfortune, are deprived of the opportunity to marry. The Reformers, in their zeal to elevate the institution of marriage, may have lost sight of the fact that in the era of the Fall, there are some people who should not be made to feel guilty for not marrying. In fact, some of these ought to be commended for having sufficient self-perception and discernment to avoid blundering into a union they cannot sustain.

What the Reformers were reacting against was a tendency to view marriage as second-best for those who could not achieve the purer and more meritorious status of celibacy. In the fourth century, Jerome had gone so far as to assign numerical value to marriage and celibacy. On a scale of 0 to 100, he assigned 100 to virginity, 60 to widowhood, and 30 to marriage. Marriage comes last in this scheme because it is a concession to the weakness of people who would derail spiritually and psychologically without the institution. Inverting all such calculations, Johann Bugenhagen (1485-1558), Luther's confessor and the pastor of the city church in Wittenberg, exclaimed, "It is faith, and not virginity, that fills paradise." This one pithy aphorism points to the totality

---

6.   Thanks to war, there is always a scarcity of men in the world. Britain lost 250,000 men in WWI, while France lost 1.6 million. In the wake of that war, there were whole communities of women who banded together for mutual comfort and companionship because they knew they were never going to find husbands.

of Reformation theology while also indicating why the Reformation opposed the medieval understanding of marriage. Bugenhagen grasped how the doctrine of justification by faith was related to the practice of allowing clergy to marry. He understood that it is faith in Jesus Christ which is our sole, sufficient salvation—not sexual self-renunciation misunderstood as another form of self-salvation.

Many modern feminists excoriate the Reformers, and Luther particularly, for regarding woman chiefly in her roles as wife and mother. They point out the drudgery of being dominated by a male, the drudgery of endless household labor and multiple pregnancies. And no doubt there was an element of drudgery. Luther's wife had six children, and that was relatively few for the time. John Wesley's mother, 200 years later, had 19, and was herself the last of 25 children. In an era when there was an infant mortality rate of fifty percent, it was common for a woman to have a child every year, or every 18 months, for the whole span of her natural fertility. Feminists today point out that when the Reformation overturned the medieval understanding and encouraged women to marry rather than seek a vocation to celibacy, it condemned them to a drudgery they would not have known had they lived in a convent.

In their failure to look upon a woman as the social equal of a man, the Reformers may indeed have undervalued women as persons. At the same time, the Reformers' approach to marriage elevated women in several respects. In the sixteenth century there were only two venues where women were spared the drudgery of married life: the bordello and the cloister. But what self-respect does a woman have in a bordello, in any era? As for the cloister, the Reformers maintained that many women had been placed there against their will. Young girls—six, seven, or eight years old—were committed by their parents to a life of celibacy; even if they did not enter the convent immediately, they would be made to do so at the appointed time whether they wanted to or not. Moreover, many nuns were easily bullied by superiors in the convent or cloister. Given these considerations, Luther always encouraged families to remove their daughters from the cloister,[7] and publicized the testimonies of escaped nuns.

It was not that Luther categorically denied the legitimacy of vows of celibacy. He never denied that there are people whom God ordains to this form of self-renunciation for purposes of service to the Kingdom. However, he insisted, we should not assume that every Christian who aspires to sanctity is thereby called to a life of celibacy, or that celibacy is inherently superior to married life. It is a different vocation, not a superior vocation. Celibacy possesses Kingdom significance because of the way it frees people in some respects for Kingdom service, but there is no spiritual value in asceticism for the sake of asceticism. For these reasons Luther spoke out against the practice of leading young people, even children, into vows of celibacy when they were too young to know what they were doing.

It is worth reflecting, at this point, on the place of celibacy in the Protestant church. Protestantism would do well to rethink the whole issue of celibacy and its legitimacy as a vocation from God. In the first place, the Reformation's descendants have failed to recognize that there are some forms of Kingdom service in which marriage is a genuine impediment and celibacy an advantage. One reason for the achievements of the early Roman Catholic missionary orders was that these orders consisted of women and men who were available for situations of unusual hardship and danger—situations to which one would hardly have the right to commit a spouse and children.

---

7.   In 1523, Leonhard Koppe, a fish merchant, spirited twelve nuns out of a convent in herring barrels. One of the women was Katharina von Bora, whom Luther subsequently married. Lucas Cranach (1472-1553), one of the famous woodcut artists of the Reformation, and his wife Barbara accommodated Katharina von Bora in their home, because a woman who left a convent was bereft: she had no employable skill, and no husband to support her. Luther tried unsuccessfully to arrange a marriage for Katharina, and when his attempts failed, he decided to marry her himself in 1525. Needless to say, he was considerably older than she. He wrote a pamphlet comparing this feat to Moses' facilitation of the escape from Egypt.

Second, whereas the Roman Catholic Church has always had something non-demeaning for unmarried people to do, in the Protestant church the unmarried person is often looked upon as awkward and is segregated from the life of the married mainstream. Lacking an understanding of vocational celibacy, Protestants are also at a loss as to how to view people who are celibate involuntarily; that is, through misfortune. Roman Catholicism, on the other hand, has a rich theology of celibacy—celibacy embraced for *any* reason. So far from resenting or chafing under the misfortune of singleness, people who want to marry but have never had the opportunity to do so are encouraged to offer their predicament up to God. To the extent that involuntary celibacy is offered up to God in a spirit of resentment-free renunciation, it has the significance of a sacrifice cheerfully offered up for the sake of Christ's Kingdom. In other words, involuntary celibacy can have the same spiritual force as vocational celibacy: the person in this situation has the same spiritual status, in Roman Catholic theology, as a Mother Teresa or Ignatius Loyola. Under the Protestant assumption that marriage is normative for everyone, however, such people risk being regarded as failures or "losers."

LUTHER'S VIEWS ON MARRIAGE

Luther understood marriage to be a mandate of God—an order of the creation and a creaturely good, like the state. He did not consider it a sacrament. A sacrament, by definition, is a means of grace, and he maintained that there could not be a means of grace available only to married people. Moreover, Luther argued, marriage is first a matter of the creation before it is a matter of the church; the institution of marriage is ordained by God for both believers and unbelievers equally. Like the state, it is a *creation* mandate and applies just as much to non-Christians as to Christians. As such, it ought to be maintained in its integrity by both church and state. Sacraments, by contrast, are administered by the church for the community of faith only.

In upholding marriage as a God-honoring institution, Luther opposed the dishonest arrangements encouraged by the medieval church in the form of secret marriage. Secret marriages were encouraged between prepubescent boys and girls as young as twelve so as to furnish a fallback should the girl subsequently become pregnant. It was thought that if young people were married before they reached puberty, they would be spared the sin of fornication. (Another reason for such marriages was to ensure that money was kept in particular families—a consideration worked out in different ways in different eras.) A major problem with this arrangement, however, was the lack of public attestation. Absent appropriate witnesses, nobody else may have known that the two young people were married, and in some cases even the parties themselves were unaware of their status. Luther and the other Reformers insisted that all marriages be publicly witnessed and notarized. The state can protect the integrity of marriage and the family only if the state knows who is married to whom.

Luther also opposed ecclesiastical impediments to marriage. One such impediment was consanguinity as far as third cousins. Abhorring incest, Luther nonetheless refused to restrict marriage where Scripture did not. Since Scripture does not forbid marriage to third cousins, Luther permitted it. Otherwise, in an era of relatively little geographic mobility, most people would have had no little difficulty finding marriageable partners within the circle in which they moved.

Luther also opposed the ecclesiastical impediment based on the "spiritual affinity" of the candidates for marriage—for example, in the case of marriage to the son, daughter, niece, or nephew of one's godparent even if the godparent was not a blood relative. Obviously, one's godparents would be people in one's parents' orbit; hence their children would be among those one met fairly often and with whom one would probably form a relationship as a young person. To prohibit them as marriage partners was to eliminate the most likely candidates.

Yet another ecclesiastical impediment to marriage was defective speech or eyesight. Luther's opposition to this restriction resonates with modernity, for any suggestion that a blind, deaf, or speech-impaired person ought not to marry would not be countenanced today. On the other hand, Luther endorsed the marriage of Christian to non-Christian—something virtually all Christians today frown upon—on the grounds that the New Testament permitted it (here he had in mind Paul's insistence that "...the unbelieving husband is consecrated through his wife...".[8]) and that it was an opportunity for evangelism.

On the question of parental permission, Luther and Zwingli always said that it should be sought. Since licit marriage was not a matter enacted merely between individuals without reference to a community, it required not only public witness but the blessing of the families involved. At the same time, this blessing should not be withheld; people should be allowed to marry the person they want to marry, and should not be steered into a prearranged marriage. Especially in the case of premarital pregnancy, the Reformers softened on the requirement of parental permission. Young people whose parents were forcing them into an unwanted marriage were advised by Luther and the other Reformers to seek help from the magistrate.

Luther exemplified his high view of marriage in his love for his wife, Katharina von Bora. He described Katie as his "lord" and used to say, "I am Aaron; she is my Moses." He spoke glowingly of her to others, praised her linguistic ability and other strengths, and never objected to her public criticism of his weaknesses, especially his poor business sense and misplaced charity.[9] When it came to writing his will, Luther broke new ground by leaving everything to his wife. In those days it was common to will everything to a trustee—necessarily male—who would then grant the surviving spouse and children allowances from the estate, according to his own discretion and after charging a fee he had fixed for himself. Given this practice, the simple fact that Luther willed

---

8. 1 Corinthians 7:14 (RSV).

9. Like John Wesley, whose brother Charles said he was "born for the benefit of knaves," Luther was so generous that he was an easy target for con artists. Always financially troubled, Luther refused any payment, however small, for his publications.

all his earthly goods to his wife—not that he had many, for he died relatively poor—was evidence of his esteem for her. Katharina, he knew, was an astute businesswoman. Although poor, the Luthers used their large house as an inn and dormitory and oasis; it was crowded with "unmarried and marriable spinsters, convalescents, derelict widows, refugee pastors, orphaned children, undergraduate boarders, ushers with their pupils, scholars, foreigners."[10] Katharina had remodeled an old cloister so as to accommodate all who appeared on its doorstep, had greatly expanded its vegetable garden in order to feed them as cheaply as possible, and in addition became so proficient at brewing beer that she was able to sell what the household did not consume. She also developed a reputation as a herbalist.

Luther insisted that, while physical attraction may initiate a relationship, it cannot be the ground of a relationship. Only a commitment born of a covenantal understanding of marriage can serve as its ground. Second, Luther insisted, there must be the persistent willingness to make sacrifices. In this regard he frequently remarked that it was when one's spouse was ill that one learned the meaning of marriage. In all of this Luther remained incurably romantic; his point, however, was that a romantic misunderstanding of marriage will not sustain a couple through the less romantic episodes of their relationship. After all, no one's marriage unfolds endlessly at the level of red-hot romance; and no one could live permanently with such unrelenting intensity in any case.[11]

---

10. Posthumous paper of E. Gordon Rupp, published in John A. Vickers; *An Anthology from the Writings of Gordon Rupp* (Peterborough: The Methodist Publishing House, no date), p. 121.

11. Not only are there are periods of dryness, there are also times when one is inclined to feel hostile towards one's spouse. Richard Hays, in his book *The Moral Vision of the New Testament*, writes on the subject of marriage that Christians must take to heart the dominical command to love their enemies, because at some point the person who shares one's bed is liable to become one's enemy. While that may seem severe, it is not far from the truth: at some point, one's spouse will oppose one's plans

Luther, like others of his era, maintained that although children are not the whole meaning of marriage, they are part of it, childlessness being a terrible affliction. Luther had six children, and they were precious to him. When his daughter Elizabeth died of a childhood disease at 18 months, Luther said, "I so lamented her death and I was exquisitely sick, my heart rendered soft and weak. Never had I thought that a father's heart could be so broken for his children's sake."[12] His other daughter, Magdalena, had tuberculosis and died in his arms when she was 13. About her Luther wrote, "The features, the words, the movement of our living and dying daughter remain engraved in our hearts. Even the death of Christ is unable to take away all of this as it should."[13] In the wake of the death of his two children, Luther said his faith would not survive the death of a third. Here was a person who had faced Johann Eck, his formidable opponent, three times, and had had a price on his head from 1521 onward. None of that threatened to eclipse God for him, but the death of his children did.[14]

While Luther taught that Christ permitted divorce following adultery, he refrained from saying that adultery necessarily terminated a marriage. In fact, Luther opposed harsh penalties for adultery because he felt the imposition of a harsh penalty would only decrease the likelihood of reconciliation. Where people are genuinely penitent, there is no point in a penalty so harsh that it impedes the reconciliation of the couple. Luther cited the instance of a godly wife who had borne her husband four children, had never been unfaithful to him, and one day

---

and announce his or her disagreement, and then it is very easy to move into a position of defensiveness in which the spouse comes to be regarded as an adversary.

12. Ozment, *Protestants*, p. 167.

13. Ibid., p. 167.

14. The story of Philip Melanchthon and his wife Barbara demonstrates a similar attitude of parental devotion. Their older daughter had several children, but as her husband was totally inept and incapable of supporting them, she came to live with Philip and Barbara in their older age. They took her in, along with her four children, and cared for the whole family well after they might have expected to have had done with child-rearing.

in a moment of weakness, stupidity, or lack of spiritual alertness, had an affair. Her husband was angry and had her publicly flogged. When Luther, Melanchthon, and Bugenhagen tried to effect reconciliation between the husband and wife, the husband was willing to take her back, but the wife, even though she owned her guilt, was so humiliated by the public punishment and so scarred by its physical severity that she would hear of no reconciliation at all. Luther faulted her husband for this and said that he should have pursued reconciliation before punishment. For chronic, willful adultery, on the other hand—not a slip, but calculated and persistent infidelity—Luther was prepared to condone rigorous deterrents.[15]

Luther recognized that even people whose standing in Christ is beyond doubt and whose godliness is transparent may be overtaken in a moment of culpable folly. King David of old, described as a man after God's own heart, was derailed by an act of adultery that haunted the rest of his life. The point, from a pastoral perspective, is that the consequences of adultery in people's lives are bad enough; there is no call to maximize the disarray or the likelihood of marital breakup by imposing additional ones when people are penitent.

A SERMON ON THE ESTATE OF MARRIAGE

A Sermon on the Estate of Marriage was Luther's 59th tract. It was written in 1519, before the Diet of Worms and the developments in 1521 that put a price on his head, but after the nailing of the *Ninety-Five Theses* to the Wittenberg church door. In short, when he penned this tract he was unambiguously a Reformer.

Luther begins by invoking the Genesis 2 account of how woman was derived from man in order to provide a suitable companion for Adam.[16] As we shall see, this notion accords with his idea of the principal purpose of marriage. (Interestingly, he does not invoke Genesis 1,

---

15.   Ozment, *Protestants*, p. 164.
16.   Lull, *Martin Luther's Basic Theological Writings*, p. 630.

where man and woman are made together in the image of God and their complementarity expresses that image.[17])

He then contrasts the solemnity and profundity of human marriage with the mating of animals, and writes, "And true though it is that because of excessive lust of the flesh, light-hearted youth pays scant attention to these matters, marriage is nevertheless a weighty matter in the sight of God."[18] Animals are fruitful and multiply, following the same command given to us, but they do so by instinct. Animal libido serves only reproduction. "Light-hearted youth," especially the relatively thoughtless, ignorant, biblically unaware young people Luther had in mind, might think the same is true of human libido—that it serves only human gratification and the reproduction of the species. Luther, however, knows that erotic love in humans subserves the union of two people. Its purpose is primarily to serve male-female union and secondarily to beget children. A little further on, he writes:

> Natural love is that between father and child, brother and sister, friend and relative, and similar relationships. But over and above all these is married love, that is, a bride's love which glows like a fire and desires nothing but the husband. She says, 'It is you I want, not what is yours: I want neither your silver nor your gold; I want neither. I want only you. I want you in your entirety, or not at all.' All other kinds of love seek something other than the loved one: this kind wants only to have the beloved's own self completely.[19]

We marry, says Luther, not because we want something our wife can give us, but because we recognize in her own person that good which we think to be essential to our own good. We want to be united with

---

17. This is not, of course, to suggest that individual persons are not made in the image of God, or that the male-female complementarity is operative only within marriage.
18. Lull, p. 630.
19. Ibid., p. 632.

her. And libido, or eros, subserves this union. It secondarily serves the reproduction of the species.[20]

Describing marriage after the Fall, Luther states that "the desire of the man for the woman and vice versa is sought after not only *for companionship and children, for which purposes alone marriage was instituted*, but also for the pursuance of wicked lust, which is almost as strong a motive"[21] (my emphasis). Note again the two purposes of marriage and the order Luther assigns them. When Eve is brought before Adam in the creation story in Genesis 2, the pronouncement of God is, "It is not good that man should be alone." God does not say, "It is not good that Adam should remain childless." The two are related, but companionship is clearly the prior concern. In the above quotation, however, Luther realistically admits that in a fallen world there are those whose motive for marrying is little more than physical gratification—highlighting the difference between his era and ours, in which there are few social sanctions for people who engage in sexual relations outside of marriage.

The point of greatest significance here is that Luther inverts the understanding of marriage that was current at the time. According to it, marriage was primarily for the begetting of children and only secondarily for companionship. Luther disagrees adamantly.

Having acknowledged the power of lust in fallen human beings, Luther adds to marriage the function of expressing libido by providing a divinely ordained outlet for it. He says, in what sounds like a rather unglamorous endorsement of marriage, "The temptation of the flesh has become so strong and consuming that marriage may be likened to a hospital for incurables which prevents inmates from falling into graver sin."[22] His pronouncement reflects the realism for which Luther

---

20. Helmut Thielicke, a Lutheran theologian, has done fine work on the difference between libido in animals and libido in humans in his *The Ethics of Sex* (Grand Rapids: Baker, 1975).

21. Lull, p. 631.

22. Ibid., p. 632.

is well known. The tertiary function of marriage as a divinely-ordained libidinal outlet was recognized by all the Reformers. They were aware that the practice of forcing people into vows of celibacy when they had no such vocation resulted in the frequent violation of those vows; we have already mentioned in previous chapters the fact that in every European town, a priest's children were readily identified and their mother despised. The Reformers knew that if they were to overturn this practice, they had to make clear that marriage is the God-ordained outlet for libidinal expression. Such gratification, while not the primary purpose of marriage, is a consideration that must be accommodated. It is unrealistic, the Reformers insisted, to pretend otherwise.

"Before Adam fell," Luther writes, "it was a simple matter to remain virgin and chaste, but now it is hardly possible, and without special grace from God, quite impossible."[23] Luther does not deny that there is a vocation to celibacy, but he believes that only those whom God's grace equips for celibacy are called to it. This raises once again the question of the person who has no vocation to celibacy but is unmarried due to lack of opportunity. Given that it is "quite impossible" to remain chaste without the grace that accompanies a call to celibacy, what are such people to do?

It is for this reason that the Roman Catholic Church has developed an ascetical theology around the issue. Protestants, on the other hand, have yet to come to terms with it. Despite the recent scandals concerning the molestation of juveniles at the hands of Roman Catholic clergy, we must beware of the facile argument that if only priests were allowed to marry, all the problems involving sexual misconduct among clergy would be solved. The Protestant church has always permitted clergy to marry, yet sexual malfeasance has scarcely disappeared. On the one hand, it can readily be acknowledged, along with Luther and the other Reformers, that problems can arise from a lifelong institutional denial

---

23.   Ibid., p. 632.

of acceptable libidinal expression. At the same time, it must not suppose that marriage settles all difficulties around human sexual ethics.

Luther then proceeds to point out a number of things about marriage that militate against the sin of lust. He writes, "First, [the doctors say] that it is a sacrament. ...It is an outward and spiritual sign of the greatest, holiest, worthiest, and noblest thing that has ever existed or ever will exist: the union of the divine and human natures in Christ."[24] There are echoes of Ephesians 5 here, but he is making the very strong statement that marriage is a sacrament *of the Incarnation*. It is only 1519 and he will subsequently move away from this view later in his life, insofar as he ceases to call marriage a sacrament at all; but at the point of writing this tract, he is viewing marriage as a sign and sacrament of the hypostatic union of the divine and human natures in Christ.

Ephesians 5 speaks of marriage as depicting the union between Christ and the church, the church being a communion of the divine and the human. And indeed, throughout Scripture, marriage is the commonest metaphor for the covenant relationship between God and his people, and adultery the commonest metaphor for idolatry and unfaithfulness to God. If marriage is a metaphor for the intimate relationship between God and his people, the metaphor tells us much about the life of faith as well as much about marriage. Surely, from a biblical standpoint, the covenant with one's spouse is undertaken in the light of God's covenant with his people; this being the case, it can then become a sign of the covenant of God with us, mirroring his covenant faithfulness into our own covenant as spouses. Any future rethinking of sacrament by the Protestant church will have to consider this 'sacramental' aspect of marriage.[25]

Enlarging on the significance of the union of which marriage is a sacrament, Luther writes, "Consider this matter with the respect it

---

24. Ibid., p. 633.

25. See the quotation at the conclusion of this chapter where Luther writes, of one's encounter with one's spouse, that "right there you are face to face with God speaking."

deserves, because the union of man and woman signifies such a great mystery...."[26] Modernity tends to get over the category of mystery too quickly. In Scripture, mystery is not something eerie or strange. The mysterious can be an everyday reality as common as the air we breathe, yet simultaneously so profound that its depth escapes comprehension. It can be a common occurrence that we point to, apprehend, and commend to others, but concerning which our language is forever inadequate. Marriage comes to mind at once as an example of such a mystery: marriage and falling in love are common, everyday events, yet there remains a profundity about the union of husband and wife that no language can capture and no married people can otherwise express. This is surely what the writer of the book of Proverbs is referring to when he includes among the four wonders of the world "the way of a man with a maiden" (Proverbs 30:19, RSV).

There is a mystery as well to the union of our life in Christ, so common and simple that any child can participate in it but so wonderful that no sociologist or psychologist of religion can grasp or explain it. We apprehend a mystery only by living it, and for this reason the ultimate category in commending it to others is not explanation or argument but *witness*. When we cannot capture in words what marriage is like, we are left saying to the inquirer, "The only way you will ever know is to taste the glories of marriage yourself." Similarly, after all our words have failed to explain our relationship with Christ, ultimately we can only urge people to come to faith themselves. All argumentation is superfluous to the committed and unpersuasive to the uncommitted.

Luther continues:

> Second, [the doctors say] that marriage is a covenant of fidelity. The whole basis and essence of marriage is that each gives himself or herself to the other, and they promise to remain faithful to each other and not give themselves to any other. By binding themselves

---

26. Ibid., p. 633.

to each other and surrendering themselves to each other, the way
is barred to the body of anyone else and they content themselves in
the marriage bed with their one companion.[27]

This is Luther at his best on marriage. Marriage is not the venue of
a contest of wills or of self-seeking or one-upmanship. Marriage is
the most intense venue of our cheerful self-surrender, without which
marriage can be neither entered into nor sustained. He mentions
"binding themselves to each other" in conjunction with "surrendering
themselves to each other", intimating that it is the repeated act of self-
surrender which *is* the bond. Where the repeated act of self-surrender
does not occur, no bond is forged; instead there is competition and a
preoccupation with rights.

There is an implicit reference here to Ephesians 5:28, where Paul says
that a man should love his wife as his own body. Paul does not say that
a man should love his wife *as if she were* his body, but to love her *as* his
body. *As if* is hypothetical, but *as* means that the husband cannot love
himself without loving his wife—that to love his wife *is* to love himself.
This means that marriage forges a union, not like two blocks of wood
joined together and glued at one end, but more like a tree graft in which
the parts that are grafted together grow as one, interpenetrated by the
essence of both trees. Once a tree graft has grown for a year or two, and
has borne fruit, any attempt to ungraft the tree destroys it.

Under this rubric—the exclusivity of marriage and the claim that
spouses have upon one another—Luther attempts to deal with the
thorny issue of clandestine marriages and their dubious status. There
were two sorts of clandestine marriage common at the time. One we
have already mentioned, the case in which people had been committed
to each other by their parents in childhood. The question, given the
consensual nature of marriage, was whether the individuals in question
were really married, since they had never consented to anything and
in many cases might even have remained unaware of their parents'

---

27.   Ibid., pp. 633-634.

arrangement until they fell in love with somebody else. Yet according to current practice they were married. The second kind of clandestine marriage involved priests who, in the wake of the Reformers' teaching, concluded from Scripture that clergy should be allowed to marry, and married secretly.[28] It was not entirely secret, of course, since another priest had to marry them; but it was kept quiet, so that in the eyes of the community they were unmarried. What was the true status of people in these situations?

Luther does not come down unequivocally on this point, writing instead, "But because the estate of marriage consists essentially in consent having been previously and freely given one to another, and also because God is wonderfully merciful in all his judgments, I will leave it all to his care."[29] In view of the complexity that had arisen in Germany as a result of these practices, Luther decided to leave the status of the participants up to God, whom he knew to be merciful. He realized that for the next generation and a half, it would be necessary to turn a blind eye to such situations until new norms were established. As far as Luther and the other Protestants were concerned, a marriage was not a marriage until it was consummated; the secret "marriages" to which parents committed their young children could therefore be repudiated in good conscience and marriage to someone else undertaken. If, on the other hand, someone's conscience required him or her to honor such a marriage, then that marriage would be accepted.

Luther's third item in the list of things about marriage that militate against the sin of lust is its fruitfulness in the form of children. He writes, "Third, [the doctors say] that marriage produces offspring, for that is the end and chief purpose of marriage."[30] To be sure, the doctors

---

28. Thomas Cranmer (1489-1556), the English Reformer, was an instance of this. He secretly married the niece of Andreas Osiander (1498-1552), a Lutheran reformer. She lived in Germany while he lived in England; they used to meet on the North Sea beach of England.

29. Lull, p. 634.

30. Ibid., p. 635.

of the church do say that producing children is the end and chief purpose of marriage, but as we have seen already, for Luther marriage's chief end and purpose was the fusing of two complementary lives; producing and raising children was the secondary purpose. Nevertheless, it was a purpose that pertained to the meaning of marriage. About raising children, he writes:

> But this at least all married people should know. They can do no better work and do nothing more valuable either for God, for christendom, for all the world, for themselves, and for their children than to bring up their children well. In comparison with this one work, that married people should bring up their children properly, there is nothing at all in pilgrimages to Rome, Jerusalem, or Compostella, nothing at all in building churches, endowing masses, or whatever good works could be named.[31]

Luther—who cherished children—insists that the most significant thing to which married people can aspire in this life, more significant than any pietistic undertaking, is to be good parents. Christian discipleship is always to be exercised in the everyday world, and the most important aspect of everyday discipleship is parenting. "Where parents are not conscientious about this," he continues, "it is as if everything were the wrong way around, like fire that will not burn, or water that is not wet." Where parents aren't conscientious about parenting, or where a society denies the significance of good parenting, it is as if the whole universe were out of order.

Were Luther alive today, he would concur that even the preferential tax status given to intact families is the state's recognition of this fact. For the same reason, Luther would reject the suggestion, heard today with increasing frequency, that the blending of families through divorce and remarriage introduces a richness superior to that of the stable, intact family established by a couple who remain committed to

---

31.   Ibid., p. 635.

each other and to their children. It is as absurd, says the Wittenberger, as fire that will not burn or water that is not wet.

What impedes the proper upbringing of children is a misunderstanding by parents that love means permissiveness. "False natural love," writes Luther, "blinds parents so that they have more regard for the bodies of their children than they have for their souls." Luther recognizes the idolatry of loving our children in a way that reduces itself to indulgence. Parents' indulgence of children is actually a form of self-indulgence, as they are sparing themselves the pain of the child's temporary disappointment or displeasure. It is, as Luther points out, a false love.[32]

In the end, Luther insists, the children in whom we have invested, whom we have loved and raised, will be our comfort: "It is they who will lighten you in your hours of death, and to your journey's end."[33] Children will be a blessing to parents in the hour of the parents' dying. Even though they may disappoint us in some respect, as we will disappoint them, our ongoing love for them and their love for us will be a great blessing.

If the Protestant church has been remiss in its treatment of single people, it has been only slightly less so in its treatment of those who, for one reason or another, have been unable to have children and therefore do not enjoy the blessing of which Luther speaks. We must learn to give inclusive attention to those who are without the comfort and support of children and grandchildren in their declining years, for whom the usual occasions for family gatherings tend to be painful reminders of

---

32.   C.S. Lewis, in his *The Four Loves* (London: Collins, 1964), invokes our love for God as a corrective for disproportionate elements in the other creaturely loves. We ought to love our spouse as we love no other human being, but we cannot expect a spouse to be to us what God alone is, and therefore our love for our spouse—and for our children—never transcends our love for God. Our love for God, and especially his love for us, will continue to correct the element of sin in our marriage and child-rearing that will otherwise loom so large as to impede if not falsify love for spouse and children.

33.   Lull, p. 637.

missed blessings and joys, or who may feel marginalized in so many conversations because they have no experience of the everyday life and milestones that belong to parenting. The church, as a community of people called and claimed by Christ, ought to be one that cherishes and nourishes marriage and children and at the same time one in which the unmarried, widowed, and childless are welcomed and embraced, as those to whom *the* Child has been given and whom the eschaton will find lacking nothing.

The last word on Luther and marriage should be accorded the Reformer himself. He followed *A Sermon on the Estate of Marriage* with *A Sermon on Marriage* in 1531. The encomium plainly has his beloved Katie in mind. (She died in 1552, Luther in 1546.)

> God's word is actually inscribed on one's spouse. When a man looks at his wife as if she were the only woman on earth, and when a woman looks at her husband as if he were the only man on earth; yes, if no king or queen, not even the sun itself sparkles any more brightly and lights up your eyes more than your own husband or wife, then right there you are face to face with God speaking. God promises to you your wife or husband, actually gives your spouse to you, saying: "The man shall be yours; the woman shall be yours. I am pleased beyond measure! Creatures earthly and heavenly are jumping for joy." For there is no jewelry more precious than God's Word; through it you come to regard your spouse as a gift of God and, as long as you do that, you will have no regrets.[34]

---

34. Luther, "A Sermon on Marriage," in *Luther's Works* (Philadelphia: Fortress Press, 1976), Vol. 51. See *Sixteenth Century Journal,* Vol. 13, No. 2 (Summer, 1982), pp. 17-42.

12

Luther and the Jewish People

B efore we examine Luther's attitude to the Jewish people, a brief study of the background against which he stood is in order. The background was dark as far as the Jews were concerned.[1] As was noted earlier, humanism was sweeping Europe at the time. Although humanism is typically looked upon as the essence of enlightenment, toleration, and simple human decency, the fact is that the humanists were largely anti-Semitic.

The most vociferous anti-Semite in Europe was no less a figure than Europe's brightest man, Erasmus.[2] For him, the Renaissance's "renovation" of Europe, with which he was preoccupied, entailed ridding the continent of Jews.[3] Erasmus was the first person to use the expression *Judenrein*, meaning "pure of Jews" or "Jew-free"—a word that has had

---

1.   See Heiko Oberman, *The Roots of Anti-Semitism in the Age of Renaissance and Reformation* (Philadelphia: Fortress Press, 1981).

2.   Bernhard Lohse, *Martin Luther's Theology* (Minneapolis: Fortress Press, 1999), pp. 336-338. Lohse notes that for Erasmus, "There would be no place for the Jews."

3.   Ibid., p. 5.

a hideous history in Nazi Germany and in modern Europe generally. Erasmus said that he loved going to France, since France had led Europe in "neatly cleansing" the realm of Jews.[4] He was especially fond of Paris, because it was *Judenrein*. This was not true, of course; for centuries there had been, as there continues to be, a large Jewish population in Paris.

While Erasmus was unambiguously anti-Semitic, the situation regarding Luther is more subtle. An anti-Semite loathes Jewish people as people, regardless of what they might say, do, or believe. Luther, however, had nothing against the Jewish people as human beings, and insisted that Christians treat them kindly.[5]

Johannes Eck, Luther's most formidable and relentless opponent, was another vehement anti-Semite.[6] Eck fumed:

> Whatever comes into the heads or dreams of these people the Reformers, they give to the world for evangelical riffraff to read. For instance, right now there is this superficially learned children's preacher [Luther] with a hoof of the golden calf in his flank, who presumes to defend the bloodthirsty Jews, saying that it is not true and not plausible that they murder Christian children and use their blood to the mockery and ridicule of the authorities and all of Christendom.[7]

Eck upheld the medieval "blood myth" about the Jewish people, while Luther insisted it was not plausible.[8] The blood myth had many features in medieval Europe, one of which was that Jewish people murdered Christian children in order to extract their blood and use it as an ingre-

4.   Lohse, *Martin Luther's Theology,* p. 95.

5.   Luther, *That Jesus Christ was Born A Jew,* p. 200.

6.   The title of Eck's anti-Semitic work was *Against the Defense of the Jews.* Heiko Oberman describes it as "...outstripping all previous Reformation publications on the theme—in crudity, spleen and slander." Oberman, *Roots of Anti-Semitism,* p. 36.

7.   Johannes Eck, *Ains Judenbuechlins Verlegung,* 1542, fol. A IV; quoted in Oberman, p. 17.

8.   For the several aspects of the blood myth see Roland de Corneille, *Christians and Jews* (New York: Harper, 1966), chapter 3.

dient in *matzo*, their unleavened bread; this was believed despite the fact that Jewish people are known to have an aversion to drinking blood. Another feature of the blood myth was that Jewish people desecrated the Lord's Supper; since the consecrated wine was deemed to be the blood of Christ, any desecration of the wine amounted to desecration of Christ's blood. And finally, Jewish men were said to menstruate, although no one claimed ever to have seen this. The implication, of course, was that Jews were inherently monstrous.

This blood myth circulated throughout medieval Europe. On account of it (but not on account of it alone) the Jewish people were expelled from country after country on the grounds of ritual murder. Luther denied that Jews committed such acts. Luther, it must be remembered, cherished the Older Testament. His exposure to the Hebrew Bible and the logic of Hebrew thought found him dismissing as ridiculous the myths that others preferred to believe. As will be seen shortly, Luther consistently maintained that the Older Testament was unsubstitutable with respect to the economy of gospel and church.

Luther was not anti-Semitic, then, in the sense of being personally hostile towards Jews, but he was certainly anti-Judaistic; that is, he had no objection whatsoever to the Jews as human beings, but believed there was no place for Jewish theological conviction because it was obsolete. The Jewish people were a theological anachronism or museum piece. In this he was espousing a position called supersessionism: the belief that while the Jews had a place in God's economy until the advent and enthronement of Jesus Christ, they no longer have such a place now that his advent and enthronement have occurred. The Jews have reached the end of the road theologically and have no future *as Jews*.

Luther always assumed that as soon as the church was rid of its theological and moral corruption—that is to say, as soon as the gospel was restored to the church—the Jewish people would recognize the church as the custodian of the gospel and flock in. To his unrelieved frustration, however, they did not. And as Luther's frustration mounted, so did his vehemence.

Four salient features can be observed in Luther's position regarding the Jewish people. The first is that Luther assumed them to be legalists. That is, he assumed that they understood the Torah as a moral code and therefore a vehicle for promoting self-righteousness. Most Christians make the same assumption; they look upon *yiddishkeit* as nothing more than works righteousness because of the way they read Paul in the Newer Testament. When Paul speaks of the Law, however, he is speaking of the Torah misunderstood and misrepresented, and his criticism of such misappropriation is sound. No informed Jewish person would agree that the Torah misunderstood is anything less than a caricature, for the synagogue would never agree that God had given the Torah to Israel as a means of promoting its defiance of God. Still, Luther and others, having heard Paul's critique of a misunderstood Torah in Romans and Galatians, read it back into the history of the Jewish people.

A second thing worth noting is that Luther said the Jewish people should be loved. On the one hand, this represents a departure for that era, given what has already been said about the prevailing anti-Semitism. On the other hand, his expressed reason for loving them is that they are potential converts. Overlooked is the commandment to love the neighbor just because the neighbor has been given to us as neighbor (and particularly as suffering neighbor), not because the neighbor is a potential convert. If we love the neighbor merely as a potential convert, are we really loving our neighbor at all?

Thirdly, Luther declares that the Hebrew Scriptures should be removed from the Jewish people, because they are misinterpreting the holy book of Christians. More than merely misinterpreting it, they are falsifying it on account of their "lies".[9] In a word, the Jews are perverting Scripture. Notice that Luther's aim here is the elimination of theological error and not the abuse of a people. The idea of depriving the Jewish people of their Scriptures is deplorable, of course, but at least Luther cannot be accused

---

9.   Oberman, p. 50, 121.

of the so-called racism of anti-Semitism. At the same time he recognizes the Older Testament as canonical for Christians.

Luther also said, fourthly, that the Jewish people should convert; as noted above, he fully expected them to do so once the gospel was restored to the church. When the Jewish people proved "recalcitrant," Luther's exasperation became incandescent. He said that if the Jews did not convert, their presence should not be tolerated, since their theological error would infiltrate the church and society and deprive people of the gospel. Notice that he did not say their *existence* should not be tolerated, only their *presence*. (How one could avoid the presence of the Jewish people without threatening their existence, however, is a matter for discussion.) In 1543, after many years of waiting for the conversion of the Jewish people, Luther wrote in *On the Jews and Their Lies*, "Now what ought we Christians to do with this rejected and damned people the Jews? We have to practice a fierce mercy in hope that we can save a few of them."[10]

But what is the force of "a fierce mercy"? What does it counsel and countenance? While Luther may have understood what he meant by the practice of a fierce mercy (something akin to today's "tough love"?), the people who came after him did not, and only too readily picked up what he had said and used it in a way that has promoted wretched treatment of the Jewish people for centuries.

Several comments can be made at this point on this summary of Luther's convictions regarding the Jewish people. The first is that although Luther himself could distinguish between anti-Semitism and anti-Judaism, few others then or now can. Anti-Semitism is abuse of the people *per se*, while anti-Judaism is a rejection of their religion as an anachronism; that is, as antiquated or obsolete. But when the anti-Judaistic message is announced, it will be heard both in the church and

---

10. Luther, *On the Jews and Their Lies*, in *Luther's Works*, Vol. 45, ed. and trans. by Walter J. Brandt (Philadelphia: Fortress Press, 1962), p. 268. In this section of his tract Luther makes seven horrific recommendations, e.g., the burning of Jewish schools.

in the general public as anti-Semitism. Throughout history, anti-Judaism has always ended in anti-Semitism.

Secondly, in his zeal for theological purity, Luther felt a need to safeguard the gospel against Jewish infiltration. If, however, the gospel is ultimately Jesus Christ in his living, sovereign efficacy, then that gospel does not need to be protected.

If we do not protect the gospel, we also do not empower it: the church is mandated to evangelize through bearing witness to the gospel, but not to convert, since conversion is exclusively the responsibility and the work of the Holy Spirit. Where the church confuses its responsibility with God's, invariably the church persecutes. The history of the church attests that when Christians grow frustrated at the seeming ineffectiveness or slowness of their work of evangelism, they often decide to try to take over the Spirit's task (conversion) and add it to their own in order to do themselves what the Spirit appears reluctant or unable to do. The result is always persecution by the church. In the book of Acts, no one is converted apart from the agency of human witness, but neither is anyone converted apart from the secret efficacy of the Holy Spirit. By usurping God's prerogative for itself in the interests of making the cause of the gospel more effective, the church hampers its effectiveness in two ways: one, its aggressiveness misrepresents Christ and drives people away; and two, it advertises its unbelief to the world, for by its action the church has declared that it no longer trusts the Lord it preaches. It does this in the name of zeal for the faith, in the name of love. Not surprisingly, however, the church's unbelief in this regard fails to overturn the unbelief of the people it engages.[11] In view of this reality, Luther's motivation for befriending Jews—"in order that *we* might convert some of them"— requires no comment.[12]

---

11. When Gunther Plaut was rabbi of the Holy Blossom synagogue in Toronto, he used to say, "Every time Christians set out to love us, they end up killing us. So we have one request to make of you: don't love us. Don't even *attempt* to love us. Just leave us alone."

12. Luther, *That Jesus Christ was Born A Jew,* p. 200 (emphasis added).

As for the place of the Jewish people in God's economy, various answers are given to this question in the church today. The issue is not, of course, whether Jewish individuals are welcome in the church. The real issue is the Jewish people as Jews, as people of faith in the Holy One of Israel, and whether they are merely recalcitrant, or in fact appointed by God, in his mysterious providence, to an ongoing existence as Jews. One's answer to this depends on one's reading of Romans 9 to 11. Paul says, finally, that he would love to see the Jewish community brought into the church through its affirmation of Jesus as Messiah and Lord, in the same way that he himself and others have been brought in. However, he recognizes as one of the mysteries of God's economy the fact that the Jewish people do not embrace Jesus as the Messiah of Israel, *in order that* the Gentiles might come to embrace him. Paul refers to this as a mystery because we cannot see any logical connection between the Jewish denial of Jesus' messiahship and the Gentiles' affirmation of it. All he can say, for now, is that in God's economy the Jews say "No" to Jesus as Messiah for the sake of the inclusion of the Gentiles in the people of God. If it is true that God has ordained this as part of his unfolding economy in reconciling the world to himself, we must reflect on what this means for a proper Christian response to the synagogue. It is a huge question. In fact, the question of the relation of the two testaments, together with the question of the relation between synagogue and church, appears to be *the* issue with which the church must wrestle now.

It may be helpful here to recall Calvin. Calvin insisted that there is one and only one mediator by which anyone may be saved, but this one mediator was known to patriarchs and prophets under the economy of the Torah and to the church under the economy of the gospel. Christians agree that it cannot be inappropriate for a Jew to become a Christian—after all, apart from Jews who became Christians (the apostles, for instance), Gentiles would not know the gospel at all. At the same time, why deny that the Jewish person who, in faith, hears the Word of God as expounded in Jeremiah, Hosea, or Amos encounters the same God who incarnated himself in Jesus of Nazareth?

Anti-Semitism did not begin with the church. There was anti-Semitism already in the ancient world. Yet anti-Semitism has been given a particular twist and force by the church. Already at the time of the writing of Romans, only 25 years or so into the existence of the church, Paul noticed that the Gentile Christians in Rome were belittling and despising the Jewish Christians. Romans 9 to 11 is an exposition by Paul of the place of the Jews in salvation history, and he reminds the Gentile Christians that, without the Jewish people, they would still be pagans, knowing nothing of the gospel or God. By the mystery of God's providence they were "later" branches grafted into a tree whose trunk and root was Jewish.

Initially, Jewish Christians outnumbered Gentile Christians, but the situation was quickly reversed. The church initially made its greatest number of converts from the *phoboumenoi*, the God-fearers who fringed the synagogue, such as Cornelius. These were Gentiles attracted to the synagogue by its monotheism and by the ethics and spiritual discipline arising from that monotheism—all vastly preferable to anything else in the ancient world. But they did not want to become Jews formally, which would entail circumcision and submission to the dietary prescriptions of the Torah. Nevertheless there were many converts to Judaism in the ancient world: in the Diaspora, i.e., outside Palestine—including Rome—only 50% of Jews were born Jews, the rest being Gentile converts. As the book of Acts indicates, this issue led to a huge dispute at the Jerusalem Council in CE 51, the church ultimately decreeing that in order to become a Christian you did not first have to become a Jew. The result was that as the church welcomed these Gentile God-fearers, the latter removed themselves from the fellowship of the synagogue because they were now able to have as Christians the ethics and the monotheism that had drawn them to the synagogue in the first place, without conversion to Judaism. This "migration" in turn gave rise to hostility between the church and the synagogue.

Part of the age-old hostility between the church and the synagogue is rooted in the earliest years of the church and in the pronouncements of the church Fathers. While the Fathers are second in authority (for most Christian communions) only to the apostles, they are not for this reason to be read uncritically. There is always an unChristian element of Platonism in their writings and no little anti-Semitism, even in those who seem to be characteristically gentle. Chrysostom (whose name means "golden-mouthed"), for example, calls the synagogue a brothel, a den of thieves so vile that it is not fit even for a pig or a goat.[13] (Note the choice of animals: in the ancient world, the goat is a symbol of lust and the pig is a symbol of uncleanness.) Much later, in the 11th century, Bernard of Clairvaux, who endeared himself to many after him through his hymn, "Jesus, Thou Joy of Loving Hearts," also wrote diabolical scurrility about the Jewish people.

There were three famous sixteenth-century scholars who had much to say about the Jewish people: Reuchlin, Erasmus, and Luther.[14] Reuchlin was fully competent in Hebrew, Greek, and Latin; Erasmus, we know, was the best linguist of his era, a superb Greek and Latin scholar, but also immensely fluent in vernacular languages. However, he had little or no facility in Hebrew, and no desire to acquire any. Luther, by contrast, never had Erasmus' or Melanchthon's consummate facility in Greek, although he could handle the language creditably; Hebrew, on the other hand, was a language he took to heart. In any case, all three of these men spoke and wrote in a world unable to make up its mind whether large-scale conversion should be forced on the Jews or whether Jewish intransigence should be regarded as God's punishment and the validation of Christian truth.

Today there are two churches in old Wittenberg, only a few hundred yards apart. One is the *Schlosskirche*, the castle church where Luther preached regularly, and where the elector Frederick maintained him. The other is the *Stadtkirche*, the city church, whose preacher was Johannes Bugenhagen. Around the *Stadtkirche* is a frieze into which is chiseled, among other things, the figure of a sow nursing her piglets. A

13.　See Roland de Corneille, *Christians and Jews*, chapter 3.

14.　See Heiko Oberman, *Roots of Anti-Semitism*, chapters 1-4.

figure whose dress identifies him as a Jew is behind the sow, with his face in the pig's anus. (One aspect of the medieval myth was that Jews ate pig excrement.) The church was built 350 years before Luther, in 1180; after World War II it was decided to preserve the frieze, at the request of the Jewish people, as a reminder of their suffering not only under Hitler but throughout the preceding centuries in Christian Europe. Clearly, anyone who might have resisted anti-Semitism in the time of Luther would have been swimming against a stream that had been coursing for centuries.

Reuchlin condemned the indiscriminate destruction of Talmudic texts, but not out of any sympathy for Jewish learning and belief.[15] As a learned humanist, he had enormous respect for any language of antiquity. Moreover, he insisted on a cabalistic interpretation of the Talmudic texts which gave them a cryptically Christian meaning. This interpretation relied on calculations using the numerical values of Hebrew letters, so that, for example, the names *El Shaddai*—the Mighty One—and *Yeshua* had the same numerical value. Nonetheless, he insisted that the Talmud stood between the Jewish people and their conversion. It was to be preserved, then, because it was a crypto-Christian document if read cabalistically, but otherwise it was an impediment to the Jewish people and their spiritual well-being. There is no suggestion in Reuchlin that Hebrew is to be esteemed as the language of the Chosen People, or that the Older Testament is to be cherished because it is necessary for understanding the New Testament. The centuries-long misery of the Jewish people, he believed, was a God-ordained punishment and could be escaped only as Jews entered the church. Throughout the Middle Ages, however, the forced conversion of the Jews always rendered Jewish converts suspect in that their "conversion" was assumed to be insincere. (In Nazi Germany, those Jews who entered the church were not thereby spared; their Jewishness was deemed to be impermeable by the waters of baptism.)

---

15. Ibid., chapter 2.

According to Reuchlin, Jews were citizens of two worlds: fellow citizens of the Holy Roman Empire and adversaries in the Kingdom of God.[16] Unless they showed signs of spiritual improvement—that is, by refraining from usury and embracing Christ—they would be regarded as having ceased to be fellow citizens of the Empire and therefore could not claim the protection of the state.

Usury was a significant cause of resentment towards the Jewish people in the Middle Ages. Jews were associated with usury for two reasons. The church, on the basis of a particular reading of Scripture, forbade Christians to lend money at interest. They were permitted to *borrow* at interest, however, giving an opportunity to the Jews to lend, since the latter were not subject to the church's prohibition against usury. Meanwhile, since they were forbidden to own land or join the trade guilds, the Jewish people could not farm or make a living as skilled tradespeople. One thing they could do was collect taxes on behalf of the monarch—medieval monarchs were always seeking tax revenues to fund wars—for which they were compensated by being allowed to keep a portion of the taxes. This was the money they lent out at interest. Of course, people characteristically resent paying taxes, and also resent having to pay interest in order to borrow money. For this reason the Jews quickly incurred the odium of their fellow citizens on both counts. It was the church that assigned the Jews the moneylending business, then despised them in turn for being moneylenders, then faulted them for charging interest in contravention of the Hebrew Bible (according to the church's understanding of biblical teaching on usury).

Erasmus referred to Jewish converts to Christianity as "half-Jewish *Marranos*."[17] *Marranos* is the Spanish word for pigs. Many Jews were converted under duress during the Middle Ages and, as noted above, their conversions were therefore suspect. Unlike Luther, who had no doubt that the baptized Jew was a genuine Christian, Erasmus

---

16. Ibid., chapter 4.
17. Ibid.

and Eck would insist that Jewish converts were still Jews, or at least half-Jews; their baptism proved nothing. Some Jews, in order to prove they were Christians, would go so far as to adopt a stance as virulently anti-Semitic as that of any of their compatriots. Their stance made no difference. Erasmus said of Pfefferkorn, a Jewish convert to Christianity and a superb scholar, "If one were to operate on him, 600 Jews would spring out."[18] Between 1507 and 1521 Pfefferkorn wrote more scurrilous pamphlets on the Jews than any other individual, but even this did not convince people like Erasmus. As far as Erasmus was concerned, it did not matter what Pfefferkorn wrote; he was still a Jew and could never be a real Christian.[19]

Even the Anabaptists, despite their protests that they were singularly victimized in the 16th century, treated the Jewish people with contempt. Hubmaier (d. 1528) spoke of the Jews as "idle, lecherous, and greedy", and referred to them as a plague.[20] He called for their expulsion and incited city authorities to molest Jews. In 1519, after Hubmaier complained of the Jewish defamation of Mary, the synagogue in Regensburg where he was a leader was razed to the ground and a chapel in honor of Mary erected in its place.

In short, the Jew was universally hated. Nobody protested, then, when the Emperor decreed at the Diet of Augsburg on September 4, 1530, that all Jewish males had to identify themselves with a yellow badge on their coat or cap. This was not a new harassment of the Jews; they had been harassed throughout the Middle Ages. It was just an administrative detail of the empire. The mark they had to wear was not a Star of David but a yellow circle.

---

18. Emmanuel Hirsch is a modern example of the same tactic. A theologian in the German university in the Nazi era, he was a Jew and a Christian. He was vociferous in his anti-Semitism, thinking to prove to the German authorities that he was a real Christian. In Hitler's era, however, a Jew was a Jew forever, even if only one-eighth Jewish.

19. Oberman, *Roots of Anti-Semitism.*, p. 77.

20. Ibid.

LUTHER'S STANCE TOWARDS THE JEWISH PEOPLE

Luther wrote six anti-Judaistic tracts in all, haunted as he was by the Jewish presence in Europe and its intractability. A difference in his writings, in both tone and content, can be discerned between 1523 (*That Jesus Christ was Born a Jew*) and 1543 (*On the Jews and Their Lies*—not his last writing on this topic but his last major one, and the writing most quoted today). In 1523 he wrote, "If the apostles who were also Jews had dealt with us Gentiles as we Gentiles have dealt with the Jews, no Christians would ever have emerged from among the Gentiles."[21] Contrast this with the following, written twenty years later when he had reached the point of frustration:

> Now what ought we Christians to do with this rejected and damned people the Jews? We have to practice a fierce mercy in hopes that we can at least save a few of them from the glowing flames. Vengeance is out of the question. Revenge [i.e., God's revenge] already hangs on their necks a thousand times worse than we could wish on them.[22]

Luther had an extremely vivid apocalyptic sense and saw himself as standing in the breach in the end times.[23] He looked upon Jewish intransigence as a collaboration with apocalyptic powers, for which the divine punishment was blindness and dispersal. But if the Jews were collaborators with apocalyptic powers, they were so no more than the pope himself, no more than the Turks or heretics against whom Luther also wanted a more severe policy. Since he regarded the Older Testament as an integral part of the Christian Scriptures, he wanted to wrest it out of Jewish hands only because the Jews persistently and consistently misinterpreted it and thereby threatened the church. His motive, in other words, was the elimination of falsehood and the pro-

---

21. Luther, *That Jesus Christ was Born a Jew,* p. 200.

22. Luther, *On the Jews and Their Lies,* p. 268.

23. See Oberman, *Luther: Man Between God and the Devil* (New Haven: Yale University Press, 1989).

tection of Christians, not a vendetta against the Jewish people because of any deluded belief that they desecrated the Lord's Supper or perpetrated ritual murder upon Christian children. He also did not impute collective guilt to the Jewish people for the death of Christ, as so many others did and still do; certainly, he would say, a few Jewish religious leaders in the first century were directly involved in putting Christ to death, but beyond that, all human beings past, present, and future were equally responsible. Moreover, Luther did not find in his anti-Judaistic beliefs any grounds for mistreating individual Jews. The problem for him was not "the Jew" but rather "the Jews".[24] Even while believing that the Jews as a people no longer had a place in God's economy, that their religion was an impediment to the gospel, and that they were under God's judgment, Luther behaved decently to the individual. He never espoused a race theory with reference to the Jews.

Despite his persistent reputation as an anti-Semite, then, Luther was not one; in fact, he was the principal opponent of what amounted to medieval anti-Semitism, since the baptized Jew had the same standing as the baptized Gentile. As has been noted earlier, however, he was anything but an opponent of anti-Judaism.

The older Luther appears harsher, as he was by then more convinced than ever of the apocalyptic nature of the time. He felt that as the Reformation forces advanced, the forces of evil posed an increasing threat to the spread of the gospel—a threat which had to be met in turn by intensified opposition from those committed to spreading that gospel. The supposed falsehoods embraced by the Jews were part of this threat, and the truth of Christianity had to be protected from such falsehood. Jewish intransigence was an impediment to the survival of the gospel, and the gospel needed to be kept alive in the face of every assault upon it. However, while Luther himself could always distinguish between anti-Semitism and the need for theological purity, his descendants could not.

---

24.   This despite Luther's "...next to the devil, the Christian has no more bitter and galling foe than a Jew." *That Jesus Christ was Born a Jew*, p. 278.

As we have seen repeatedly, it was Luther himself who insisted tirelessly on "first-commandment righteousness", the idea that the first commandment of the Decalogue bespeaks the gospel, whose polar correlate is justification by faith. Yet Luther, recognizing first-commandment righteousness for Christians, denied its possibility for Jews.

LUTHER'S *THAT JESUS CHRIST WAS BORN A JEW*

Throughout much of this tract, which Luther wrote in 1523 when he was still sanguine of the Jews' conversion in the wake of the Reformation, there runs the thread of Christian indebtedness to the Jewish people. The title itself makes two points: one, that Luther recognized the Jewishness of Jesus, and two, that there must have been people who did not, whom he was now attempting to correct. He hoped that by doing so he would "win some Jews to the Christian faith".[25] In the third paragraph of his tract he writes:

> Our fools, the popes, bishops, sophists, and monks—the crude asses' heads—have hitherto so treated the Jews that anyone who wished to be a good Christian would almost have had to become a Jew. If I had been a Jew and had seen such dolts and blockheads govern and teach the Christian faith, I would sooner have become a hog than a Christian.[26]

Luther acknowledges the centuries-old mistreatment of the Jewish people, and clearly believes that his own attitude towards them is qualitatively different. He continues:

> They have dealt with the Jews as if they were dogs rather than human beings. They have done little else than deride them and seize their property...When the Jews then see that Judaism has such strong support in Scripture and that Christianity has become a mere babble without reliance on Scripture, how can they possibly compose themselves and become right good Christians?

---

25. Luther, *That Jesus Christ was Born a Jew*, p. 200.
26. Ibid.

Notice Luther's statement that Judaism has scriptural support. Later in the same tract he will claim that the scriptural support for Judaism in the Old Testament has been superseded by the addition of the New Testament. He does not say that the Old Testament has *itself* been superseded, for the Scripture that lies at the heart of the restoration of Christianity not only includes the Old Testament but is four-fifths Old Testament; he will say, rather, that the New Testament, having revealed the true meaning of the Old Testament, has rendered the synagogue obsolete and the Jewish community's adherence to it a political threat. Nevertheless, the Judaism of the Jewish people must be met with careful instruction rather than summary dismissal. Otherwise, "[t]hey will only be frightened further away from [the Christian faith] if their Judaism is so utterly rejected that nothing is allowed to remain and they are treated only with arrogance and scorn." The Jews' *yiddishkeit* should be allowed to remain, lest they be driven away from the church and from the gospel; but once they are brought into the church and have understood the gospel, their Jewishness would simply be pointless and should be dropped. Once again we see that Luther's kindly regard for the Jews, though genuine, serves the agenda of conversion.

Luther recognizes our debt as Christians to the Jewish people. "When we are inclined to boast of our position," he writes, "we should remember that we are but Gentiles, while the Jews are of the lineage of Christ. We are aliens and in-laws; they are blood relatives, cousins, and brothers of our Lord."[27] Three passages of Scripture come immediately to mind. One is Romans 9:4-5, one is Romans 9-11 as a whole, and the other is Ephesians 2:11-22. In Ephesians 2:11-22 Paul says that, thanks to the death of Christ, Gentiles who have embraced Jesus Christ in faith have been admitted to the commonwealth of Israel. Obviously the Apostle believes, first of all, that admission to the commonwealth of Israel is salutary, and second, that such a commonwealth still exists. Whether Luther draws this conclusion is, in the light of subsequent statements, another question.

---

27.   Ibid., p. 201.

In a similar vein, however, he writes:

> The second promise of Christ was to Abraham, Genesis 22[:18], where God said, "In your seed shall all the Gentiles be blessed." If all the Gentiles are to be blessed, then it is certain that otherwise, apart from this seed of Abraham, they were all unblessed and under a curse.[28]

Luther maintains that we can be blessed and our curse relieved through the promise to Abraham only as we embrace Abraham's son, Jesus Christ, in faith. What he did not see is that we can own Jesus Christ, *the* son of Israel, only as we own at the same time the sons and daughters of Israel. Christians have denied the Jewishness of Jesus not explicitly, lest they appear ridiculous, but implicitly by reading past those elements of the gospel story that depict him as Jewish. For example, informed by the King James translation, we talk about the menorrhagic woman reaching out and touching the "hem" of Jesus' "garment," not registering the fact that this garment would have to be the tallith or prayer shawl worn by every Jewish male as an undershirt. The tallith had four *zithzith* or tassels at the four corners, representing the four corners of the earth to which the Word of God extended. These tassels were left fringed, and it is this fringe that the menorrhagic woman touches. Similarly, we fail to grasp the significance of the fact that the only physical information we are given about Jesus was that he was circumcised. It does not matter to our faith whether he was slender or stout, tall or short, but the apostles insist it means everything that he is a son of Israel.[29] In other words, the Jewishness of Jesus is essential to the faith of Gentiles.

---

28.   Ibid., p. 203.

29.   In Zechariah 8:23 we read the moving words, "In those days, ten men from the tribe of every nation will take a Jew by the robe and say, 'Let us go with you, for we have heard that God is with you.'" The ten people from the tribe of every nation are plainly Gentiles. In glorious fulfillment of this prophecy, Gentile believers have grasped the robe of Jesus Christ, having heard that God is with him uniquely because

Further on, Luther writes, "While we are on the subject, however, we wish not only to answer the futile liars who publicly malign me in these matters"—that would be Johann Eck and company—"but we would also like to do a service to the Jews on the chance that we might bring some of them back to their own true faith, the one which their fathers held."[30] He considers that the fathers of the Jews he sees in Germany owned a true faith. Clearly, he has in mind a faith in the Holy One of Israel that is nonlegalistic, yet he assumes that the faith of their descendants is necessarily legalistic.[31] Rather inconsistently, while Luther was quick to declare that the "faith" of much (if not most) of the church on the eve of the Reformation was a form of legalism or self-righteousness, he did not conclude that the gospel inherently promotes self-righteousness. Instead he maintained that fallen humanity always inclines towards legalism and self-righteousness. If the faith of the Jewish fathers was not inherently legalistic, then Luther's assumption that contemporary Judaism is inherently legalistic is questionable if not groundless.

In the next paragraph he says:

> In the first place, that the current belief of the Jews and their waiting on the coming of the Messiah is erroneous is proved by the passage in Genesis 49[:10-12] where the holy patriarch Jacob says, "The scepter shall not depart from Judah, nor a teacher from those at his feet, until the *Shiloh* comes; and to him shall be the gathering of his nation. He will bind his foal to the vine and his ass to the choice vine. He will wash his garments with wine, and his mantle with the blood of grapes.

Luther returns tirelessly to this passage in Genesis 49, which he takes to be proof that Jesus is the Messiah. "Therefore," he says, "Jewish waiting for the Messiah is erroneous. But what is inherently erroneous in spiritual

---

he *is* God. How can we grasp the robe of this Jew while disdaining the robe of our Jewish neighbor?

30. Luther, *That Jesus Christ was Born a Jew*, p. 213.

31. "'The Jews' were simply a cipher for one who justifies oneself" (Lohse, op. cit., p. 345).

matters is also without excuse." If Jewish belief is inherently erroneous, and therefore inherently without excuse, then coercive treatment of the Jews in matters of faith is legitimate. The Jewish people, according to Luther, read their Scripture in a way that is indefensible. From the passage in Genesis 49 "it necessarily follows that Shiloh must first die, and thereafter rise again from the dead. For since he is to come from the tribe of Judah, he must be a true, natural man, mortal like all the children of men."[32] Luther then proceeds for the next five pages with a highly convoluted and somewhat wrenched argument demonstrating the fulfillment of the prophecy in Genesis 49 and alternating, in his interpretation, between spiritualization and a denunciation of spiritualization. He concludes:

> Now to be temporal and to reign eternally are two mutually contradictory concepts. Therefore it had to turn out that he died temporally and departed this life and again that he rose from the dead and became alive in order that he might become an eternal King. For he had to be alive if he were to reign, because one who is dead cannot reign.[33]

In any case, however, he writes that the Jews "will not listen to this interpretation until they first accept and acknowledge the fact that Christ must have come in accordance with this prophecy. Therefore we will let the matter rest until its own good time."[34] To which a reasonable response is, would to God that Christians *had* let the matter rest! The church's inability to let the matter rest is what has allowed its frustration to erupt in persecution.

Yet even Luther does not let the matter rest. In the next paragraph he writes, "Now I ask the Jews, when was there ever such a man of Jewish ancestry to whom so many nations were subject as this Jesus Christ?" He is writing out of European Christendom, of course; in Western

---

32. Luther, *That Jesus Christ was Born a Jew*, p. 214.
33. Ibid., p. 219.
34. Ibid., p. 220.

Europe, at least, all nations recognize this Jew to be the Messiah of God. Luther is appealing to history to corroborate a theological statement. The theological statement is that Jesus is the Messiah promised in Genesis 49, and the historical corroboration of that statement is the fact that all nations recognize him. Today, however, history would not be thought to furnish this corroboration; one visit to the Asian countries would reveal that the most populous nations of the world do *not* recognize Jesus as the Messiah. In any case, Luther's resort to history is a strategy doomed to failure, for history can only refute a claim to revelation; it can never confirm one. God cannot be read off the face of history. Had Jesus' body been discovered in his tomb, such a discovery would have refuted the claim that God had raised him from the dead, but an empty tomb does not of itself confirm that he did. In the same way, history in the form of the continued existence of poverty, wars, and disease refutes any claim that the messianic age is manifestly here, but history cannot confirm that Jesus is the Messiah.

Moreover, the very attempt to prove a theological assertion by invoking history is an instance of the theology of glory, a theological perversion that Luther elsewhere deplores. His characteristic *Theology of the Cross* repudiates the four features of the theology of glory, one of which is that the truth of God can be inferred from historical occurrence. The gospel that we are the beneficiaries of God's everlasting love can never be proven from history, says Luther in that document, because every time we look at what is going on in the world, what we see tends to lead us to the opposite conclusion. Yet in his argument about Genesis 49, where a theology of glory seems to work to his advantage, he supports it.

He engages in the same sort of argument with regard to the fulfillment of prophecies about the city of Jerusalem. Referring to Daniel 9:26, a text that prophesies the abiding desolation of Jerusalem, he writes, "The city today is still the ruin it was before, so that no one can deny that this prophecy and the actual situation before our eyes coincide perfectly."[35]

---

35. Luther, *That Jesus Christ was Born a Jew,* 227.

Here we see again the weakness of an appeal to history, for the present-day state of affairs would refute Luther out of his own mouth. Jerusalem is not now a desolate ruin; it is thronged with people in the wake of the creation of a Jewish state in 1948. The city thrives.

Summing up on the next page, he writes, "Now let someone tell me, where will one find a prince or Messiah or king with whom all this accords so perfectly as with our Lord Jesus Christ? Scripture and history agree so perfectly with one another that the Jews have nothing they can say to the contrary." In other words, historical perception ought to constrain the Jews to believe that Jesus is the Messiah. But as the church has always insisted, in accord with the New Testament—and as Luther himself recognizes elsewhere—it is only through the work of the Holy Spirit, an act of God, that any person can acknowledge that Jesus is Lord. The church forbids anyone to say "Jesus is Lord" based on a perceived agreement between Scripture and history. "Jesus is Lord" can be asserted, according to Scripture, only because the Holy Spirit constrains this confession in defiance of the perceived *disagreement* between Scripture and history.

Towards the end of the tract Luther returns to the theme of treating the Jewish people kindly lest we jeopardize our chances of winning them over. He asks, "So long as we thus treat them like dogs, how can we expect to work any good among them?" Of course, the real reason for not treating people like dogs has nothing to do with whether we expect to "work good among them"; we ought to refrain from treating people like dogs because they are not dogs. In any case, Luther continues:

> If we really want to help them, we must be guided in our dealings
> with them not by papal law but by the law of Christian love. We
> must receive them cordially and permit them to trade and work
> with us that they may have occasion and opportunity to associate
> with us, hear our Christian teaching, and witness our Christian life.
> If some of them should prove stiff-necked, what of it? After all, we
> ourselves are not all good Christians either.[36]

---

36.   Ibid., p. 229.

According to Luther the Jewish people ought not to be punished socially because such punishment removes them from the hearing of the gospel. Once again, however, when the Jews appeared to be intransigent with respect to the gospel, this exhortation not to punish them socially was rescinded.

Luther was haunted by a Judaism which did not yield before the church's efforts, and his frustration consumed him. In his penultimate tract written in 1543, three years before his death, he writes,

> Therefore this work of wrath proves that the Jews, surely rejected by God, are no longer his people, and neither is he any longer their God. ...If there were but a spark of reason or understanding in them they would surely say to themselves, 'O Lord God, something has gone wrong with us. Our misery is too great, too long, too severe. God has forgotten us!'[37]

Since they did not do so, Luther lamentably concluded, "they are venomous, bitter, vindictive, tricky serpents, assassins, and children of the devil."[38]

Here we have four dangerous ideas: first, that the Jews are rejected by God, which is in direct opposition to what Paul says in Romans 9-11. Second, that we can conclude this from world events. Third, that the Jews fail to acknowledge their Messiah because they are irrational or devoid of reason—as if careful analysis of the facts could bring anyone to confess Jesus as Lord. Fourth, that the Jewish people are possessed by the devil. If the Jews are rejected by God, devoid of understanding, and demon-possessed, it is not difficult to justify mistreating them—and that is exactly what has happened, regardless of Luther's intent. At the war crimes trial in Nuremberg in 1945, the notorious Nazi Rudolph Streicher based his defence largely on the later writings of Luther. These words had been seeping into the consciousness of the German people for 400 years.

---

37. Luther, *On the Jews and Their Lies*, p. 139.
38. Ibid., p. 277.

Luther makes one more point. In the same tract of 1543, he refers to the Jews' "insane boasting" that they are the Chosen People. What does it mean to be the Chosen People? Everywhere in Scripture, to be singled out by God is to be visited with extraordinary suffering. Certainly this was true of Jesus Christ. According to the apostles he is singled out *par excellence*: he alone is the Incarnate One, the Atoning One, and the Messiah of Israel, and he has been singled out for an anguish (the dereliction) known to him alone. If it is true that to be chosen by God is to be singled out, and to be singled out is to be visited with extraordinary suffering, it is ludicrous to regard as "an insane boast" any claim to be the Chosen People.

The treatment of the Jewish people in Europe after the Reformation era is tragic. Luther, as we have seen, did not invent the mistreatment; the tragedy is that he did nothing to relieve it. His anti-Judaism remains problematic. Despite his motivation—"we would also like to do a service to the Jews on the chance that we might bring some of them back to their own true faith, the one which their fathers held"[39]—the character of what he achieved approaches the hellishness he imputed to them. We can only wonder at his expecting to do "a service to the Jews" or return them "to their own true faith" while speaking of their rabbis as "those night herons and screech owls", and of one of their most venerated thinkers, Rabbi Akiba, as "the old fool and simpleton."[40] And when he intoned "We do not give a fig for their crazy glosses,"[41] no one should be surprised that his descendants heard, "We ought not give a fig for *them*."

---

39. Luther, *That Jesus Christ was Born a Jew*, p. 213.
40. Luther, *On the Jews and their Lies*, pp. 244, 235.
41. Ibid., p. 196.

Printed in the United States
128482LV00001B/175-219/P